Mill on God

The Pervasiveness and Elusiveness of Mill's Religious Thought

ASHGATE STUDIES IN THE HISTORY OF PHILOSOPHICAL THEOLOGY

ALAN P.F. SELL

MILL ON GOD

Mill on God is Professor Sell's latest impressive study in a long list of substantial theological writings, and historical and philosophical works on religion. Drawing upon several of Mill's classic philosophical texts, his posthumous publications on religion, and a range of informal communications, Sell has produced easily the best available introduction to Mill's religious thought, the intellectual context of his religious views, and the reception of his ideas and arguments. This combative and elegant work of historical and philosophical interpretation teases out the important ambiguities and tensions in Mill's thoughts, and amply demonstrates the centrality of his concern with religion.

James E. Crimmins, International Academic Advisor and
Professor of Political Science, Huron University College, Canada

John Stuart Mill (1806–73) was the most influential nineteenth-century British philosopher. Highly regarded by many in his own day, his writings on logic, economics and moral philosophy have been widely studied ever since. His religious writings have received less attention yet were highly controversial when originally published. They have continued to provoke philosophers of religion. This is especially so with respect to Mill's ideas on immorality, and his dramatic posing of the problem of evil.

Based upon a study of Mill's intellectual environment, life, critics contemporary and subsequent, and the relation of his religious writings to the rest of his corpus, Alan Sell presents an invaluable introduction to, and exploration of, Mill's religious thought. Despite Mill's widespread failure to satisfy believers and non-believers alike, Sell shows that in his religious writings he raises issues of continuing importance, not least that of the appropriate starting-point for Christian apologetics. This comprehensive study represents an invaluable resource for students and scholars of philosophy, intellectual history and theology as well as for those more generally interested in Mill.

ASHGATE STUDIES IN THE HISTORY OF PHILOSOPHICAL THEOLOGY

Ashgate Studies in the History of Philosophical Theology provides students and researchers in the field with the means of consolidating and re-appraising philosophy of religion's recent appropriation of its past. This new Ashgate series offers a focused cluster of titles presenting critical, authoritative surveys of key thinkers' ideas as they bear upon topics central to the philosophy of religion. Summarizing contemporary and historical perspectives on the writings and philosophies of each thinker, the books concentrate on moving beyond mere surveys and engage with recent international scholarship and the author's own critical research on their chosen thinker. Each book provides an accessible, stimulating new contribution to thinkers from ancient, through medieval, to modern periods.

Series Editors

Dr Martin Stone, Katholieke Universiteit Leuven
Professor Peter Byrne, King's College, London
Professor Edwin M. Curley, University of Michigan
Professor Carlos Steel, Katholieke Universiteit Leuven

Other Titles in the Series

Hegel's God
A Counterfeit Double
William Desmond

Mill on God

The Pervasiveness and Elusiveness of Mill's Religious Thought

ALAN P.F. SELL

ASHGATE

© Alan P. F. Sell 2004

Published by
Ashgate Publishing Limited
Gower House
Croft Road
Aldershot
Hampshire GU11 3HR
England

Ashgate Publishing Company
Suite 420
101 Cherry Street
Burlington, VT 05401-4405
USA

Ashgate website: http://www.ashgate.com

British Library Cataloguing in Publication Data
Sell, Alan P. F. (Alan Philip Frederick)
    Mill on God : the pervasiveness and elusiveness of Mill's
    religious thought. - (Ashgate studies in the history of philosophical
    theology)
    1.Mill, John Stuart, 1806-1873 - Religion
    I.Title
    210.9'2

Library of Congress Cataloguing-in-Publication Data
Sell, Alan P. F.
    Mill on God : the pervasiveness and elusiveness of Mill's religious thought
    / Alan P.F. Sell.
        p. cm. -- (Ashgate studies in the history of philosophical theology)
    Includes bibliographical references (p.) and index.
    ISBN 0-7546-1665-7 (alk. paper) -- ISBN 0-7546-1665-5 (pbk. : alk.
    paper)
        1. Mill, John Stuart, 1806-1873--Religion. I. Title. II. Series.

B1608.R44S45 2004
210'.92--dc22

                                                                2003057769

ISBN 0 7546 1666 5 Pbk
ISBN 0 7546 1665 7 Hbk

Typeset in England by Author & Publisher Services, Calne, Wiltshire SN11 9DQ
Printed in England by MPG Books Ltd, Bodmin, Cornwall

Contents

Preface   vi
Abbreviations   viii

1   Variations on an A-theistic Theme   1
2   The Omnipresence of God   27
3   Mill's Substitute Religion   69
4   Theism, Theology and Christ   119
5   Conclusion: Pervasiveness and Elusiveness   173

References   181
Index of Persons   195
Select Index of Subjects   201

Preface

It would not be at all surprising if this book differed in method and style from others in the series of which it is a part. For, unlike many other philosophers, John Stuart Mill did not publish substantial, closely-argued, tomes on theistic and religious issues in general, or even on the Religion of Humanity which he hoped would replace all other religions. We simply do not have from Mill major works specifically on religion, through whose arguments we might proceed in blow-by-blow fashion. Apart from his posthumous and relatively brief *Three Essays on Religion*, Mill's views on God and religion have to be tracked through his many publications and letters. I hope to show that when this task is undertaken it becomes clear both that God and religion are pervasive themes in his writings, and that these themes are, for reasons to be explained, frequently treated in an elusive manner. This very elusiveness in large part explains the diversity of critical responses to Mill's religious thought. Indeed, the attempt to detect Mill's real intentions when writing on God and religion, when coupled with a consideration of these diverse responses, constitutes a not insignificant part of the interest of his religious thought. All of which is to say that in the case of Mill, perhaps more than in that of most other philosophers, we need to examine his religious writings in the context of his times, and with reference to the varied judgments they elicited. This historical rooting need not, and will not, preclude reference to more recent critics of Mill. On the contrary, by viewing the course of criticism from Mill's day to the present it will become clear that, however it may be with some other issues which he discussed, where God and religion are concerned Mill's heirs are ever with us. If his Religion of Humanity has so far failed to become established, it is abundantly clear that Mill's writings on religion clamantly raise that old, yet ever new, question of apologetic starting-points.

In writing this book I have been greatly assisted by colleagues at following libraries: The British Library (and its Newspaper Library at Colindale); Dr. Williams's Library, London; The Hugh Owen Library, University of Wales, Aberystwyth; The National Library of Wales; The Open University Library; and The United Theological College Library, Aberystwyth. I thank them all.

I am grateful to Martin Stone for inviting me to accept the challenge of writing this volume, and to Sarah Lloyd and her colleagues at Ashgate Publishing for their unfailing courtesy and efficiency.

As time goes on I become increasingly appreciative of the philosophical foundations laid by my first teachers of the subject: Dorothy M. Emmet, Eric Gilman and Desmond Paul Henry.

Alan P.F. Sell
Milton Keynes

Abbreviations

CW	*Collected Works of John Stuart Mill*
DAB	*Dictionary of American Biography*
DHT	*The Dictionary of Historical Theology*
DMBI	*A Dictionary of Methodism in Britain and Ireland*
DNCBP	*Dictionary of Nineteenth-Century British Philosophers*
DSCHT	*Dictionary of Scottish Church History and Theology*
MR	*Mill on Religion. Contemporary Responses to Three Essays on Religion*
ODNB	*Oxford Dictionary of National Biography*

Chapter 1

Variations on an A-theistic Theme

Perhaps the most important sign in the above title is the hyphen. Taught by his father, James Mill,[1] young John Stuart Mill was not plied with dogmatic atheism but, as we shall see, he was raised in an educational environment from which God, as a matter of his father's policy, was excluded. By the psychological traumas of his early manhood Mill was led to query the adequacy of the Benthamite doctrine in which he had been reared, and to make intellectually broadening adjustments to his thought which led him to a more eclectic, if not always a more consistent, position. While Mill never reneged on his anti-supernaturalism, and while he never ceased to abominate what he took to be Christianity's reliance upon postmortem rewards and punishments as inducements to morality, his attitude towards religion perceptibly softened as the years passed – especially following the death of his wife, Harriet.

This book represents an attempt to justify the bald statements just made. I hope to show that religious and theological considerations, far from being confined to the posthumous *Three Essays on Religion* (1874), permeate many of Mill's books, essays and letters. This is the case to such a degree that the fairly common omission of this dimension of his thought from otherwise wide-ranging studies of his philosophy is as remarkable as it is questionable.[2] It will become clear that some of Mill's best known writings – *Utilitarianism*, for example – are incompletely construed if Mill's religious intentions are overlooked and his philosophical arguments are treated in abstraction from his authorial motivations. In order to achieve as rounded a view of the situation as possible I shall not only investigate Mill's texts, but shall attempt to set him in his immediate intellectual context, and to pay particular heed to the reception his ideas have received from both friendly and hostile critics from his day to our own.

I

If Mill's religious thought has been neglected by many professional philosophers, biographers have found in Mill a subject as intriguing as he is on occasion elusive. The general biographical work has been so efficiently done that we may restrict our attention to Mill's intellectual development. Here the sources are his voluminous writings, especially his *Autobiography*, begun in the winter of 1853–4, significantly revised in 1861, and finally

1

amended in 1869–70. Mill's account of his life has been much studied, not least from the point of view of its factual reliability and completeness.[3] Certainly he does not provide an exhaustive account of his life, least of all of his family. Indeed, the entire omission of his mother from the final version of the *Autobiography* has frequently been remarked upon, not least by Joseph Parker who, in his witty satirical tract, *Job's Comforters*, puts the following words into Mill's mouth:

> When I die there will be found in my desk the manuscript of my Autobiography, and so sustained was I by philosophic reflection during its composition, that never once in its pages have I mentioned my mother! Nobody could know from my Autobiography that I ever had a mother! That is what I call self-control! Other people talk of their mothers, and their mothers' influence, and their mothers' prayers, and their mothers' example, but I never own the relationship; I keep on the airy highlands of philosophy, and avoid the close and relaxing valleys of sentiment.[4]

Parker is correct as to the absence of Mill's mother, but his speculation as to the reason for it, though enjoyable, is inaccurate. The more mundane truth is that Mill wrongly felt that his mother and sisters had snubbed his bride-to-be, Harriet Taylor, now widowed, prior to their wedding.[5]

There is much to be said for R.H. Hutton's general verdict upon the *Autobiography*:

> On the whole, the book will be found, I think, even by Mr. Mill's most strenuous disciples, a dreary one. It shows that in spite of all Mr. Mill's genuine and generous compassion for human misery and his keen desire to alleviate it, his relation to concrete humanity was of a very confined and reserved kind, – one brightened by few personal ties, and those few not, except in about two cases, really hearty ones.[6]

Criticisms apart, the *Autobiography* does provide a useful guide to the changes through which Mill's thought passed, and this is our primary concern. In broad terms this is the story of one who came to question the adequacy of the doctrines in which he was reared; who suffered a psychological-*cum*-emotional crisis which prompted a broadening of his intellectual sympathies; and who emerged with revised and somewhat enlarged convictions and a new confidence.[7]

It will make for clarity if we consider in turn Mill's education, his mental crisis, his recovery, the death of his father, and his wife. These are among the more important stimuli to his intellectual development.

II

In the opinion of E.M. Chapman, 'The opening pages of the "Autobiography" tell the story of a prodigy at once so fascinating and so abnormal as well-nigh to threaten even an experience-philosopher's disbelief in miracle.'[8] The reference here is to Mill's education by his father, James, the Benthamite utilitarian. Let us first follow Mill's own account of his studies. As if in agreement with Chapman, Mill explains that among his reasons for writing his *Autobiography* was that of giving an account of 'an education which was unusual and remarkable' in that so much ground was covered in the early years which in normal educational arrangements are 'little better than wasted'. In a period of intellectual transition he also wishes to depict for the interest and benefit of others 'the successive phases of [a] mind which was always pressing forward, equally ready to learn and to unlearn either from its own thoughts or from those of others'. Finally, he wishes to acknowledge those to whom he is intellectually and morally indebted.[9]

Mill records his birth date, 20 May 1806, and proceeds at once to introduce his father who, though licensed to preach in the Church of Scotland, was never ordained, 'having satisfied himself that he could not believe the doctrines of that or of any other Church'.[10] To his other duties James Mill added the education of his children, to which pursuit he devoted 'a considerable part of almost every day'.[11] Mill began to learn Greek and arithmetic at the age of three, remembering the latter for its 'disagreeableness'; on morning walks with his father he would recount the previous day's learning; and between the ages of four and seven he was reading the histories of William Robertson, David Hume and Edward Gibbon. His favourite histories were those of Robert Watson and Nathaniel Hooke. He felt a 'lively interest' in Frederic of Prussia, but 'when I came to the American War, I took my part, like a child as I was (until set right by my father) on the wrong side, because it was called the English side'.[12] The parenthesis is revealing of James Mill's unbounded confidence in the rightness of all he said and did. Mill read Thomas M'Crie's *Life of Knox*, and William Sewell and John Rutty's histories of the Quakers. More popular reading came by way of occasional gifts from relatives – among them his favourite, *Robinson Crusoe* – or his father's borrowings from others.

At the age of eight Mill began Latin, concurrently teaching it to his younger sister, Wilhelmina, with other siblings joining in in their turn. Mill recalls that this 'was a part which I greatly disliked; the more so, as I was held responsible for the lessons of my pupils, in almost as full a sense as for my own'.[13] Large slabs of Greek literature followed and, as if all this were not enough, Mill voluntarily plundered books to write his own histories. His father encouraged this 'useful amusement' but never asked to see what his son wrote: 'so that I did not feel that in writing it I was accountable to anyone, nor had the chilling sensation of being under a critical eye'[14] – a further ominous choice of words. The writing of verse was 'one of the most disagreeable of my [statutory] tasks'.[15] At about the age of twelve Mill was introduced to theoretical chemistry (experimentation not being available to him – sadly, in his view), and he was simultaneously plunged into Aristotle's *Organon*, proceeding thence to Hobbes, and to a well-remembered walk on Bagshot Heath during which his father drilled him in syllogistic principles. Plato and Demosthenes followed, and these had to be read aloud to James Mill for their elocutionary usefulness: 'Of all things which he required me to do, there was none which I did so constantly ill, or in which he so perpetually lost his temper with me.'[16] None of which detracted from his delight in his father's *History of India*, published in 1818. In the following year James Mill put his son through a course in political economy; 'The path was a thorny one even to him …'[17]

At the age of fourteen Mill went to France for a year. On his return, 'my studies went on under my father's general direction,' but 'he was no longer my schoolmaster'.[18] Looking back upon the education he received, Mill insists that it 'was not an education of cram. My father never permitted anything which I learnt, to degenerate into a mere exercise of memory. He strove to make the understanding not only go along with every step of the teaching, but if possible, precede it.'[19] Even so, we are not altogether surprised to read that 'I was always too much in awe of him to be otherwise than extremely subdued and quiet in his presence.'[20] As a result of his father's abhorrence of self-conceit, Mill thought of himself as intellectually backward, though he did notice that others did not view him as such. He was 'carefully kept' from too much contact with other boys, and no holidays were allowed 'lest the habit of work should be broken, and a taste for idleness acquired'.[21] This is consistent with James Mill's view that the mind, *tabula rasa*, receives sense impressions on the basis of which it forms associations of ideas. The educator is the one who can regulate what goes in, as it were. James Mill made no bones about this: '[A]s all the actions of man are produced by his feelings or thoughts, the business of education is, to make certain feelings or thoughts take place instead of others.'[22] Hence the rigour of James's educational method and the restricted nature of the experiences it sanctioned. The nearest Mill comes to adverse criticism of the strict regime he had endured is the remark that his education had prepared him rather to know than to do, and that his father had too often 'expected effects without causes'.[23]

James Mill's strongly held convictions were even more important in Mill's formation than the 'book learning' he acquired. 'I was brought up from the first,' he tells us, 'without any religious belief, in the ordinary acceptation of the term.'[24] He explains that while his father found Butler's *Analogy* compelling against the deists, it did not answer the question of the origin of anything at all. He thus adopted the agnostic position that we could know nothing of such things. Alexander Bain records how surprised George Grote was when he first heard James Mill express this view, which went further than the deistic position with which he was familiar.[25] But John is at pains to point out that his father was not a dogmatic atheist: indeed, he regarded such a position as absurd. Moreover, James's rejection of religious belief

> was not ... primarily a matter of logic and evidence: the grounds of it were moral, still more than intellectual. He found it impossible to believe that a world so full of evil was the work of an Author combining infinite power with perfect goodness and righteousness. His intellect spurned the subtleties by which men attempt to blind themselves to this open contradiction.[26]

We shall find more than an echo of this view when we come to Mill's own diatribe against Nature's cruelties.[27]

James Mill was a stern critic of religion as such. He regarded it as morality's enemy, since it encouraged the setting up of 'factitious excellencies, – belief in creeds, devotional feelings, and ceremonies, not connected with the good of human kind, – and causing these to be accepted as substitutes for genuine virtues'. Above all, he could not stomach the religious way of making morality 'consist in doing the will of a being, on whom it lavishes all the phrases of adulation, but whom in sober truth it depicts as eminently hateful':[28]

> Think (he used to say) of a being who would make a Hell - who would create the human race with the infallible foreknowledge, and therefore with the intention, that the great majority of them were to be consigned to horrible and everlasting torment.[29]

Few were as understanding of James Mill at this point as the Unitarian philosopher, C.B. Upton, who argued that

> the Protestant Church no less than the Catholic, has throughout its history enjoined belief in propositions, some of which are at variance with logical necessity, others with the natural conscience, and others again with the claims and affections and the affirmations of direct spiritual experience. It was Mr. James Mill's fate to encounter the full force of this unnatural development of theological doctrine, and, confounding as he did the spirit of the Christian faith with the dogmas of Scotch Presbyterianism, he came at length to the not unreasonable conclusion, 'that the *ne plus ultra* of wickedness is embodied in what is commonly presented to mankind as the creed of Christianity'.[30]

On the other hand W.G. De Burgh justifiably posed his rhetorical question, confident of a negative reply: 'When James Mill ... declared that the God of Christianity was the supreme embodiment of evil, had he even studied to enlarge his view beyond the confines of a contemporary travesty of Calvinism?'[31]

In connection with his father's views on Christianity it must in fairness be said that John Mill demurs. Without correcting his father he nevertheless expresses his opinion that 'The time … is drawing near when this dreadful conception of an object of worship will no longer be identified with Christianity.'[32] The fact remains that James Mill could not understand how Christians could believe in 'an Omnipotent Author of Hell', whilst deeming the same one to embody perfect goodness.

It is difficult not to detect a whiff of the denied dogmatic atheism in the ferocity of James Mill's remarks. As Packe has truly said of him, 'Characteristically, he reached conclusions which were sharp, swift, and final. Characteristially, he never dreamed that they were wrong or incomplete.'[33] When Mill goes on to say that 'It would have been wholly inconsistent with my father's ideas of duty, to allow me to acquire impressions contrary to his convictions and feelings respecting religion,' the impression of dogmatism is enhanced to such a degree that we seem to have a mirror image of those (allegedly) closed Calvinistic minds of which James Mill had had quite enough. It verges on the ironic when Mill almost immediately adds that his father 'taught me to take the strongest interest in the Reformation, as the great and decisive context against priestly tyranny for liberty of thought.'[34] We also note a significant curtailment of what might, at least from its breadth if not from its manner, have been described as a liberal education.

When Mill goes on to say 'I am thus one of the very few examples, in this country, of one who has, not thrown off religious belief, but never had it: I grew up in a negative state with regard to it,'[35] we have the clue to a certain tiresomeness in his subsequent writings which is characteristic of many fashionable pundits, then as now, who debunk Christianity while showing little sign that they have paid close, still less scholarly, attention to its more competent representatives. Mill simply had not read the texts – indeed, he had been kept from them, and he never made good the deficiency. Both he and his father worked with stereotypes of Christian teaching rooted in its more unacceptable expressions. To put it otherwise, Mill could not always bring himself to follow his stated policy, namely, that it is 'a more healthful exercise of the mind to employ itself in learning from an enemy, than in inveighing against him'.[36] It is part of my purpose to justify this stern judgment, and I shall return to it in the Conclusion. It is not, however, denied that some expressions of the Christian faith were (and still are) abominable, or that one of the blessings of the English Enlightenment (and one of the beneficial legacies of the oft-despised eighteenth-century 'Arians', for example) was its encouragement of a moral critique of dubious theology.[37] What may be queried is whether Mill succeeded, or even seriously attempted to succeed, in the first duty of the honourable critic, namely, that of seeking to 'get under the skin' of the quarry by the expenditure of effort and the employment of imaginative sympathy.[38]

Mill proceeds to characterize his father as a Stoic, as professing 'the greatest contempt' for passionate emotions, and as one who regarded right and wrong, good and bad 'as qualities solely of conduct ... he refused to let his praise or blame be influenced by the motive of the agent'.[39] We are not therefore surprised to learn that 'The element which was chiefly deficient in his moral relation to his children, was that of tenderness.'[40] In view of his father's hold on him even after many years, it is equally no surprise that Mill partially excuses his father for this deficiency on the ground that most Englishmen do not readily display their feelings, and thereby starve them.

Mill met his father's greatest friend, David Ricardo, and also the politician, Joseph Hume, who hailed from the same part of Scotland as James Mill. But Bentham was the one of whom Mill saw most, and he was the one to whom he was intellectually most indebted. Mill informs us that 'my father was the earliest Englishman of any great mark, who thoroughly understood, and in the main adopted, Bentham's general views of ethics, government, and law'.[41] Mill then recalls his visit to France: 'the greatest, perhaps, of the many advantages which I owed to this episode in my education, was that of having breathed for a whole year the free and genial atmosphere of Continental life'.[42] Perhaps loyally, Mill does not mention any relief at being out of his father's reach for a period, though he does level the mild charge of narrowness against one who found it difficult to appreciate continental liberalism because of the inhibition imposed by the fact that James was not exempt from the prejudice of 'judging universal questions by a merely English standard'.[43]

During the winter of 1820–21 Mill became acquainted with his father's new friend, the jurist John Austin, a friend of Bentham's. With Austin he studied Roman law, but what most strikingly engaged his interest was Pierre Étienne Louis Dumont's translation of Benthamism in his *Traité de Législation*. Mill could never remember a time when he was not taught 'the greatest happiness' principle, but now 'it burst upon me with all the force of novelty' that Bentham was right:

What thus impressed me was the chapter in which Bentham passed judgment on the common modes of reasoning in morals and legislation, deduced from phrases like 'law of nature', 'right reason', 'the moral sense', 'natural rectitude', and the like, and characterized them as dogmatism in disguise imposing its sentiments upon others under cover of sounding expressions which convey no reason for the sentiment, but set up the sentiment as its own reason. It had not struck me before that Bentham's principle put an end to all this. The feeling rushed upon me, that all previous moralists were superseded, and that here indeed was the commencement of a new era in thought ... When I laid down the last volume of the *Traité* I had become a different being. The 'principle of utility', understood as Bentham understood it ... gave unity to my conception of things. I now had opinions, a creed, a doctrine, a philosophy; in one among the best senses of the word, a religion; the inculcation and diffusion of which could be made the principal outward purpose of my life.[44]

It was at this period in his intellectual development that Mill became aware of David Hartley's associationism, on which his father based his *Analysis of the Phenomena of the Human Mind*, written between 1822 and 1829. He also read, 'as I felt inclined', Berkeley, Hume, Reid, Stewart and Brown. Philip Beauchamp's *Analysis of the Influence of Natural Religion on the Temporal Happiness of Mankind* (1822), greatly interested him. Beauchamp was a pseudonym of James Mill's friend, George Grote, to whom Bentham entrusted the task of shaping a quantity of his not very orderly notes into publishable form. The denunciation in the resulting volume of the claim that a religion may be useful even if its doctrines are untrue no doubt influenced Mill's subsequent argument to the same effect in 'Utility of Religion', which was written by 1858. Not, indeed, that Mill went all the way with Bentham/Grote, to whom religion was pernicious, and for whom its demise could not come quickly enough. Bentham, after all, wished to rid human minds of any trace of religion,[45] though, as Mill later observed to John Morley, from the dream that 'if only you broke up the power of the priests and checked superstition, all would go well', men like his father 'were partially awakened by seeing that the French Revolution which overthrew the Church still did not bring the millennium'.[46] As we shall see, Mill was quite open to the possibility that traditional religion would survive for some time to come – even that some of its features were useful; and far from wishing to reject religion altogether he came to advocate a new one, the Religion of Humanity.[47]

III

We need not follow Mill in his career at the East India Company where, yet again, he was under the eye of his father who was his superior there; nor need we delay over the debating societies with which he was involved and the friends he made there, or over his earliest published articles. It is imperative, however, that we turn our attention to his breakdown of 1826. There can be no doubt that Mill's mind and emotions were in turmoil; there can equally be no doubt that those around him would have been hard put to realize this. He took no time off work. Outwardly everything was as it always was; inwardly Mill was struggling for intellectual and emotional survival.

I do not think that the significance of Mill's breakdown has been sufficiently recognized by some of his critics. For example, the Lutheran theologian, C. A. Stork, writes:

> Mr. Mill has written some very eloquent passages on the benumbing and cramping effects of receiving our beliefs on tradition; but the best illustration of what he has so well portrayed, in the abstract, he has himself furnished in the history of the adoption of his own beliefs concerning religion. No man of equal

capacity … was to the end of his life more influenced by the lessons imbibed in his youth. He was, as far as his religious opinions are concerned, a 'made man'.[48]

There is here an echo of the opinion of the erstwhile Benthamite turned Coleridgian, John Sterling, and others, with whom Mill struck up a friendship following his mental crisis, for Sterling told him that they 'had looked upon me as a "made" or manufactured man, having had a certain impress of opinion stamped on me which I could only reproduce'.[49] But what Stork overlooks is Mill's attempt, never completely successful no doubt, to 'unmake' himself and to become his own man.[50] The struggle that this entailed almost certainly goes some way towards accounting for his breakdown. I say, 'almost certainly', because speculation upon the causes of a person's breakdown is fraught with risk, especially when the person is long since deceased. Lonely, starved of parental affection, overworked, beginning to doubt the adequacy of his inherited Benthamism yet not wishing to go against his father under whose stern eye he continued both at home and at work, Mill succumbed. His friend, Alexander Bain, offers a vignette calculated to make the most self-possessed jumpy. Of James Mill he writes,

> at home he did not care to restrain the irritability of his temperament. In his advancing years, as often happens, he courted the affection of the younger children, but their love for him was never wholly unmingled with fear, for, even in his most amiable moods, he was not to be trifled with. His entering the room where the family was assembled was observed by strangers to operate as an immediate damper. This was not the worst. The one really disagreeable trait in Mill's character, and the thing that has left the most painful memories, was the way that he allowed himself to speak and behave to his wife and children before visitors.[51]

It is hardly surprising that James Mill was described as the 'most consistent and most unpleasant of the Utilitarians'.[52] Such a one was not the person to whom the depressed would naturally turn, and in this Mill was no exception. In what must surely be the most pathetic lines in the *Autobiography* he confides,

> Advice, had I known where to seek it, would have been most precious … But there was no one on whom I could build the faintest hope of such assistance. My father, to whom it would have been natural to me to have recourse in any practical difficulties, was the last person to whom, in such a case as this, I looked for help. Everything convinced me that he had no knowledge of any such mental state as I was suffering from, and that even if he could be made to understand it, he was not the physician who could heal it.[53]

Mill further explains that he did not wish to cause his father the distress of thinking that his educational method had failed, and further points out that he had no other friends to whom he could unburden himself.

Among the most sympathetic comments from the Christian side is that of the former Bampton Lecturer, W.J. Irons. He writes of Mill's training, 'excluded from the ways of men', and continues:

> Shut out too much from common homes and habits, he seemed scarcely one of his kind. There is a gentle self-contemplation in his life which touches the reader at times profoundly, as it gives us glimpses of what he might have been. Our feeling concerning him is deepened by the fact that he really wrestled with the ruinous predestinarian philosophy, and only succumbed to it as a materialist for want of the *à priori*, which had withered in him from his earliest hours. It was with him, then, no mere theory to be 'without God'.[54]

Mill found himself in 'a dull state of nerves' which (interestingly) he surmised might be akin to that 'in which converts to Methodism usually are, when smitten by their first "conviction of sin"'.[55] He began to question the ideology in which he had been reared. He came to feel that associationism, the doctrine that concepts of objects are inferred from sensations associated with their perception, relied upon praise and blame, reward and punishment, in order that approved desires and aversions might be engendered. But this now seemed artificial and, what is more, habitual analysis in such matters tended to 'wear away the feelings'.[56] Invoking a nautical image, he diagnosed his condition thus: 'I was ... left stranded at the commencement of my voyage, with a well equipped ship and rudder, but no sail; without any real desire for the ends which I had been so carefully fitted out to work for: no delight in virtue or the general good, but also just as little in anything else.'[57] This inability to feel was what most distressed him.

From this predicament he began to be rescued by J.-F. Marmontel's *Memoirs*, in which the author recounts the death of his father and his own boyish resolve to fend for his family. This moved Mill to tears, his burden began to be lightened, and he was never again as miserable as he had been.[58] He at once began to review his Benthamite utilitarianism. While still believing that happiness was the test of all conduct and the rule of life, he now concluded that happiness should not be the direct end aimed at: 'Those only are happy (I thought) who have their minds fixed on some object other than their own happiness; on the happiness of others, on the improvement of mankind ... Aiming thus at something else, they find happiness by the way.'[59]

We shall return to Mill's revision of his Benthamism in Chapter 3, for it is bound up with his qualified reception of Comte's ideas; but for the present we must register the fact that Mill's mental crisis with its attendant intellectual adjustments focused a wider concern than the purely personal. The times were changing, and many writers, Mill among them, found themselves caught in a pincer movement between a scientific determinism inherited from the eighteenth century on the one hand and a Romantic libertarianism in ethics on the other.[60] Hence Mill's outburst:

during the later returns of my dejection, the doctrine of what is called Philosophical Necessity weighed on my existence like an incubus. I felt as if I was scientifically proved to be the helpless slave of antecedent circumstances; as if my character and that of all others had been formed for us by agencies beyond our control, and was wholly out of our own power.[61]

Happily for Mill a broader range of literary interests began to intrude as he went in eager quest of emotional sustenance which would balance his long-standing commitment to rationality. Indeed, 'The cultivation of the feelings became one of the cardinal points in my ethical and philosophical creed.'[62] This remark needs to be placed in context. Mill was not altogether deprived of what we might term at least *quasi*-Romantic feelings prior to his mental crisis. Writing of Bentham's stately home, Ford Abbey, Somerset, he says that his visit there was

> an important circumstance in my education. Nothing contributes more to nourish elevation of sentiments in a people, than the large and free character of their habitations. The middle-age architecture, the baronial hall, and the spacious and lofty rooms, of this fine old place, so unlike the mean and cramped externals of English middle class life, gave the sentiment of a larger and freer existence, and were a sort of poetic cultivation, aided also by the character of the grounds in which the Abbey stood; which were riant and secluded, umbrageous, and full of the sound of falling waters.[63]

No doubt this is couched in Mill's post-crisis language, but, as A.O.J. Cockshut has pointed out, 'It is striking to find Mill sharing the "medieval" sentiments of Horace Walpole, Walter Scott and some romantic poets.'[64]

Such uncharacteristic paeans apart, Mill himself conceded that for two or three years he was little more than a 'mere reasoning machine' of the Benthamite kind.[65] He chided the Benthamites for their 'neglect both in theory and practice of the cultivation of feeling' and their 'undervaluing of poetry, and of Imagination generally as an element of human nature'.[66] His father

> cared little for any English poetry except Milton (for whom he had the highest admiration), Goldsmith, Burns, and Gray's 'The Bard', which he preferred to his *Elegy*: perhaps I may add Cowper and Beattie. He had some value for Spenser ... The poetry of the present century he saw scarcely any merit in, and I hardly became acquainted with any of it till I had grown up to manhood, except the metrical romances of Walter Scott, which I read at his recommendation and was intensely delighted with.[67]

The general impression Mill conveys is of one whose sensibilities were unmoved by the Augustans, whose appetite for poetry was whetted by Scott, and who thought there must be something more. There was: Wordsworth, whose poems he read for the first time in the autumn of 1828, later testifying,

these poems addressed themselves powerfully to one of the strongest of my
pleasurable susceptibilities, the love of rural objects and natural scenery; to
which I had been indebted not only for much of the pleasure of my life, but quite
recently for relief from one of my longest relapses into depression.[68]

But what is particularly significant for the subsequent development of Mill's
thought is his account of the further benefit he derived from Wordsworth's
poems:

> What made Wordsworth's poems a medicine for my state of mind, was that they
> expressed, not mere outward beauty, but states of feeling, and of thought
> coloured by feeling, under the excitement of beauty.[69]

Here is the Romantic 'inwardness' to balance the Enlightenment rationalism
in which he had been reared. It is not simply that he can value the beauties
of nature as if this were simply one more among many accomplishments; it
is that *he* can do so. He can feel. It is a quasi-spiritual awakening. But it is
also in part a reaction against his father, and this was tempered as the years
went by.[70] Certainly 20 years later we find him inveighing against the
cruelties of nature in the first of what became his *Three Essays on Religion*.
We shall return this text in Chapter 4, but what interests us now are the
reactions of two of that essay's critics, both of whom refer to Wordsworth.
The writer in *The British Quarterly Review* declares that 'Nature' shows 'no
signs of the spiritual progress which [Mill] describes in his autobiography as
a result of his study of Wordsworth's poetry. He certainly never learned to
look at Nature with the eyes of Wordsworth; and in this essay he proclaims
war to the knife against her.'[71] The Scottish theologian, John Tulloch,
concurs: 'Nature, so far from being to him an object of admiration, as it was
to Wordsworth … was, on the contrary, a cruel and mischievous power.'[72]
These assertions require to be qualified in two ways: first, Wordsworth's
nature is not always pretty and benign, it is sometimes stark and threatening.
Secondly, Mill's outburst is fundamentally against a God who can make such
a cruel nature; and in so far as he personifies nature and levels charges
against 'her', he is none the less so far a Romantic expressing feelings, albeit
feelings of a strongly disapproving kind. We may also note that in the
roughly contemporary second of his *Essays on Religion* Mill found no
difficulty in more temperately affirming that

> Religion and poetry address themselves, at least in one of their aspects, to the
> same part of the human constitution: they both supply the same want, that of ideal
> conceptions grander and more beautiful than we see realized in the prose of
> human life.[73]

A final debt Mill owed to Wordsworth was the conviction that, in the poems,
'I seemed to draw from a source of inward joy, of sympathetic and
imaginative pleasure, which could be shared in by all human beings; which

had no connexion with struggle or imperfection, but would be made richer by every improvement in the physical or social condition of mankind.'[74] In a word, the poems made him sensitive to the feelings of others, and by so doing became a spur in his quest for social reform. Far from diverting his attention from 'the common feelings and common destiny' of human beings, Wordsworth's poetry greatly increased his interest in those things.[75] So enthused was Mill by all of this that as early as January 1829 we find him on his feet delivering a two-and-a-half-hour speech at the London Debating Society in defence of Wordsworth against his friend John Arthur Roebuck's championing of Byron.[76] From that time relations between the two cooled, for though Roebuck was not a 'vulgar' Benthamite or utilitarian, 'he never could be made to see that [poetry and the fine arts, which he loved] have any value as aids in the formation of character'.[77] That they undoubtedly had such a role to play lay at the heart of Mill's new-found convictions, as witness his *On Liberty* (1859) and *Utilitarianism* (1862). In the latter he counters the view that that philosophical stance renders its exponents cold and unsympathizing, and declares that the sympathies and artistic expressions of people, and their 'beauties of character', are all relevant to the morality or otherwise of their actions.[78] From 1828 the importance of self-culture was among Mill's prominent themes. Not surprisingly, in an essay of 1832 we find him agreeing that more important than what is done is the spirit in which it is done, and hastening to add: 'Nor is this mere mysticism; the most absolute utilitarianism must come to the same conclusion.'[79]

If Wordsworth unlocked Mill's hitherto constricted feelings, Coleridge influenced him over a fairly wide range of topics. We shall, for example, consider Coleridge's views concerning the credence to be paid to doctrines widely held over many centuries, and his account of Church–state relations in the next chapter. For the present it suffices to associate Coleridge with Wordsworth as a further contributor to Mill's 'awakening'. Coleridge, too, had been stopped in his intellectual tracks. The son of a Church of England clergyman, he had passed through Unitarianism – and had considered ministry in that tradition – before returning to the Anglican fold. More to our present point, whereas he had informed Robert Southey in 1794 that 'I am a complete necessitarian' – indeed, one who goes further than Hartley in holding that thought is corporeal, that is, motion, by 1801 he could tell Thomas Poole that 'I have not only *completely extricated the notions of time and space*, but have overthrown the doctrine of associationism, as taught by Hartley, and with it all the irreligious metaphysics of modern infidels – especially the doctrine of necessity.' By 1804 he could count Wordsworth and Southey as his converts from the necessitarian fold.[80]

For Coleridge Mill had high praise:

> Few persons have exercised more influence over my thought and character than Coleridge has ... I consider him the most systematic thinker of our time, without

excepting even Bentham ... On the whole, there is more food for thought – and the best kind of thought – in Coleridge than in all other contemporary writers.[81]

Mill particularly valued Coleridge's tolerance of views other than his own, and the efforts he expended to ensure that he had fairly grasped the positions of those who differed from him. But Mill's praise was tempered by disagreement. He had previously written to John Sterling expressing his preference, against that of his friend, for Schleiermacher's location of the basis of religion in 'sentiment and moral expediency', rather than for Coleridge's view that the Christian mysteries are the highest truths of reason.[82] Nevertheless, in a letter to Edward Lytton Bulwer, Mill urges that utilitarians of varying stripes should unite in holding 'Feeling at least as valuable as Thought, & Poetry not only on a par with, but the necessary condition of, any true & comprehensive Philosophy'.[83] Moreover, when Mill elsewhere affirms that 'Truth is *sown* and germinates in the mind itself, and is not to be struck *out* suddenly like a fire from a flint by knocking another hard body against it,'[84] we cannot fail to detect the relative erosion of a self-described 'reasoning machine' by powerful Romantic streams.

The question how far Mill successfully married the positivist with the Romantic has exercised critics from his day to ours. What cannot be denied is that, in the wake of Mill's mental crisis, Coleridge no less than Wordsworth exercised a profound influence upon him in affective and methodological terms. Chapman's engaging conclusion is as follows:

> It is easy to imagine the dissatisfaction of his father with some of the companions whom John Mill found in the Utilitarian and Speculative Societies; and it is by no mean difficult to understand Mrs. Grote's evident desire to box his ears when, to the scandal of the straiter members of the Benthamite sect, he suddenly appeared as an expositor of the philosophy of Coleridge. The brilliant disciple had broken his leading strings; and though a Utilitarian still, had entered into strange relations with idealism and the poetry of Wordsworth, which to the Grotes were as the daughters of Heth to Isaac and Rebekah.[85]

But Mill may not have been quite the traitor he appeared to be, for he did not swallow the poets whole. Mill's Romanticism was tempered at the point at which feeling conflicted with phenomenalism, and he reverted to an eighteenth-century mode of thought. In his essay on 'Coleridge' he proclaims his empiricism in no uncertain terms.[86] He contrasts Locke and Aristotle with Coleridge and the German philosophers since Kant and declares,

> The nature and laws of Things in themselves, or of the hidden causes of the phenomena which are the objects of experience, appear to us radically inaccessible to the human faculties. We see no ground for believing that anything can be the object of our knowledge except our experience, and what can be inferred from our experience by the analogies of experience itself; nor is there

any idea, feeling, or power in the human mind which, in order to account for it, requires that its origin should be referred to any other source.[87]

As to the interpretation of the mental crisis as such, commentators, not surprisingly, divide. A few examples will illustrate the diverse responses to Mill's predicament. R.H. Hutton was among the least sympathetic:

> Surely a profound sense of the inadequacy of ordinary human success to the cravings of the human spirit was never followed by a less radical moral change. That it resulted in a new breadth of sympathy with writers like Coleridge and Wordsworth, whose fundamental modes of thought and faith Mr. Mill entirely rejected, but whose modes of sentiment, after this period of his life, he somehow managed, not very intelligibly, to make room, is very true...But as far as I can judge, all this new breadth was gained at the cost of a certain haze which, from this time forth, spread itself over his grasp of the first principles which he still professed to hold. He did not cease to be a utilitarian, but he ceased to distinguish between the duty of promoting your own happiness and of promoting anybody else's, and never could make it clear where he found his moral obligation to sacrifice the former to the latter ... He did not cease to declaim against the prejudices engendered by the intuitional theory of philosophy, but he made it one of his peculiar distinctions an an Experience-philosopher, that he recommended the fostering of new prepossessions, only distinguished from the prejudices he strove to dissipate by being, in his opinion, harmless, though quite as little based as those in ultimate or objective truth ... The result of the moral crisis through which Mr. Mill passed at the age of 20 may be described briefly, in my opinion, as this, – that it gave him *tastes* far in advance of his philosophy, foretastes in fact of a true philosophy; and that this moral flavour of something truer and wider, served him in place of the substance of anything truer and wider, during the rest of his life.[88]

To the extent that the concluding judgment here is accurate, it is sad.

If, to Hutton, Mill was left in a methodologically contradictory state, to his friend Morley, Mill had been spared a much worse fate than that:

> The wonder is that the reaction against such an education as that through which James Mill brought his son, – an education so intense, so purely analytical, doing so much for the reason and so little for the satisfaction of the affections, – was not of the most violent kind. The wonder is that the crisis through which nearly every youth of good quality has to pass ... did not land him in some of the extreme forms of transcendentalism.[89]

What the entire episode, indeed the entire *Autobiography*, revealed to C.A. Stork was 'the history of a fruitless search after something to take the place of God'.[90]

IV

Having, as we have seen, distanced himself from some of his father's more angular views, and having begun to esteem poetry and take due account of the affective, Mill's next turning-point came with James' Mill's death on 23 June 1836. It is not too much to say that by the early 1840s Mill had to a considerable extent reverted to his pre-1826 epistemology, for he now held that any intuitive capabilities of the mind, while they may be prevenient, do not carry conviction in the way that empiricism does. Moreover, he now holds with the Radicals that people must be permitted to come by truth in their own way and in their own time, and that Coleridge's view of authoritative guidance in these matters is wanting.[91]

But if Mill underwent an epistemological reversion (though it was not complete), this did not entail his leaving the feelings behind. He remained indebted to the Romantics for that, and as late as 1867 we find him exhorting the students at St. Andrews thus:

> Who does not feel a better man after a course of Dante, or Wordsworth, or, I will add, of Lucretius of the *Georgics*, or after brooding over Gray's *Elegy*, or Shelley's 'Hymn to Intellectual Beauty'? ... All the arts of expression tend to keep alive and in activity the feelings they express.[92]

It is remarkable, considering the character and attitudes of his father, that Mill should compose what amounts to a panegyric following his death. He thinks that his father would have made a distinguished contribution to Parliament[93] – 'A characteristic misjudgement,' snorts A.O.J. Cockshut: 'It is hard to think of a man of ability more certain to be a political failure than James Mill.'[94] Mill rates James highly as a thinker: he 'united the great qualities of the metaphysicians of the eighteenth century, with others of a different complexion, admirably qualifying him to complete and correct their work'.[95] 'During his later years,' Mill writes elsewhere, his father 'was quite as much the head and leader of the intellectual radicals in England, as Voltaire was of the *philosophes* in France.'[96] Indeed, 'In the power of influencing by mere force of mind and character, the convictions and purposes of others, and in the strenuous exertion of that power to promote freedom and progress, he left, as far as my knowledge extends, no equal among men, and but one among women.'[97]

Enter Harriet, whom Mill, far more than any other person before or since, deemed to be the paramount influence upon his thought. They met in 1830, she being the wife of a London druggist, John Taylor.[98] Taylor was a faithful Unitarian, and the Unitarians, overall the most radical of the English Dissenters, float in and out of Mill's story on a number of occasions. Mill contributed to their journal, *The Monthly Repository*, whose editor was William Johnson Fox; Coleridge, as we have seen, had been within their orbit for a time, while Mill's acquaintance, F.D. Maurice, a university friend of John Sterling, was raised among them. James Martineau was their rising intellectual star, and he had broken from the necessarianism of Hartley, Priestley and Thomas Belsham in which he had been bred, and, influenced by Coleridge, the American William Ellery Channing and the Scot, Carlyle, he came to elevate conscience as *The Seat of Authority in Religion* (the title of his book of 1890) and to develop an ethical theism which beat a track between determinism and materialism on the one side and the post-Hegelian absolute idealists' synthetic unity on the other. Martineau's change of philosophical stance did not go unnoticed by Mill: 'Are not your general metaphysical opinions a shade or two more German than they used to be?' he gently enquired.[99]

Reflecting upon his life, Mill is at pains to point out the propriety of his friendship with Harriet Taylor prior to their eventual marriage: 'though we did not consider the ordinances of society binding on a subject so entirely personal, we did feel bound that our conduct should be such as in no degree to bring discredit on her husband, nor therefore on herself'.[100] The myopia in the phrase 'entirely personal' is astonishing given that 'in professional circles, in the chapel, and in his club' John Taylor became 'a figure of ribald fun'.[101] Bain assures us that the liaison was not a subject which Mill's friends raised with him.[102] It is not fanciful to suppose that Mill's assertion of the 1850s was born of personal experience: 'When once the means of living have been obtained, the far greater part of the remaining labour and effort which takes place on the earth, has for its object to acquire the respect or the favourable regard of mankind; to be looked up to, or at all events, not to be looked down upon by them.'[103] This seems the more self-serving – even hypocritical – when we consider that three sentences earlier Mill had pronounced that 'Through all departments of human affairs, regard for the sentiments of our fellow-creatures is in one shape or other, in nearly all characters [but evidently not in the case of himself and Harriet where J. Taylor was concerned], the pervading motive.'[104]

The hapless John Taylor was released by premature death in 1849,[105] and in April 1851 Mill was married 'to the lady whose incomparable worth had made her friendship the greatest source to me both of happiness and of improvement, during many years in which we never expected to be in any closer relation to one another', thereby deriving from 'that evil my own greatest good'.[106] As early as 1833 the smitten Harriet had eulogized Mill thus: 'Oh this being, seeming as though God had willed to show the type of the possible elevation of humanity. To be with him wholly is my ideal of the noblest fate.'[107] Mill more than repaid the compliment. Indeed, he cannot write of Harriet without exaggeration. In thought and intellect Shelley 'was but a child compared with what she ultimately became';[108] she was 'more of a poet than [Carlyle], more of a thinker than I';[109] and so on *ad nauseam*. It would be difficult to deny the accuracy of C.B. Crane's prediction: 'I think that [Mill's] exchange of a servile homage paid to his father for an infatuated devotion paid to the woman who subsequently became his wife, will take its place among the chief curiosities of literature.'[110]

As to Harriet's influence on Mill's ideas (something of which Mill seems completely to have convinced himself) the consensus of biographers and critics alike is that, as regards the practical implications of some of the subject matter of Mill's *Political Economy* and *Liberty*, she added a dimension to his thought;[111] and we have his own testimony that, whereas before he met her he had thought it right in an abstract way that women and men should enjoy equality in life, it was she who showed him the practical bearing of this theoretical stance in relation to actual disabilities suffered by women.[112]

V

As we proceed we shall meet Harriet again, as well as others, notably Comte, who influenced Mill's religious thought. For the present we shall do well to prepare ourselves for what follows by addressing two questions. First, what was the intellectual air which Mill breathed in so far as it bore upon religion and God? A mere list of some of the constituents of it will suffice. In addition to the increasing impact of Romanticism, to which we have already paid some attention, there flowed down from the eighteenth century the continuing influence of the theistic 'evidences' and arguments. There was the significant growth of Methodism in its various branches; this, coupled with the numerical post-Evangelical Revival gains of Old Dissent enabled the entire body of Nonconformists to achieve parity of membership with the Church of England as the century proceeded. There was the rise and spread of the Oxford Movement, the agitation for Catholic Emancipation, and arguments (and societies) in favour of the disestablishment of the Church of England. In addition, modern biblical criticism coupled with modern historical method played their part in stirring up debate among Christians, as did the growing influence of evolutionary thought. Atheism and agnosticism came to be more openly proclaimed, secularism in some of its aspects assumed organizational shape, and materialism and naturalism came to be increasingly opposed by post-Hegelian idealists, some of them absolutists, some personalists, some Christian, others not. Not the least remarkable fact about Mill is that notwithstanding his a-theistic upbringing he had something to say on all of these issues, as we shall see.[113]

Our second question returns us to Mill himself. On the basis of our study so far, what is our interim characterization of his mode of thought? It is clear in the first place that it oscillates between theoretical positions, with the result that he can land himself in contradiction. These oscillations are partly attributable to the impact of differing intellectual influences upon him at different times, and partly owing to a pragmatic streak in him which inclines him to seek consensus among people of diverse opinions as a basis for social reform. Thus, if religion is useful to some, let it alone for now; it will be superseded in time. Herein lies the greatest difference between Mill and his father. For James always worked from his chosen Benthamite principles, allowing none of his son's moderation of them, but rather wielding them as principles of exclusion where alternative ideas were concerned. John Mill set down his own policy in the course of his remarks on Puseyism:

> We not only esteem it a more healthful exercise of the mind to employ itself in learning from an enemy, than in inveighing against him; but, we believe, that the extirpation of what is erroneous in any system of belief is in no way so much promoted as by extricating from it, and incorporating into our own systems, whatever in it is true.[114]

He elsewhere underlines the point: 'When I had taken in any new idea, I could not rest till I had adjusted its relation to my old opinions, and ascertained exactly how far its effect ought to extend in modifying or superseding them.' But this does not imply the wholesale rejection of the old, for 'I never allowed it to fall to pieces, but was incessantly occupied in weaving it anew.'[115] This, as we have seen, was his particular intention following his discovery of the feelings. Indeed, John Morley considered that 'Perhaps the sum of all his distinction lies in this union of stern science with infinite aspiration, of rigorous sense of what is real and practicable with bright and luminous hope.'[116]

Mill even seemed to believe (however unrealistically) that by following the path of tolerant eclecticism it would eventually be possible to supersede intellectual sectarianisms and reach a position which would stand eternally secure:

> I looked forward, through the present age of loud disputes but generally weak convictions, to a future which shall unite the best qualities of the critical with the best qualities of the organic periods; unchecked liberty of thought, unbounded freedom of individual action in all modes not hurtful to others; but also, convictions as to what is right and wrong, useful and pernicious, deeply engraven on the feelings by early education and general unanimity of sentiment, and so firmly grounded in reason and in the true exigencies of life, that they shall not, like all former and present creeds, religious, ethical, and political, require to be periodically thrown off and replaced by others.[117]

Some of Mill's critics, however, felt that he could speak in this way only because he avoided the close analysis of first principles on the one hand and specific practical remedies on the other. I think that in 1859 James Martineau accurately described the nature of Mill's method:

> The great mass of Mr. Mill's labour has been devoted to what may be termed the *middle ground* of human thought, below the primary data which reason must assume, and short of the applied science which has practice for its end. At the

upper limit shunning the original postulates of all knowledge, and at the lower its concrete results, he has addressed himself to its intermediary processes, and determined the method for working out derivative, but still general truths.[118]

A.D. Lindsay suggests a possible cause of this state of affairs: 'Mill's open-mindedness was too large for the system he inherited; his power of system-making too small for him to construct a new one.'[119]

So much for Mill's method. As to his manner, R.H. Hutton was blunt: 'He was too strenuously didactic to be in sympathy with man, and too incessantly analytic to throw his burden upon God.'[120] There is something to be said for both parts of this judgment, though, in view of what we know of Mill's personal generosity and his hopes for humanity, the first part is unduly harsh. As for the second part: certainly nobody was less of a 'God-botherer' than John Stuart Mill. The question remains, how far did God bother him?

Notes

1   For James Mill (1773–1836) see DNCBP, MR, ODNB; Alexander Bain, *James Mill. A Biography*, London: Longmans, 1882. James was still a churchgoer when he met Bentham, and did not 'come out' as an agnostic until 1816. His children were all baptized, John went to church as a small boy, and the girls continued to attend with their mother. For Bain (1813–1903) see DNCBP, MR, ODNB. Cf. M.St.J. Packe, *The Life of John Stuart Mill*, London: Secker and Warburg, 1954, p.25. This is the most comprehensive biography of Mill.

2   A prominent example in this connection is John Skorupski's *John Stuart Mill*, London: Routledge, 1989, whose author, albeit with regret, omits discussion of Mill's *Three Essays on Religion*. Lest my reaction be dismissed as only to be expected from one known to have religious inclinations, we may note that A.G.N. Flew, himself somewhat less than a defender of the Faith (though well versed in it), likewise regretted Skorupski's omission of the religious dimension. See *The Philosophical Quarterly*, XLI, no. 162, January 1991, 97–8. In his review of Skorupski's book, J.B. Schneewind explains that the author ignores religion among other subjects 'because his theme is the purely philosophical aspects of Mill's thought'. See *The Philosophical Review*, CI, no. 4, October 1992, 873. This goes further than Skorupski's own statement (op.cit., xii) that Mill's *Three Essays on Religion* 'do not break new paths in our understanding of what religion is. Nor are they essential to Mill's philosophy in the way that Hume's *Dialogues Concerning Natural Religion* are central to his'. The following observations are pertinent: 1. Schneewind, after the manner of a twentieth-century professional philosopher, speaks anachronistically. In Mill's day philosophy was not the 'professionally pure' entity which some think it has subsequently become, and his 'philosophy' cannot easily be abstracted from his wider thought in the way implied here. Ross Harrison is equally anachronistic. In his review of Alan P.F. Sell (ed.), *Mill on Religion. Contemporary Responses to Three Essays of Religion*, in *The British Journal for the History of Philosophy*, VII, no. 2, June 1999, 387, he declares that 'Only Bain and Stephen of the philosophers are included here.' If he had assimilated the information provided in what he calls my 'useful biographical notes' he would have known that of the 32 respondents included in the volume seven are anonymous, but *eight* were employed as teachers of philosophy for at least part of their careers. The remainder are divines, literary figures and the like: 'freelances' or 'amateurs' from the modern 'professional' point of view, no doubt; but so were J.H. Stirling, Herbert

Spencer and Mill himself. 2. It is part of my purpose to show that, far from being confined to the *Three Essays*, Mill's religious thought pervades his writings. It is a motivating force of a number of his works, and our study of these works is hampered if we do not see why he undertakes them. In the 'Introduction' to a collection of papers gathered under the title, *The General Philosophy of John Stuart Mill*, Aldershot: Ashgate Publishing, 2002, Víctor Sánchez-Valencia observes that there are few (relatively recent) essays on Mill's religious thought. This fact, he says, indicates that 'Mill's main significance for contemporary philosophers lies in his ethical and epistemological writings' (Ibid., xxix). No doubt Alan Millar, 'Mill on religion', in J. Skorupski, *The Cambridge Companion to Mill*, Cambridge: CUP, 1998, pp.176–202, appeared too late for inclusion in the foregoing work; but the editor's judgment may otherwise stand. There is thus a balance to be redressed lest Mill be denuded of some of his most pressing concerns.

3   Studies of the *Autobiography* include W. Thomas, 'John Stuart Mill and the uses of autobiography', *History*, LVI, no. 188, October 1971, 341–59; R.D. Cumming, 'Mill's history of his ideas', *Journal of the History of Ideas*, XXV, no. 2, April–June, 1964, 235–56; Carolyn A. Barros, *Autobiography. Narrative of Transformation*, Ann Arbor: University of Michigan Press, 1998, ch. 4. For an account of the writing and revisions of the *Autobiography* see John M. Robson and Jack Stillinger's 'Introduction' to CW, I.

4   J. Parker, *Job's Comforters. Scientific Sympathy*, London: Hodder and Stoughton, 1874, pp.19–20. Mill did not altogether avoid the 'relaxing valleys of sentiment', as we shall see. For Parker (1830–1902), Congregational minister of London's City Temple, see MR, ODNB, *The Congregational Year Book*, 1903, 208 (b)–(e); *A Preacher's Life. An Autobiography and an Album*, London: Hodder and Stoughton, 1899; Albert Dawson, *Joseph Parker, D.D. His Life and Ministry*, London: S.W. Partridge, 1901; William Adamson, *The Life of the Rev. Joseph Parker*, Glasgow: Inglis, Ker, 1902.

5   For this less than improving tale see M.St.J. Packe, *The Life of John Stuart Mill*, pp.348–57, London: Secker and Warburg, 1954.

6   Richard Holt Hutton, 'John Stuart Mill's Autobiography', in his *Criticisms on Contemporary Thought and Thinkers selected from The Spectator*, London: Macmillan, 1894, I, pp.181–2. For Hutton, the erstwhile Unitarian who turned Anglican, see MR, DNCBP, ODNB; Alan Ruston, *The Inquirer. A History and Other Reflections*, London: Inquirer Publishing Co., 1992.

7   Eugene August has reminded us, with reference to Carlyle's *Sartor Resartus*, Tennyson's 'In Memoriam' and Newman's *Apologia Pro Vita Sua*, how frequently the pattern running from loss of faith, via scepticism to a new faith recurs in Victorian literature. See his *John Stuart Mill: A Mind at Large*, London: Vision, 1976, pp.246–7. We should, of course, remember that what may appear to us as a regularly-repeated pattern, even a stereotypical one (cf. religious conversion experiences), does not imply that the accounts of those who underwent the experiences are insincere, however much they may be couched in the 'language of Canaan' approved by the circle concerned.

8   Edward Mortimer Chapman, *English Literature and Religion 1800–1900*, London: Constable, 1910, p.319.

9   J.S. Mill, *Autobiography*, CW, I, p.5.

10   Ibid., p.7.

11   Ibid. James Mill's motives in educating his son at home were almost certainly mixed. On the one hand he wished to control what his son received; on the other hand Oxford and Cambridge universities were not highly esteemed by some, notably Bentham, on account of their laxity. A number of prominent people, Macaulay among them, were educated privately.

12   Ibid., p.11.

13   Ibid., p.13.

14   Ibid., p.17.

15   Ibid.
16   Ibid., p.27.
17   Ibid., p.31.
18   Ibid., p.33.
19   Ibid., p.35.
20   Ibid., p.37.
21   Ibid., p.39.
22   See W.H. Burston (ed.), *James Mill on Education*, Cambridge: CUP, 1969, p.52.
23   J.S. Mill, *Autobiography*, CW, I, p.39.
24   Ibid., p.41.
25   A. Bain, *James Mill. A Biography*, pp.90–91.
26   J.S. Mill, *Autobiography*, CW, I, p.43.
27   See ch. 4 below.
28   J.S. Mill, *Autobiography*, CW, I, p.43.
29   Ibid.
30   C.B. Upton, 'Mr. Mill's Essays on Religion. – II', *The Theological Review*, XII, 1875, 261. For Charles Barnes Upton (1831–1920) see DNCBP, MR; *The Inquirer*, 27 November 1920, 596, and 30 June 1923, 419–20.
31   W.G. De Burgh, *From Morality to Religion*, London: Macdonald & Evans, 1938, p.279.
32   J.S. Mill, *Autobiography*, CW, I, p.43. There is, of course, another face of Calvinism than James Mill's crude depiction of it. But there is no smoke without fire and, no doubt, he had been sorely tried by some Calvin*ists*. There is also a considerable swathe of Christianity which is not Calvinistic.
33   M.St.J. Packe, *The Life of John Stuart Mill*, p.14.
34   Ibid., p.45.
35   Ibid. A number of commentators have questioned how far it was possible for Mill, living when he did, to be as insulated from knowledge of the Christian religion as he here implies. See, for example, the Congregational theologian A.M. Fairbairn, *Studies in Religion and Theology. The Church: In Idea and in History*, New York: Macmillan, 1910, p.612. For Fairbairn, see DHT, DNCBP, DSCHT, ODNB; Alan P.F. Sell, *Dissenting Thought and the Life of the Churches. Studies in an English Tradition*, Lewiston, NY: Edwin Mellen Press, 1990, ch. 19; W.B. Selbie, *The Life of Andrew Martin Fairbairn*, London: Hodder and Stoughton, 1914; Elaine Kaye, *Mansfield College. Its Origin, History and Significance*, Oxford: OUP, 1996.
36   J. S. Mill, 'Puseyism, I', from *The Morning Chronicle*, 1 January 1842, 3, in CW, XXIV, p.812.
37   See further, Alan P.F. Sell *Philosophy, Dissent and Nonconformity 1689–1920*, Cambridge: James Clarke, 2004, ch. 3; idem, *Dissenting Thought and the Life of the Churches*, ch. 7.
38   The aforementioned A.G.N. Flew, for example, cannot be faulted on this score. The territory of Christian theology is rightly open to all comers. The unlettered believer who thinks of God is having theological thoughts, as are atheist and humanist critics of theological discourse. The fact remains that where an intellectual critique is called for the conventions of normal scholarly debate should apply. I do not, for example, presume to instruct Richard Dawkins on disputed points in zoological theory on the ground of my having visited a few zoos over the years.
39   J.S. Mill, *Autobiography*, CW, I, p.51.
40   Ibid., p.53.
41   Ibid., p.55.
42   Ibid., p.59.
43   Ibid., p.63.
44   Ibid., pp.67, 69.
45   See further, James E. Crimmins, 'Bentham on religion: atheism and the secular society', *Journal of the History of Ideas*, XLVII, January–March 1986, 95–110; ibid.,

Secular Utilitarianism: Social Science and the Critique of Religion in the Thought of Jeremy Bentham, Oxford: Clarendon Press, 1990. In his article Crimmins says (p.99), 'At the heart of the confidence with which Bentham condemned religion was the scientific framework of his view of the world. To this source can also be traced his failure to comprehend the inner spirit which motivates the truly religious person.' As to the first sentence: Bentham is one of a long line of similarly motivated critics of religion. As to the second, it is not simply that such persons fail 'to comprehend the inner spirit which motivates the truly religious person'; it is that, frequently without argument, they unwarrantably delimit the epistemological and linguistic territory in such a way that only their claims to knowledge or their uses of language are deemed justifiable or appropriate. See further, Alan P.F. Sell, *Confessing and Commending the Faith: Historic Witness and Apologetic Method*, Cardiff: University of Wales Press, 2002, ch. 3.

46 See J. Morley, *Recollections*, London: Macmillan,1917, I, p.67. For Morley (1838–1933) see DNCBP, ODNB.

47 The Lutheran theologian, C.A. Stork, was among others who gave due weight to this consideration. See his, 'Mr. Mill's *Autobiography* as a contribution to Christian evidences,' *Quarterly Review of the Evangelical Lutheran Church*, IV, 1874, 266. For Stork (1838–1883) see Abdel Ross Wentz, *Gettysburg Evangelical Lutheran Seminary, I. The History 1826–1926*, Harrisburg, PA: The Evangelical Press, [?1927], pp.406–9.

48 C.A. Stork, 'Mr. Mill's Autobiography', 264.

49 J.S. Mill, *Autobiography*, CW, I, p.163. For Sterling (1806–44) see ODNB.

50 The Baptist theologian, C.B. Crane, overlooks the same point when he writes of Mill, 'He was not born; he was made. He was the product of culture, and that not the best. He was his father's son; but he was even more his father's manufacture. James Mill is the explanation of John Stuart Mill.' See 'John Stuart Mill and Christianity', *The Baptist Quarterly* (Philadelphia), VIII, 1874, 350. Crane does concede that Mill surmounted his upbringing sufficiently to make some contributions to thought which, though 'partial and imperfect', are real. I would more cautiously suggest that James Mill is a large part of the explanation of the virtual clone his youthful son was, and a considerable motivation towards what the son became as he progressively distanced himself from his father. For Cephas Bennett Crane (1833–1917) see MR; William Cathcart, *The Baptist Encyclopaedia*, Philadelphia: Louis H. Everts, 1881; *The National Cyclopaedia of American Biography*, XVI, New York: James T. White, 1937; *Who Was Who in America*, I.

51 A. Bain, *James Mill. A Biography*, 334.

52 Quoted by E.M. Chapman, *English Literature and Religion 1800–1900*, 319.

53 J.S. Mill, *Autobiography*, CW, I, p.139.

54 W.J. Irons, *An Examination of Mr. Mill's Three Essays on Religion*, London: Robert Hardwicke, 1875, p.31. For Irons (1812–83), Church of England clergyman and son of the Independent minister and hymn writer, Joseph Irons, see MR, ODNB.

55 J.S. Mill, *Autobiography*, CW, I, p.137.

56 Ibid., p.141.

57 Ibid., p.143.

58 In his edition of *The Autobiography of John Stuart Mill*, Krumlin, Halifax: Ryburn Publishing, 1992, A.O.J. Cockshut observes, 'The obvious significance of the fact that reading about the death of a father was a source of recovery was never mentioned by Mill. It is actually possible that he never even thought of it' (p.237).

59 J.S. Mill, *Autobiography*, CW, I, pp.145, 147.

60 Cf. Bernard Semmel, *John Stuart Mill and the Pursuit of Virtue*, New Haven: Yale University Press, 1984, pp.9, 23. We recall that one of Mill's motives in writing his *Autobiography* was that of depicting a mind in transition in an age of transition.

61 J.S. Mill, *Autobiography*, CW, I, pp.175, 177.

62 Ibid., p.147.

63   Ibid., p.57.
64   A.O.J. Cockshut (ed.), *The Autobiography of John Stuart Mill*, 229.S
65   J.S. Mill, *Autobiography*, CW, I, p.111.
66   Ibid., p.114.
67   Ibid., p.19.
68   Ibid., p.151.
69   Ibid.
70   In retrospect Mill thought that, in reaction and relief, he may have treated Bentham too harshly and Coleridge too leniently in his essays of 1833 and 1840, respectively. See his *Autobiography*, CW, I, pp.225, 227.
71   *The British Quarterly Review*, LXI, no. cxxi, January 1875, 272.
72   J. Tulloch, *Movements of Religious Thought in Britain during the Nineteenth Century* (1885), reprinted Leicester: Leicester University Press, 1971. For Tulloch (1823–86) see DNCBP, DSCHT, MR, ODNB; Mrs. Oliphant, *A Memoir of the Life of John Tulloch, D.D., LL.D*, Edinburgh: Blackwood, 1889.
73   J.S. Mill, 'Utility of Religion', CW, X, p.419. Karl Britton points out that the first phrase here repeats a phrase used by Harriet in a letter to Mill. See 'John Stuart Mill on Christianity', in John M. Robson and Michael Laine (eds.), *James and John Stuart Mill. Papers of the Centenary Conference*, Toronto: University of Toronto Press, 1976, p.31.
74   J.S. Mill, *Autobiography*, CW, I, p.151.
75   Ibid., p.153.
76   See Edward Alexander, *John Stuart Mill: Literary Essays*, Indianapolis: Bobbs-Merrill, 1967, pp.343–55; Karl Britton, 'J.S. Mill: A debating speech on Wordsworth, 1829', *Cambridge Review*, LXXIX, March 1958, 418–23. For Roebuck (1801–79) see ODNB.
77   J.S. Mill, *Autobiography*, CW, I, p.155.
78   Idem, *Utilitarianism*, CW, X, p.221.
79   Idem, 'On genius', CW, I, pp.329–30.
80   See E.H. Coleridge (ed.), *Letters of Samuel Taylor Coleridge*, London: Heinemann, 1895: Letter of Coleridge to Southey of 11 December 1794, I, 113; Letter of Coleridge to Poole of 16 March 1801, I, 348–9; Letter of Coleridge to Poole of 15 January 1804, II, 454.
81   Letter of Mill to John Pringle Nichol of 15 April 1834, CW, XII, p.221.
82   Letter of Mill to John Sterling of 12 July 1833, CW, XII, p.168. The words 'sentiment and moral expediency' are Sterling's, in a letter to Mill of 10 June 1833. They do not adequately reflect Schleiermacher's position.
83   Letter of Mill to Bulwer of 23 November 1836, CW, XII, p.312. We shall return to Mill's modifications of utilitarianism in Chapter 3.
84   Letter of Mill to Carlyle of 18 May 1833, CW, XII, p.163.
85   E.M. Chapman, *English Literature and Religion*, 325–6.
86   In *The Philosophy of J.S. Mill*, London: OUP, 1953, p.73, R. P. Anschutz reminds us that Mill 'always pronounced himself an adherent of the School of Experience as against the School of Intuition. Nevertheless, he always used the term *empiricism* to denote a theory which he did not hold', because to him it denoted unscientific surmise. But from his own mouth he shows himself to be an empiricist as that term is commonly understood.
87   J.S. Mill, 'Coleridge', CW, X, pp.128–9.
88   R.H. Hutton, 'John Stuart Mill's Autobiography', 179–81. The entire passage is worth reading as illustrative of the conventions of Victorian reviewing. These were widely understood by all concerned, and it was not uncommon for those savaged in the periodicals to be on the best of terms in life with their supposed enemies. A not altogether imperfect analogy with latter-day all-in wrestlers comes to mind.
89   J. Morley, 'Mr. Mill's Autobiography', in his *Critical Miscellanies*, London: Macmillan, 1898, p.57. For Morley (1838–1922) see DNCBP, ODNB.
90   C.A. Stork, 'Mr. Mill's Autobiography', 264.

91   See further, Karl Britton, *John Stuart Mill*, Harmondsworth: Penguin Books, 1953, pp.34–5. As early as 1832, Mill had, in Romantic fashion, demoted authority: 'Knowledge comes only from within; all that comes from without is but *questioning*, or else it is mere *authority*.' See 'On genius', CW, I, p.332.

92   J.S. Mill, *Inaugural Address Delivered to the University of St. Andrews*, CW, XXI, p.254.

93   Idem, *Autobiography*, CW, I, p.205.

94   A.O.J. Cockshut (ed.), *The Autobiography of John Stuart Mill*, 241.

95   J.S. Mill, 'Bentham' (1838), CW, X, p.80.

96   Idem, *Autobiography*, CW, I, p.213.

97   Ibid.

98   See further, F.A. Hayek (ed.), *J.S. Mill and Harriet Taylor*, London: Routledge, 1951; H.O. Pappé, *John Stuart Mill and the Harriet Taylor Myth*, Parkville: Melbourne University Press, 1960.

99   Letter of J.S. Mill to Martineau of 12 May 1841, quoted by C.B. Upton, *Dr. Martineau's Philosophy: A Survey*, London: Nisbet, 1905, p.23. See further Alan P.F. Sell, *Commemorations. Studies in Christian Thought and History* (1993), reprinted Eugene, OR: Wipf & Stock, 1998, chs 1, 10. For Martineau (1805–1900) see also DNCBP, ODNB; James Drummond and C.B. Upton, *The Life and Letters of James Martineau*, 2 vols, London: Nisbet, 1902. The Unitarian body was not a little strained as older Priestleyites and newer followers of Martineau sought to move forward in the wake of the religious liberty accorded to them in 1813. See H.L. Short, 'Presbyterians under a new name', in C.G. Bolam, *et al.*, *The English Presbyterians. From Elizabethan Puritanism to Modern Unitarianism*, London: Allen and Unwin, 1968, pp.219–86.

100   J.S. Mill, *Autobiography*, CW, I, p.237.

101   M.St.J. Packe, *The Life of John Stuart Mill*, 320.

102   A. Bain, *John Stuart Mill. A Criticism with Personal Recollections* (1882), reprinted Bristol: Thoemmes Press, 1992, p.166. Pages 163–73 of this work amply indicate the discomfort felt by Mill's friends.

103   J.S. Mill, *Autobiography*, CW, I, p.411.

104   Ibid.

105   See M.St.J. Packe, *The Life of John Stuart Mill*, 338–9.

106   J.S. Mill, *Autobiography*, CW, I, p.247.

107   Hugh S.R. Elliot (ed.), *The Letters of John Stuart Mill, With a Note on Mill's Private Life by Mary Taylor* [Harriet's granddaughter], 2 vols, London: Longmans, 1910, I, p.xli.

108   J.S. Mill, *Autobiography*, CW, I, p.195.

109   Ibid., p.183.

110   C.B. Crane, 'John Stuart Mill and Christianity', 351.

111   See, for example, Joseph Hamburger, *John Stuart Mill on Liberty and Control*, Princeton: Princeton University Press, 1999, pp.24–7; M.St. Packe, *The Life of John Stuart Mill*, 316–17. That this was Mill's own opinion too is clear from the *Autobiography*, CW, I, pp.255, 257, 259.

112   J.S. Mill, *Autobiography*, CW, I, p.253 n.

113   A complete bibliography for the topics listed in this paragraph would be vast. Some works will be noted as appropriate in subsequent chapters.

114   J.S. Mill, 'Puseyism – I', 1842, CW, XXIV, p.812.

115   Idem, *Autobiography*, CW, I, pp.163, 165. In his paper, 'J.S. Mill as a nineteenth-century humanist', Rhetorica, X, no. 2, Spring 1992, 165–91, John F. Tinkles likens Mill to the humanists in that 'Mill's whole political system – perhaps his whole society – is a kind of constantly contested rhetorical controversy. The social debate, or conflict of interests, is kept on an even keel so long as it avoids the *determinatio* of any single authority' (p.186).

116   J. Morley, 'The death of Mr. Mill', in his *Critical Miscellanies*, III, 40–41.

117 J.S. Mill, *Autobiography*, CW, I, p.173.
118 J. Martineau, 'John Stuart Mill', *Essays, Reviews and Addresses*, London: Longmans, 1891, III, p.495; reprinted from the National Review, 1859.
119 A.D. Lindsay, 'Introduction' to Mill's *Utilitarianism, Liberty, and Representative Government*, London: Dent, n.d., p.viii.
120 R.H. Hutton, 'John Stuart Mill's Autobiography', 182.

Chapter 2

The Omnipresence of God

The title of this chapter may appear to signal a doctrinal treatise concerning one of God's incommunicable attributes. In fact it is intended to suggest that, whether we read Mill's published works or his letters, God, or at least religion, is not far away. In Chapters 3 and 4 we shall consider those of his writings which are overtly concerned with religion; but now, through a topical approach to Mill's religious ideas, I shall attempt to demonstrate that, even in those books whose titles seem at first glance to be far removed from religious interests, those interests lie not far below the surface, and on occasion they come into view, either to advance the argument or to illustrate a point. Following some general remarks on Mill's attitude towards religion in general, I shall in turn consider what he has to say about necessity and liberty, epistemology as it bears upon religious questions, and institutional religion.

I

The popular notion that an atheist cannot but be an immoral person is a long time dying: to this day it surfaces in sermons of the more grotesque kind. In Mill's early years the idea was powerfully present to many minds, not least to some of the most sophisticated. Thus, for example, the philosopher Henry Sidgwick attributed his own 'strict silence' on theological questions to the fact that, 'while I cannot myself discover adequate rational basis for the Christian hope of happy immortality, it seems to me that the general loss of such a hope, from the minds of average human beings as now constituted, would be an evil of which I cannot pretend to measure the extent'.[1] He did not suppose that the dissolution of the social order would necessarily result from the loss of religious belief, though the danger of such a dissolution would be seriously increased; and he thought it likely that in time 'average human beings' would not find the hope of future happiness so necessary a resource to sustain them in the trials of life.[2] But he was clearly concerned about the consequences of a divorce of morality from its alleged religious sanction.

The Unitarian writer, Henry Shaen Solly, an ardent advocate of a rational faith, was concerned at the point of practice. Of Mill he writes, he thinks that the new Christian duties having been once manifested to humanity, will be a secure possession to the race, whatever may have been their source. No doubt they do not need miraculous credentials, and shine by their own light as long as they are practised, but it is difficult to believe that they would be long in existence if men ceased to draw strength to discharge them from religion.[3]

The religious sanction was bolstered by the law against blasphemous libel. This 'included denying the being or providence of the Almighty, contumelious reproaches of Christ, and all profane scoffing at the holy scripture or exposing it to contempt and ridicule'.[4] All of which prompted Mill, on his father's advice, to hold back his anti-religious opinions. The time was not ripe for them: 'In giving me an opinion contrary to that of the world my father thought it necessary to give it as one which could not prudently be avowed to the world.'[5] Things of importance which Mill wished to say on other subjects would not be heard if he antagonized potential hearers over religion in general and Christianity in particular.[6] As Mill wrote to Comte,

> You are doubtless aware that here an author who should openly admit to antireligious or even antichristian opinions, would compromise not only his social position, which I feel myself capable of sacrificing to a sufficiently high objective, but also, and this would be more serious, his chance of being read. I am already assuming great risks when, from the start, I carefully put aside the religious perspective and abstained from rhetorical eulogies of the wisdom of Providence, customarily made even by unbelievers among the philosophers of my country.[7]

To Comte this was intolerable dissembling which indicated either moral weakness or lack of firm convictions; hence his later expostulation, 'true freedom is not granted; it is seized'.[8]

Mill admits that his father's advice concerning the advisability of reticence on religious matters 'was attended with some moral disadvantages; though my limited intercourse with strangers, especially such as were likely to speak to me on religion, prevented me from being placed in the alternative of avowal or hypocrisy'.[9] As the years went on, however, this self-denying ordinance became increasingly irksome, as may be inferred from his dismay at 'A state of things in which a large portion of the most active and inquiring intellects find it advisable to keep the general principles and grounds of their convictions within their own breasts, and attempt, in what they address to the public, to fit as much as they can of their own conclusions to premises which they have internally renounced.' An inhibited society of this kind, he was convinced, 'cannot send forth the open, fearless characters, and logical, consistent intellects who once adorned the thinking world'.[10] Such a society cannot easily receive fresh ideas either. Having explained that Comte's religion has no God, Mill comments,

In saying this, we have done enough to induce nine-tenths of all readers, at least in our own country, to avert their faces and close their ears. To have no religion, though scandalous enough, is an idea they are partly used to: but to have no God, and to talk of religion, is to their feelings at once an absurdity and an impiety. Of the remaining tenth, a great proportion, perhaps, will turn away from anything which calls itself by the name of religion.[11]

Mill published these words in 1865, the year in which he entered Parliament. It is not surprising, therefore, that during his candidacy for election he made it known that 'On one subject only, my religious opinions, I announced from the beginning that I would answer no questions.'[12]

Mill's carefulness in this matter did not prevent some from suspecting him of atheism: indeed it encouraged such speculation. Thus, for example, he felt it necessary to defend himself against adversely critical remarks passed upon his *An Examination of Sir William Hamilton's Philosophy* (1865) by defying 'any one to point out in my writing a single passage that conflicts with what the best religious minds of our time accept as Christianity'.[13] Three years later, when Mill was tarred with the atheistic brush for having supported the parliamentary candidature of the noted secularist, Charles Bradlaugh, he advised Frederick Bates that 'If any one again tells you that I am an atheist, I would advise you to ask him, how he knows and in what page of my numerous writings he finds anything to bear out the assertion.'[14] Of course, there may be, and in Mill's case there sometimes is, a distinction between the views an author expresses in private and those that appear in print. It may therefore be that Mill's reticence is at work here. Not, indeed, that he could justly be accused of dogmatic atheism; but in his retort to Bates he does not distinguish between that and practical atheism – a charge he would find it more difficult to deflect.

By 1873, Mill could advert to so great an advance in liberty of discussion that few would hold their unpopular opinions from the world, or advise others to do the same. Indeed,

On religion in particular the time appears to me to have come, when it is the duty of all who being qualified in point of knowledge, have on mature consideration satisfied themselves that the current opinions are not only false but hurtful, to make their dissent known; at least, if they are among those whose station, or reputation, gives their opinion a chance of being attended to. Such an avowal would put an end, at once and for ever, to the vulgar prejudice, that what is called, very improperly, unbelief, is connected with any bad qualities either of mind or heart. The world would be astonished if it knew how great a proportion of its brightest ornaments ... are complete sceptics in religion.[15]

Remarks of this kind were wounding to some, as witness a writer in the [Aberdeen] *Daily Free Press* of 20 October 1874: 'The publication a year ago of his autobiography revealed two things – the extreme heterodoxy of Mr. Mill's religious beliefs and the pusillanimity – for it is difficult to see how a milder epithet can be applied to it – with which during his lifetime he concealed these beliefs from the world.'[16] For quite different reasons the freethinker, B.V., found Mill's argument for reticence unacceptable, and wished that Mill had declared his hand earlier: 'Had the early Reformers and Freethinkers availed themselves of the excuse sanctioned by John Stuart Mill, we should now be under the absolute despotism of the Holy Roman Catholic Church.'[17]

Mill had long hoped that the more open discussion of religious issues would become possible, for by this means religion would the more easily be discredited:

> for exactly in proportion as the received systems of belief have been contested, and it has become known that they have many dissentients, their hold on the general belief has been loosened, and their practical influence on conduct has declined: and since this has happened to them notwithstanding the religious sanction which attached to them, there can be no stronger evidence that they were powerful not as religion, but as beliefs generally accepted by mankind.[18]

Indeed, Mill contends that the source of the sense of public obligation is in Greek and Roman, not Christian, thought; and similarly, 'in the morality of private life, whatever exists of magnanimity, highmindedness, personal dignity, even the sense of honour, is derived from the purely human, not the religious part of our education, and never could have grown out of a standard of ethics in which the only worth, professedly recognised, is that of obedience'.[19] However it may be with non-Christians, we may note in passing that Mill loads his argument here with the phrase, 'the only worth', whereas elsewhere he recognizes the importance of other Christian virtues, supremely that of love. Furthermore, while it cannot be denied that some Christians have exemplified the following perversion, Mill is unfair in taking it as a true characterization of Christian ethical teaching and practice:

> Christian morality (so called) has all the characters of a reaction; it is, in great part, a protest against Paganism. Its ideal is negative rather than positive; passive rather than active; Innocence rather than Nobleness; Abstinence from Evil, rather than energetic Pursuit of Good; in its precepts … 'thou shalt not' predominates unduly over 'thou shalt'.[20]

Mill moves immediately to a further charge, namely, that Christian morality is a 'carrot and stick' affair: 'It holds out the hope of heaven and the threat of hell, as the appointed and appropriate motives to a virtuous life: in this falling far below the best of the ancients, and doing what lies in it to give human morality an essentially selfish character.'[21] While, again, it is undeniable that Christians have thought and spoken in these terms, Mill has recourse to the most bizarre version of Christian ethical theory. The teleological thrust can never justifiably be removed from Christian ethics, but the deontological claim is also to be acknowledged; and post mortem rewards are most satisfactorily construed as consequences of living in a God-honouring way, not as the reason for so living. In a less bilious mood Mill himself virtually implies this: 'If there is any one requirement of Christianity less doubtful than another, it is that of being spiritually-minded; of loving and practising good from a pure love, simply because it is good.'[22] Again, 'What is really true is, that Christianity considers no act as meritorious which is done from mere worldly *motives*.'[23]

Mill, then, is stoutly opposed to any suggestion that in the absence of religious sanctions morality will crumble. This long-standing view, which he had imbibed as a youth from 'Philip Beauchamp's' *Analysis of the Influence of Natural Religion on the Temporal Happiness of Mankind*, explains his resentment of any Christian attempt to annexe morality. Such resentment surfaces, for example, in Mill's early review of Robert Blakey's *Essays on Moral Good and Evil* (1833), where the nub of his adverse criticism is that 'of all those theories, whether ethical or metaphysical, whether declaring what our *conduct should* be, or what our *feelings are*, none surely is so utterly destitute of plausibility as Mr. Blakey's own doctrine, that virtue is *constituted* by the will of God'.[24] This would mean, Mill continues, that

> God does not *declare* what is good, and *command* us to do it, but that God actually makes it good. Good is whatever God *makes* it. What we call evil, is only evil because he has arbitrarily prohibited it. The countless myriads to whom he has never signified his will, are under no moral obligations. This doctrine takes away all motives to yield obedience to God, except those which induce a slave to obey his master.[25]

Mill proceeds to turn Blakey's appeal to Scripture on its head. Blakey holds that the Bible presents a perfect morality: it tells us what to do, not why. But Mill retorts, 'if we are capable of recognising excellence in the commands of the Omnipotent, they must possess excellence independently of his command; and excellence discoverable by us without revelation; for whatever reason can recognise when found, reason can find'.[26] Moreover,

> the simple-hearted men who gathered themselves around the founder of Christianity, far from believing the doctrines to be excellent because they came from God, believed them to come from God because they found them to be excellent ... Christianity had perished with its founder if Mr. Blakey's theory had been true. The world has acknowledged him as sent of God, has believed him to *be* God, because there *was* a standard of morality by which man could test not the word of man merely, but what was vouched for as the word of God ... It was out of the hardness of their hearts that they needed signs. Had all been right within, the precepts themselves would have sufficed to prove their origin.[27]

Mill is thus opposed to 'the infinitely mischievous tendency of a theory of moral duty, according to which God is to be obeyed, not because God is good, nor because it is good to obey him, but from some motive or principle which might have dictated equally implicit obedience to the powers of darkness.'[28] When Mill returned to the theme some 20 years later he added the consideration that 'there is a very real evil consequent on ascribing a supernatural origin to the received maxims of morality. That origin consecrates the whole of them, and protects them from being discussed or criticized', and it makes unworthy received injunctions as binding upon the conscience as 'the noblest, most permanent and most universal precepts of Christ'.[29]

In his letters Mill goes further: religious claims can be positively immoral. The following two examples will illustrate the point. First, he writes,

> I confess it is as revolting to me as it was to Coleridge to find infinite justice represented as a sort of demoniacal rage that must be appeased by blood & anguish but provided it has that, cares not whether it be the blood and anguish of the guilty or the innocent.[30]

That similarly grotesque explications of the atonement can be heard to this day cannot be denied, and in making his protest Mill stands in the line of those eighteenth-century 'Arians' who were so frequently discredited by the orthodox for their attempts to develop a critique of theological assertions which they deemed to be immoral.[31] The orthodox remedy for this orthodox failure resides in the refusal to drive a wedge between the Father and the Son, and to allow full force to Paul's claim, '*God* was *in Christ* reconciling the world to himself' (II Corinthians 5: 19). I cannot further delay over this crucial theological point, except to say that Mill's preferred view of the atonement is that 'the sufferings of the Redeemer were ... an indispensable means of bringing about that change in the hearts of sinners, the want of which is the real & sole hindrance to the universal salvation of mankind'.[32] This view, Abelardian in origin, on the one hand has all the attractiveness of that moral influence theory of the atonement and, on the other hand, is liable to the charge that it reduces the Cross to the place where something is merely shown, not done.[33]

Secondly, Mill comments upon the phrase 'the righteous judgments of one who visits the sins of the fathers upon the children':

> To such a degree does religion or what is so called, pervert morality. How can morality be anything but the chaos it is now, when ideas of right & wrong, just & unjust, must be wrenched into accordance either with the notions of a tribe of barbarians in a corner of Syria three thousand years ago, or with what is called the order of Providence; in other words, the course of nature, of which so great a part is tyranny & iniquity – all the things which are punished as the most atrocious crimes when done by human creatures, being the daily doings of nature through the whole range of organic life.[34]

Here we have a harbinger of what was to become Mill's most devastatingly expressed anti-theistic argument. We shall return to this in Chapter 4. For now we may conclude this discussion of Mill's claim that morality can survive the loss of religious sanctions by noting the query of his friend John Morley, who wondered whether Mill would have been better advised not to show the nullity of such sanctions, but rather to demonstrate that 'their efficaciousness costs in other ways more than it is worth'.[35]

For all his querying of religious, and especially Christian, morality, it is clear that when Mill applauds religion it is generally because of its beneficial influence upon morality. Not, indeed, that Christianity 'delivers a code of morals, any more than a code of laws', but it 'influences the conduct by shaping the character itself: it aims at so elevating and purifying the desires, that there shall be no hindrance to the fulfilment of our duties when recognised'.[36] By the time he writes to Arthur W. Greene in 1861, Mill has concluded that historical criticism has caused the 'evidences of the supernatural part of Jewish and Xtian history' to collapse, with the result that 'almost all theologians deserving the name (in Protestant countries) now rest the proof of the divine origin of Xtianity not so much on external evidence as on the intrinsic excellence of its ethics or (as some think) the philosophical truth of its metaphysics'.[37] If we overlook the *ad hominem* reference to theologians 'deserving the name' and the overstatement regarding apologetics,[38] this remains at least a mild tribute to Christian ethics. Seven years later Mill reminds a correspondent that

> the special characteristic of Xtianity as opposed to most other religions is that it insists that religion does affect this world; making charity to our fellow-creatures & good actions the criterion of a good man. Now this is also the fundamental doctrine of those who are called Atheists as well as of those whose religious opinions are founded on individual convictions & are not therefore altogether in accordance with any of the sects. Honesty, self-sacrifice, love of our fellow-creatures, & the desire to be of use in the world, constitute the true point of resemblance between those whose religion however overlaid with dogmas is genuine, & those who are genuinely religious without any dogmas at all.[39]

This statement is redolent of Mill's practical desire to find common ground on which people of good will may march together in the real world to useful ends. He says as much in introducing the words just quoted: 'I have long thought that what we now want in the present stage of the world is a union among all those men (& women) who are deeply impressed with the fundamental essence of religion, *in so far as religion affects this world*.'[40] His statement is also, as the faintly patronizing swipe at dogmas suggests, a further example of his cavalier attitude towards first principles in the interest of such cooperation. From the point of view of most Christian writers of his day, and of many since, his characterization of Christian ethics is reductionist and unrealistic in that it takes no account of that other type of common ground, namely, that all too often the estimable virtues are simply not willed. That is to say, it is frequently not the case that people do not know what they should do: they do not need further information; they do not wish to do what they know they ought to do: they need to be reorientated by grace and empowered to act aright.[41] In a word, Mill betrays no understanding of the fact that Christian morality comprises a grateful response to what God has done in Christ, to which the casually dismissed 'dogmas' testify.

Although Mill thinks highly of widely shared values he is quick to rebuke the Church for failing to live up to its ethical principles. Archdeacon John Allen had accused him of undervaluing 'what teachers of religion can effect'. Mill denies this:

> I rate it most highly, but what they *do* effect I rate very low. An example of what they might do has been given lately by the Independent Church at Totnes, in severely rebuking those of its members who have been implicated in bribery, and only not expelling them from its communion because they expressed the deepest penitence, and determination never to offend in that manner again. This gave me the rare satisfaction of finding an existing Church, or branch of a Church, who are actually Christians.[42]

It is not easy to accuse a confirmed 'outsider' of forgetting that the Church comprises sinners, when so many 'insiders' parade a false and hypocritical piety and seem to think that they are better than everyone else: an attitude reinforced in Mill's day by the conviction to which I adverted earlier, namely, that by definition an atheist is, like the psalmist's 'impious fool' who 'says in his heart there is no God',[43] an immoral person.

But while Mill can applaud what he takes to be the moral sensitivity encouraged, and the virtues extolled, by religion, he nevertheless contends that 'some of the greatest improvements ever made in the moral sentiments of mankind have taken place without it and in spite of it'.[44] Indeed,

> one of the hardest burdens laid upon the other good influences of human nature has been that of improving religion itself. The improvement, however, has taken place; it is still proceeding, and for the sake of fairness it should be assumed to be complete. We ought to suppose religion to have accepted the best human morality which reason and goodness can work out, from philosophical, christian, or any other elements.[45]

This ostensibly generous judgment hides the further reductionist claim that the inspiration of religious morality is mundane: the very point that many religious persons would dispute, and which Mill does not stay to argue.[46] Even so, it is on the basis as stated that Mill attempts to show that any benefits of religion may be acquired without it, and hence that the claim that religion is useful even if its claims cannot be substantiated is redundant. Of mankind at large he tartly wrote, 'If their religion is false it would be very extraordinary that their morality should be true.'[47] He here seems to overlook the extolling of Christian morality in which, as we have seen, he elsewhere indulged. Undeterred, he concludes that those great effects on human conduct, which are commonly ascribed to motives derived directly from religion, have mostly for their proximate cause the influence of human opinion ... The effect of religion has been immense in giving direction to public opinion: which has, in many most important respects, been wholly determined by it. But without the sanctions superadded by public opinion, its own proper sanctions have never, save in exceptional characters, or in peculiar moods of mind, exercised a very potent influence, after the times had gone by, in which divine agency was supposed habitually to employ temporal rewards and punishments.[48]

The situation, in short, is that in his more generous moods Mill extols Christian morality, whilst eschewing its supernatural basis. As an older writer put it, Mill 'wavers ... between the notion that religion is simply ethical, and the conception of it as a knowledge or experience that reflects the presence of a real object; and he makes, indeed he attempts, no synthesis of these elements in the religious consciousness'.[49] On a related matter the same writer argues that on the one hand Mill 'sees "the principal worth of all religions whatever" in the "ideal conception of a Perfect Being" to which men habitually refer as the guide of their conscience', while, consistently with his repudiation of the intuitionism of Hamilton and Mansel, he declares that 'Whatever relates to God ... I hold to be a matter of inference; I would add, of inference *à posteriori*.' God, he now thinks, can be known as a concrete reality.[50] The upshot is that moral experience and the idea of God attested by natural facts are left 'in a mutual isolation, which deprives both of any definite religious character'.[51] To Hamilton and Mansel we shall return shortly; but for the present we must say a little more about Mill's anti-supernaturalism.

In one sense of 'supernatural' Mill does not rule it out. He deems it compatible with positivist modes of thought to believe that if the universe had a beginning this was a supernatural occurrence, for 'the laws of nature cannot account for their own origin'.[52] Much more frequently, however, his objection to the supernatural is consistent with his empiricism and materialism. He told Comte that 'I would be filled with hope if I believed that the time had come when we could frankly hoist the flag of positivism and succeed, shake off every shred of the doctrines of the past (except for their historical value) and refuse all the concessions, even tacit, to theories of the supernatural.'[53] Elsewhere, however, he distinguishes between religion and poetry, for religion 'is the product of the craving to know whether these imaginative conceptions have realities answering to them in some other world than ours'.[54] But Mill soon forgets this ontological quest. As Lipkes says, his distinction is jettisoned and 'religion comes to consist in the "elevated feelings" themselves'.[55]

Among other charges which Mill levels against religion (especially Christianity) are that it is dogmatic, intellectually and morally constricting, backward and frequently hypocritical. I shall have more to say about specific doctrines later. My concern now is with the dogmatic attitude which Mill professes to abhor – notwithstanding that he fairly frequently manifests it himself. He deplores the fact that many dogmas are intellectually confusing, they pervert the moral sense and they foster sectarianism:

> Thus the most genuinely pious among the Catholics are often the most bitter against the protestants, those among the C[hurch] of E[ngland] against Dissenters, those among the Dissenters against Deists, &c &c. This is comparatively speaking an old evil, & one which it is comparatively difficult to remove, because when people hold very strongly particular dogmas it is natural that they shd specially dislike those who hold with equal intensity to other dogmas specifically contradictory to their own.[56]

By contrast, Mill finds the attitude of his friend the Unitarian William Johnson Fox, editor and proprietor of *The Monthly Repository*, exemplary. He has, said Mill, 'divested [the *Repository*] of its sectarian character so completely as to have lost the support of almost all the Unitarians. His religion, of the most unobtrusive kind, is what the religion of all denominations would be, if we were in a healthy state – a religion of *spirit*, not of *dogma*, and catholic in the best sense'.[57] This, of course, would be the catholicity of those whose deepest convictions are, paradoxically, non-specifiable.

Mill has little patience with Anglican clergymen, for they are required to assent to fixed Articles of Religion – something which he regards as a damaging engagement 'to remain stationary'.[58] This circumstance, with its attendant hypocrisy, irritated Mill from his earliest writings to his latest. In 1823 we find him declaring that, owing to the baneful work of dogmaticians, religion, 'instead of a spirit pervading the mind, becomes a crust encircling it, nowise penetrating the obdurate mass within, but only keeping out such precious rays of precious light or genial heat as might haply have come from elsewhere'.[59] It greatly disturbs him that 'the intellectual grounds of [religious belief] should require to be backed by moral bribery or subornation of the understanding'.[60] Hypocrisy is the inevitable consequence, as when

> those who have not a trace of religious feeling or religious conviction of any kind whatever but who have not the smallest wish to sacrifice a particle of worldly consequence & success are confirmed in the opinion that if they allowed the world in general to know the true state of their mind on religious matters they would become objects of opprobrium & deep seated dislike such as they see the outspoken men of their own opinions to be.[61]

Interestingly, however, in increasingly latitudinarian times Mill sides with those Anglican clergymen 'who elect to remain in the national church, so long as they are able to accept its articles and confessions in any sense or with any interpretation consistent with common honesty, whether it be the generally received interpretation or not', because otherwise religious teaching and worship would be left in the hands of those with the narrowest minds.[62]

Mill is never more scornful of dogma than when his mind turns towards the Calvinism in which his father had been bred and concerning which he himself had scarcely heard a good word spoken during his formative years. Indeed, one of Mill's Christian critics, the Baptist Cephas Crane, himself no lover of Calvinism, went so far as to say that 'what Mr. Mill knowingly rejected was not the genuine Christianity, but that wretched travesty of it, that horrible hyper-Calvinism, that ghastly skeleton, which his grim father had lighted upon in some dismal theological crypt'.[63] Mill's accusation is that, according to Calvinism,

> the one great offence of man is self-will. All the good of which humanity is capable is comprised in obedience. You have no choice; thus you must do, and no otherwise: 'whatever is not a duty, is a sin'. Human nature being radically corrupt, there is no redemption for any one until human nature is killed within him. To one holding this theory of life, crushing out any of the human faculties, capacities, and susceptibilities, is no evil: man needs no capacity, but that of surrendering himself to the will of God: and if he uses any of his capacities for any other purpose but to do that supposed will more effectually, he is better off without them. This is the theory of Calvinism.[64]

Against such a travesty it ought only to be necessary to expostulate in pantomime fashion, 'Oh no it isn't!' We need not deny that some Calvinists may have spoken or written in this way, but they are not representative of Calvinists as a whole. To the charge of determinism I shall return shortly. Suffice it here to say that, according to Calvinism no less than to Catholicism, human nature is, by grace, capable of restoration, it is not killed; the *imago dei*, though defaced, is not obliterated. Joseph Parker took offence at Mill's 'caricature' of Calvinistic anthropology, pointing out that Mill and Calvin use 'human nature' in different senses. Mill thinks materialistically, Calvin thinks of the apostle Paul's 'old Adam' who does need to be vanquished so that the new person in Christ may flourish.[65] The upshot is that the suppression of human faculties, capacities and susceptibilities is no part of the Calvinistic ethic; and the idea that human beings retain the one capacity of self-surrender to God undercuts the Calvinist conviction that any response to God's grace made by human beings can be only one *enabled* by God the Holy Spirit.

Since Mill adduces no evidence for what is little more than hearsay, he need not at this point be countered by evidence, though there is plenty of it. From the eighteenth century onwards, under the twin motives of a moral critique of untoward doctrinal statements and a missionary desire to have an evangel proclaimable to the ends of the earth, significant adjustments were being made to Calvinism in its more scholastic modes. In this revisionary work the Baptist Andrew Fuller and the Congregationalist Edward Williams were pioneers, and in Mill's own time John McLeod Campbell in Scotland and R.W. Dale in England were prominent.[66] To none of this does Mill pay any heed whatsoever. In view of this we may feel that there are grounds for querying W.G. Ward's tribute to Mill: 'Of Mr. Mill certainly, if of any man living, it may truly be said, that he aims at doing the fullest justice to every school of thought, however remote from his own.'[67]

It appears that what particularly irks Mill is that believers are content to rest in dogmas rather than to adduce rational grounds for their convictions. He has no patience with those

> who think it enough if a person assents undoubtingly to what they think true, though he has no knowledge whatever of the grounds of the opinion, and could not make a tenable defence of it against the most superficial objections ... This is not the way in which truth ought to be held by a rational being. This is not knowing the truth. Truth, thus held, is but one superstition the more, accidentally clinging to the words which enunciate a truth.[68]

Are all apologists? There seems little room here for the childlike, for whom the Gospel is. Mill is never more objectionable, or unrealistic, than when he ascends his aristocratic pedestal and views the rest of humanity from an Olympian height. On such occasions he is frequently at his most dogmatic, which makes the following a priceless example of the pot calling the kettle black: 'The smallest rag of dogmatic religion is enough, in the opinion of its professors, to entitle them to call themselves infinitely higher and worthier than those who profess no dogmatic belief. But ... all my own experience and observation lead me to an exactly opposite conclusion.'[69]

All of which underscores Mill's charge that Christianity is intellectually constricting. He looks forward to the forthcoming appearance of Coleridge's *Confessions of an Inquiring Spirit* (1840), a work 'altogether smashing the doctrine of plenary inspiration, and the notion that the Bible was *dictated* by the Almighty, or is to be exempt from the same canons of criticism which we apply to books of human origin'.[70] But he clearly feels himself to be in a minority, and seven years later he writes to his French friend, Gustave D'Eichthal, 'nobody here is yet ripe for reading a serious discussion of the Bible. We are all either bigots or Voltairians. In ten years I think we shall have made some way, between our neo-Catholic school at [Oxf]ord & the German Rationalists who are beginning to be *secretly* read here'.[71]

What is Mill's remedy for the unhappy state of affairs in which dogma is imposed, hypocrisy encouraged, the intellect constricted and moral sensibilities stunted? Part of his answer is to propagate a positivist alternative:

> The best thing to do in the present state of the human mind is to go on establishing positive truths ... & leave Xtianity to reconcile itself with them the best way it can. By that course, in so far as we have any success, we are at least sure of doing something to improve Christianity.[72]

The problem is that too many talented people are uselessly occupied:

> If it were possible to blot entirely out the whole of German metaphysics, the whole of Christian theology, and the whole of the Roman and English systems of technical jurisprudence, and to direct all the minds that expand their faculties in these three pursuits to useful speculation and practice, there would be talent enough set at liberty to change the face of the world.[73]

Although, as C.L. Ten has pointed out, the Mill of the 1820s 'was fearful of any power that might be exercised without the control of public opinion', from 1829, under the influence of Saint Simonian ideas, he took a more optimistic, albeit aristocratic view.[74] Thus he wrote to his friend John Sterling in 1831: 'In the present age of transition, everything must be subordinate to *freedom of inquiry*: if your opinions, or mine, are right, they will in time be unanimously adopted by the instructed classes, and *then* it will be time to found the national creed upon the assumption of their truth.'[75] Later, he felt sufficiently encouraged to say, 'I believe that our times are most favourable for any new doctrine capable of sustaining thorough discussion ... everyone is shouting high and low for new principles.'[76] As he explained to Alexander Bain in connection with *On Liberty*,

> we ought to convert all we can. We *must* be satisfied with keeping alive the sacred flame in a few minds when we are unable to do more - but the notion of an intellectual aristocracy of *lumières* while the rest of the world remains in darkness fulfils none of my aspirations – & the effect I aim at by the book is, on the contrary, to make the many more accessible to all truth by making them more open minded.[77]

Yet still there lingers a trace of the older aristocratic notion, for Mill goes on to say that as far as the religious are concerned, 'I am not anxious to bring over any but really superior intellects & characters to the whole of my own opinions – in the case of all others I would much rather, as things are now, try to improve their religion than to destroy it.'[78]

However impractical it may appear to us who have hindsight, Mill never lost the vision presented to him by Harriet, of a time when religion and poetry 'must be superseded by morality deriving its power from sympathies and benevolence and its reward from the approbation of those we respect'.[79] In *On Liberty*, for example, we find him confident that

> As mankind improve, the number of doctrines which are no longer disputed or doubted will be constantly on the increase ... The cessation, on one question after another, of serious controversy, is one of the necessary incidents of the consolidation of opinion.[80]

Not all were as sanguine in Mill's own day; indeed, some were highly sceptical that his goal would be achieved by mutual discussion, and elsewhere Mill himself expressed caution concerning unrestricted free debate.[81] None was more teasing than a writer in the *Dublin University Magazine* who gently enquired, 'Would Mr. Mill conceive it to be advantageous to the formation of his maid-servant's enlightened opinion upon the excellence of chastity, that she should be invited to spend her Sunday afternoon in earnest controversy upon the matter with a profligate dragoon from Kensington barracks …?'[82]

II

'I do not know whether then or at any other time so short a book ever instantly produced so wide and so important an effect on contemporary thought as did Mill's *On Liberty*.'[83] So wrote John Morley and, for reasons whether positive or negative, many have endorsed his opinions.

In the opening words of *On Liberty* Mill makes it clear that 'The subject of this Essay is not the so-called Liberty of the Will, so unfortunately opposed to the misnamed doctrine of Philosophical Necessity; but Civil, or Social Liberty: the nature and limits of the power which can be legitimately exercised by society over the individual.'[84] I cannot so easily forgo a brief treatment of the bracketed topics, however, for everything which Mill proceeds to say concerning individual self-development both presupposes the individual's competence to make free choices, and is eroded by a necessarian undertow from which he never completely freed himself.[85] As he looked back upon the periods of dejection which he suffered from time to time in the wake of his breakdown, Mill recalled that the doctrine of philosophical necessity 'weighed on my existence like an incubus'.[86] At last, however, influenced now by the German idealist/Romantic writers Wilhelm von Humboldt, Goethe and Fichte, and by his then current friendship with Thomas Carlyle, Mill

> perceived, that the word Necessity, as a name for the doctrine of Cause and Effect applied to human action, carried with it a misleading association; … I saw that though our character is formed by circumstances, our own desires can do much to shape those circumstances; and that what is really inspiriting and ennobling in the doctrine of freewill, is the conviction that we have real power over the formation of our own character; that our will, by influencing some of our circumstances, can modify our future habits or capacities of willing.[87]

As he wrote to Alexis de Tocqueville, 'I have found peace in these ideas' for 'they alone have fully satisfied my need to put intellect and conscience into harmony.'[88] If Mill found peace, Stanley Jevons was disquieted: '[Mill] clearly reprobates the doctrine of Free Will, and expressly places himself in the camp of Necessity; but he objects to the name Necessity, and explains it away so ingeniously, that he unintentionally converts it into Free Will'.[89]

Mill reaffirmed his position eleven years later: 'The doctrines of free will and necessity rightly understood are both true. It is necessary, that is, it was inevitable from the beginning of things, that I should freely will whatever things I do will.'[90] Accordingly, in his *Logic*, Mill recommended that the term 'necessity' no longer be used with reference to causation, for it 'involves much more than uniformity of sequence; it implies irresistibleness'.[91] When it is used in this latter sense we have 'one of the most signal instances in philosophy of the abuse of terms'.[92]

In the opinion of some of Mill's critics we also have a signal instance of Mill, the 'automatist' back-tracking.[93] For what may be lost in Mill's phraseology is, as Drummond and Upton point out, his continuing conviction that moral decisions remain the inevitable consequents of the antecedent psychological states.[94] By contrast, to James Martineau 'it appeared self-evident that there can be no real basis for moral responsibility apart from the possession by the human soul, in its moral determinations, of a power of free choice between equally possible alternatives'.[95] The comparison between Mill and Martineau on this point is more than ordinarily interesting, since both of them struggled with the 'incubus' of necessity, and both were influenced by German, and, in Martineau's case, by French, thinkers. The latter's own account of his conversion will underline the point that, although they shared a common struggle and found a similar relief, they did not emerge from the tunnel at exactly the same point:

> the more I scrutinised the physical science assumptions, which I had carried as axioms into philosophy, the less I could rest in them as ultimate and valid for all thought. Above all, I had to concede to the self-conscious mind itself, both as knowing and as willing, an autonomous function distinct from each and all the phenomena known and changes willed, – a self-identity, as unlike as possible to any growing aggregate of miscellaneous and dissimilar experiences … It was the irresistible pleading of the moral consciousness which first drove me to rebel against the limits of the merely scientific conception … The secret misgivings which I had always felt at either discarding or perverting the terms which constitute the vocabulary of character, – 'responsibility', 'guilt', 'merit', 'duty', – came to a head and insisted upon speaking out and being heard; and to their reiterated question, 'Is there then no *ought to be* other than *what is*?' I found the negative answer of Diderot intolerable, and all other answers impossible. This involved a surrender of determinism, and a revision of the doctrine of causation: or rather … a recall of the outlawed causes from their banishment and degradation to the rank of antecedents … The effect I cannot describe but as a new intellectual birth.[96]

Clearly more in sympathy with Martineau than with Mill at this point, Charles Douglas found Mill 'left amid the antinomies of determinism and indeterminism, because his conception of the self is inadequate and irrelevant'. Mill's idea that we make our character 'if we will' by changing our circumstances is 'abstract and mechanical; and it ignores the fact that the will to be different is itself a change of character – that character is modified from within, by the volitions which express it'.[97] A related range of questions was more recently posed by Karl Britton:

> How … can Man be free to make genuine moral choices if his character is determined (in the end) by external forces? And, still more difficult, how can he be free to discriminate correctly between right and wrong, if his morality is imposed upon him by tradition and early education? … How can man be free to describe the world correctly, if his perceptions, and his responses to his perceptions, are determined by external stimulation and internal habits and associations? Mill never really faces these questions.[98]

So much for some general considerations regarding free will and determinism. Before leaving the topic, however, it is necessary to spell out a little more clearly Mill's view of foreknowledge in relation to free will. This has implications for his religious views and, somewhat surprisingly, occasions the most understanding remarks he ever made concerning Calvinism. What we may describe as Mill's regular view of that brand of the Christian faith is epitomized in the remark, quoted earlier, that according to Calvinism, 'the one great offence of man is self-will … You have no choice; thus you must do, and no otherwise'.[99] However, to the Anglican-turned-Roman Catholic, W.G. Ward, Mill wrote, 'I am not aware of having ever said that foreknowledge is inconsistent with free will. That knotty metaphysical question I have avoided entering into, & in my Logic I have even built upon the admissions of free will philosophers that our freedom be real though God foreknows our actions.'[100] With particular reference to Calvinism he declares,

> not only the doctrine of necessity, but Predestination in its coarsest form – the belief that all our actions are divinely preordained – though, in my view, inconsistent with ascribing any moral attributes whatever to the Deity, yet if combined with the belief that God works according to general laws, which have to be learnt from experience, has no tendency to make us act in any respect otherwise than we should do if we thought our actions really contingent. For if God acts according to general laws, then, whatever he may have preordained, he has preordained that it shall take place through the causes on which experience shows it to be consequent: and if he has predestined that I shall attain my ends, he has predestined that I shall do so by studying and putting in practice the means which lead to their attainment.[101]

It is necessary only to add that belief in 'predestination in its coarsest form' is not a *sine qua non* of Calvinism, and is untypical of Calvin himself; and that, while the majority of Calvinist thinkers have been necessarians, a number have been libertarians. This is possible because of the distinction between the philosophical doctrines of free will and determinism and the theological doctrine of predestination, concerning which William

Cunningham, himself a staunch Calvinist, declared, 'Predestination implies that the end or result is certain, and that adequate provision has been made for bringing it about. But it does not indicate anything as to what must be the nature of this provision in regard to the different classes of events which are taking place under God's government, including the volitions of rational and responsible beings.'[102]

Against the background thus sketched we may return to *On Liberty*. To the tract is prefixed a quotation from von Humboldt's *The Sphere and Duties of Government*: 'The grand, leading principle, towards which every argument unfolded in these pages directly converges, is the absolute and essential importance of human development in its richest diversity.'[103] We shall do well to keep the positive thrust of these words in mind for, as we shall see, it has been a frequent criticism of *On Liberty* that in it Mill is concerned with negative freedom only. The quotation is followed by a dedication to the late Harriet, 'the inspirer, and in part the author, of all that is best in my writings'. While sceptical because of Mill's tendency to eulogize Harriet, a number of scholars do at least admit that she probably did contribute to this text, especially in the area of practical illustrations of the theme. Mill's own view is that

> The *Liberty* is likely to survive longer than anything else that I have written (with the possible exception of the *Logic*), because the conjunction of her mind with mine has rendered it a kind of philosophic text-book of a single truth, which the changes progressively taking place in modern society tend to bring out into ever stronger relief: the importance, to man and society, of a large variety in types of character, and of giving full freedom to human nature to expand itself in innumerable and conflicting directions.[104]

We should note the phrase '*full* freedom' because of the criticism that, for all his liberal talk, Mill had firm ideas concerning acceptable and unacceptable exercises of freedom.

Mill states his underlying principle thus: 'the sole end for which mankind are warranted, individually or collectively, in interfering with the liberty of action of any of their number, is self-protection ... Over himself, over his own body and mind, the individual is sovereign'.[105] He proceeds at once to qualify this assertion by restricting its application to human beings 'in the maturity of their faculties'. He next makes it clear that he is not thinking in terms of any abstract rights the individual may have. On the contrary, 'I regard utility as the ultimate appeal on all ethical questions; but it must be utility in the largest sense, grounded on the permanent interests of a man as a progressive being.'[106] The context of his discussion is one in which there is 'in the world at large an increasing inclination to stretch unduly the powers of society over the individual, both by the force of opinion and even by that of legislation'.[107] This Mill regrets, though, again as we shall see, some were soon to accuse him of invoking the force of opinion against expressions of freedom of which he disapproved.

Mill emerges as a powerful advocate of freedom of thought. He is opposed to the arbitrary assumption of infallibility, but equally sceptical concerning those who wish to side-step the question of the truth of beliefs in favour of their usefulness. This, we recall, is the main thrust of his essay 'Utility of religion'. In *On Liberty* he points out that the question of the utility of an opinion is as much a point of discussion as its truth; indeed, 'The truth of an opinion is part of its utility. If we would know whether or not it is desirable that a proposition should be believed, is it possible to exclude the consideration of whether or not it is true?'[108] Mill exhorts his readers not to deny a hearing to opinions they condemn, not least because a currently vilified opinion may become a generally accepted one in the future. Among his illustrations of this point is that of Saul, the persecutor of Christians, who became Paul the apostle. Mill opposes the persecution of people on the ground of their religious convictions, and he is no less opposed to those who accept their beliefs on authority alone, and have no grounds for them: that way lies superstition. He further argues that, once creeds become hereditary and are accepted passively, religion becomes simply a matter of form. Worse still, 'the creed remains as it were outside the mind, incrusting and petrifying it against all other influences addressed to the higher parts of our nature ... doing nothing for the mind or heart, except standing sentinel over them to keep them vacant'.[109] This, he is convinced, is what has happened to the majority of those who believe the doctrines of Christianity – a class of propositions which, be it noted, he immediately reduces to 'the maxims and precepts contained in the New Testament'.[110] These, he continues,

> are considered sacred, and accepted as laws, by all professing Christians. Yet it is scarcely too much to say that not one Christian in a thousand guides or tests his individual conduct by reference to those laws. The standard to which he does refer it, is the custom of his nation, his class, or his religious profession.[111]

We observe that on this occasion it is Mill who gives no grounds for his conviction. He grants that believers of a sectarian disposition pay more heed to their doctrines as long as they are challenged, but 'Both teachers and learners go to sleep at their post, as soon as there is no enemy in the field.'[112]

As to the relation between Christianity and morality, Mill, while valuing the principles taught by Christ, contends that these are not the whole of morality and, as we have already seen, he refuses to allow Christianity to annexe morality to itself:

> If Christians would teach infidels to be just to Christianity, they should themselves be just to infidelity. It can do truth no service to blink the fact ... that a large portion of the noblest and most valuable moral teaching has been the work, not only of men who did not know, but of men who knew and rejected, the Christian faith.[113]

At the heart of *On Liberty* is Mill's appeal on behalf of the liberty of the individual. Against the socialist tendencies of the Saint-Simonians and the cooperative ventures of Robert Owen, and influenced by the American Unitarian writer, William Ellery Channing,[114] Mill pits the individual against what he deems to be unwarrantable societal impositions: 'It is desirable ... that in things which do not primarily concern others, individuality should assert itself.'[115] He was deeply concerned that 'In our times, from the highest class of society down to the lowest, every one lives as under the eye of a hostile and dreaded censorship.'[116] Accordingly, 'the strongest of all the arguments against the interference of the public with purely personal conduct, is that when it does interfere, the odds are that it interferes wrongly, and in the wrong place'.[117] It should not be forgotten that

> The notion that it is one man's duty that another should be religious, was the foundation of all the religious persecutions ever perpetrated, and if admitted, would fully justify them ... It is a determination not to tolerate others doing what is permitted by their religion, because it is not permitted by the persecutor's religion. It is a belief that God not only abominates the act of the misbeliever, but will not hold us guiltless if we leave him unmolested.[118]

We are now in a position to discuss the main thrust of Mill's position on liberty in so far as it bears upon religious questions in relation to others of his works, and to consider some of the criticisms which have been levelled against him. First, Mill is utterly persuaded that people must be free to choose for religion or for infidelity; that no obstacles to such choices are permissible; and that no punishments are legitimate consequent upon such choices. He never reneged upon his view expressed as early as 1825, that

> Nothing can be more certain, than that it is unsafe for [people] to permit any but themselves to choose for them in religion. If they part with the power of choosing their own religious opinions, they part with every power. It is well known with what ease religious opinions can be made to embrace every thing upon which the unlimited power of rulers and the utmost degradation of the people depend.... Permit any man, or any set of men, to say what shall and what shall not be religious opinions, you make them despotic immediately.[119]

The implication is that infidelity no less than religious faith must be tolerated:

> In an age when the slightest difference of opinion on [religion] was deemed a perfectly sufficient reason for bringing the unhappy minority to the stake, it was not wonderful that Infidelity should also be considered a crime. But now, when a Churchman no more thinks of persecuting a Calvinist, or a Calvinist of persecuting a Churchman, than we think of punishing a man because he happens to be taller, or shorter, than ourselves; it is truly strange that there should be any one who can so blind himself as not to see, that the same reasons which make him a friend to toleration in other cases, bind him also to tolerate Infidelity.[120]

Hence, for example, Mill's dismay when in 1823 the pawnbroker Mr
Connell was fined in Ireland not for refusing to give evidence, or for
withholding a solemn affirmation that what he would say would be true, but
for refusing to take the oath, the terms of which violated his principles.[121]
Mill later stated his general response to such matters in these terms: 'The
man, be he Christian or Atheist who endures torture or ignominy because he
will not swerve from his convictions is to me a martyr, and I should detest
myself if I could not venerate him as he deserves.'[122] Hence also Mill's
attitude towards the secularist Charles Bradlaugh, to which reference has
already been made. All of which underlines the distance between Locke and
Mill on the question of toleration, for Locke was not in favour of according
atheists (or Roman Catholics) toleration under the law;[123] reminds us that
Joseph Priestley, yet another Unitarian (a disproportionate number of whom
influenced Mill), was in the van in arguing for toleration for all;[124] and
explains both the stance of those of Mill's critics who thought that he had
gone too far in denying the state the right to punish atheists,[125] and the
pleasure of Bain and Grote at Mill's openness on the issue of irreligious
opinions.[126]

Other criticisms flowed thick and fast. Edward Lucas observed in *The
Dublin Review* that in this essay of two hundred pages 'the reader looks in
vain for a definition' of 'liberty'. Rubbing salt in the wound, he continues,
'This is the more astonishing because, in one of the early chapters of his
book on Logic, Mr. Mill himself lays down what is tolerably self-evident
that the first rule of logic is to see that terms be accurately defined.'[127] He
further expresses puzzlement that when enquiring what is the principle of
utility to which all appeal on ethical questions is to be made, we are told that
utility is 'founded on the permanent interests of man as a progressive being.
Now we have always supposed that an ultimate appeal must be to a first
principle. But no; here we have an ultimate appeal based on something as
unsubstantial as itself, viz., upon "permanent interests", which are neither
explained nor even alluded to further, except to say that they are founded on
the progressive character of human nature.'[128] All of which is to explain
what is vague by what is vaguer still.

Joseph Parker was equally perplexed by Mill's refusal adequately to
analyse crucial terms in his argument. It is central to Mill's case that power
may legitimately be exercised over individuals only in order to prevent harm
to others. Does Mill mean moral harm, or physical harm (asks Parker), and
in any case what of the fact that people differ so radically over what
constitutes harm?[129] Again, Parker finds a contradiction in the fact that
whereas Mill opens by affirming 'utility as the ultimate appeal on all ethical
questions', he shortly answers an objection by complaining that 'This mode
of thinking makes the justification of restraints on discussion not a question
of the truth of the doctrines but of their usefulness.'[130]

A number of Mill's early critics denied one of his basic assumptions,
namely, that individuality was being stifled by conformism. James Fitzjames

Stephen robustly found Mill 'distinctly wrong' in supposing that 'originality of character is ceasing to exist'. On the contrary, 'There probably never was a time when men who have any sort of originality or independence of character had it in their power to hold the world at arm's length so cheaply.'[131] By way of tempering such criticisms, Peter Nicholson has reminded us, first, that Mill was well aware that he lived in a period of transition, and that according to his autobiographical reflections his objective in *On Liberty* was to utter cautions appropriate to a future period in which old creeds had been replaced by new; and, secondly, that some of Mill's contemporary critics were more than somewhat myopic as regards the socio-intellectual constraints which they took for granted.[132]

A still more frequent charge has been that Mill, oddly, turns out to be a libertarian of a dubiously rule-bound kind.[133] Joseph Parker may set the scene for us. He quotes Mill as saying both that 'All that makes existence valuable to anyone, depends on the enforcement of restraints upon the actions of other people', and 'Mankind are greater gainers by suffering each other to live as seems good to themselves, than by compelling each to live as seems good to the rest.' These assertions, he declares, once again reveal Mill as in self-contradiction.[134] If Parker found Mill self-contradictory within a single volume, James Orr offered the same criticism from a broader base:

> This writer, who has no choice but to be a Necessitarian, is yet an enthusiastic advocate of 'Liberty'. In his essay on that subject he claims for every man the right to think and act for himself, uninfluenced by authority or the opinions of others; while in the essay on 'The Utility of Religion' his thesis is that the benefits at present got from religion might all be secured by a system of rules, if only sufficiently reinforced by authority, education and social opinion.[135]

The latter point here is echoed in *On Liberty* when Mill contends that 'The right inherent in society to ward off crimes against itself by antecedent precautions, suggests limitations to the maxim, that purely self-regarding misconduct cannot properly be meddled with in the way of prevention or punishment.'[136]

I shall return to the question-begging phrase, 'purely self-regarding misconduct' shortly, but first it is proper to point out that on occasion Mill shows himself to be thoroughly aware of the tension between his utilitarian principle and his commitment to constraints both legal and social (disapproval, ostracism, and the like) upon the conduct of individuals: 'It is a most painful position to a conscientious and cultivated mind, to be drawn in contrary directions by the noblest of all objects of pursuit, truth, and the general good.'[137] In keeping with this tension, Joseph Hamburger has sought a *via media* between Cowling's rigorist interpretation of Mill and that of those ultra-liberals who present him as an unreconstructed libertarian. He presents Mill 'as he presented himself, as advocating both social controls *and* liberty'.[138] As in other connections, Mill did not stay to smooth out the joins in his theory, which is as much dictated by practical as by theoretical concerns. Hence Plamenatz's just verdict that what Mill is

> concerned to do is not to show that there are good utilitarian grounds for the non-interference he advocates, but to determine the limits of the interference which he regards as permissible. It is in this sense that Mill, in his *Liberty*, in [*sic*] untrue to his professed utilitarian principles. He leaves undone all those things that a utilitarian ought to do, but what he does is as well worth doing as anything he ever attempted.[139]

In the opinion of A.D. Lindsay (not to mention a number of theologians who wished to take due account of sin), Mill's 'fault was to believe too strongly in the improvability of society by education and political machinery'.[140] I find it difficult to disagree with this. Hamburger adds the point that Mill's oscillation between theory and practice, utilitarian principle and sociolegal repression results from the uneasy blend in his thought of Enlightenment empiricism in its form sceptical of authority, and his Coleridgian requirement of societal stability and order.[141] My way of stating the point in its bearing upon ethics is to say that the legacy of the eighteenth-century understanding of the orders of society with their implications for 'my station and its duties' consorted uneasily with Mill's Romantic notion of human society as an organism. This explains both the somewhat aristocratic credence he places in society's 'elders and betters' and his dim view of the standards and insight of the *plebs* ('the present low state of the human mind'[142]) and his vision of a harmonious society the like of which none of us has yet seen.

This reference to society returns me to the question-begging phrase, 'purely self-regarding misconduct' – or conduct. A long line of criticism accuses Mill, in the interests of asserting individual liberties, of overlooking the societal aspects of ethics. With what justification, it is asked, do we suppose that any action is purely self-regarding? Do not all actions have social implications? Of Mill's critics, if W.L. Courtney succinctly recommended that 'the difference between self-regarding and social acts ... be ... relegated to the limbo of detected impostures',[143] R.H. Hutton pressed these questions as strongly as anyone else. He argues that

> Social indifference will result, not in individual vitality, but in individual indifference ... In spite of Mr. Mill's authority, we hold that if his object be, as he states, to encourage the growth of those more bold and massive types of character which he mourns over as extinct, it will be more wise, as well as more practicable, to select as his means to that end the purifying of social judgments from their one-sidedness than to attempt the complete suspension of them on certain tabooed subjects.[144]

Warming to his theme, Hutton predicts that

An aggregate of individually free minds, if they are to be held asunder from natural social combinations by the stiff framework of such a doctrine as Mr. Mill's, would not make in any true or deep sense a free society or a free nation ... It is strange that, while Mr. Mill lays so much and such just stress on the liberty of individual thought and expression, he should quite ignore the equally sacred liberty of social and national thought and expression.[145]

Mill's mistake is to regard society only as an arbiter between individuals, and not as an organism having a 'common life of which all its members partake'. Hence, Mill's sole guard against social bigotry is 'to erect, by common consent, every individual human mind into an impregnable fortress, within the walls of which social authority shall have no jurisdiction'.[146]

As H.S. Jones has remarked, 'it is striking that much of Hutton's argument would have gone down well with the author of *Representative Government* [i.e. Mill]'.[147] This is simply another way of saying that on other occasions and in other places Mill redresses the disturbed balance. In this connection R.W. Church emerges as a harbinger of Jones, for in his 1860 review of *On Liberty* he refers to Mill's essay on Coleridge, in which he 'set forth the importance of that complex social phenomenon called national character' and showed himself alert to the importance of 'a strong and active bond of cohesion ... which comes with the mutual sympathy of men, who feel themselves one in purpose and in their view of life and its ends'.[148] Indeed, Church almost quotes Mill, who declared that an 'essential condition of stability in political society, is a strong and active principle of cohesion among the members of the same community and state'.[149] We might also note that one of Mill's criticisms of Bentham's philosophy was that

A theory ... which considers little in an action besides that actions's *own* consequences ... will be most apt to fail in the consideration of the greater social questions – the theory of organic institutions and general forms of polity; for those (unlike the details of legislation) to be duly estimated, must be viewed as the great instruments of forming the national character; or carrying forward the members of the community towards perfection, of preserving them from degeneracy.[150]

This accords well with his practice in the political and social arenas: in connection with Catholic Emancipation, for example, where he has no compunction about appealing to the judgment of 'the public mind'.[151]

Mill's phrase, just quoted, 'carrying forward the members of the community towards perfection', prompts two further observations concerning Mill's view of liberty. First, many of his critics have complained that uppermost in his mind is negative liberty, that is, the freedom of the individual not to be unwarrantably interfered with from without. But the quoted words have a positive ring. Indeed, Bernard Semmel has gone so far as to argue that *On Liberty* 'was in fact a tract whose major purpose was to advocate the positive freedom of self-development ... of the German philosophers'.[152] It is not, indeed, difficult to find statements in the text which bear out this interpretation: 'The only freedom which deserves the name, is that of pursuing our own good in our own way, so long as we do not attempt to deprive others of theirs, or impede their efforts to attain it.'[153] But it seems to me that what was of equal importance to Mill was the conviction that the objective could be reached only by the route of negative freedom: there must be no untoward imposition upon the individual from others or from the state. As Noel Annan said of this tract, 'It is a solemn reminder how important it is to keep alive the idea of *negative* liberty, that is to say the right to allow people to go their own way even if it is to hell.'[154] In my judgment Richard Vernon achieves the proper balance:

> As for the notion of negative freedom, we must distinguish between two things at least: the definition of freedom, and the reasons for valuing it. There is no problem in seeing in Mill an appropriately 'negative' definition of freedom, as the absence of coercive restraint ... But there is no reason why the case for advocating negative freedom should not include its contribution to a positive conception of human virtue.[155]

Secondly, Mill's phrase about members of the community being carried forward towards perfection throws into relief conviction which underlies Mill's entire socio-ethical position, namely, that humanity is in progress.[156] Indeed, what he believes about progress provides the context for the articulation of his utilitarian creed: 'I regard utility as the ultimate appeal on all ethical questions; but it must be utility in the largest sense, grounded on the permanent interests of man as a progressive being.'[157] But all is not as straightforward as it seems, for in this connection, as in others, it is difficult to pin Mill down precisely. On the one hand he values freedom of thought and discussion, because absolute intellectual certainty is an elusive commodity; on the other hand he looks forward to a time of settled convictions – indeed to the age of the Religion of Humanity, but even then there is something which makes him suspicious of the existentially static. The following assertions exemplify each attitude. On *freedom of thought and discussion valued*:

> To call any proposition certain, while there is any one who would deny its certainty if permitted, but who is not permitted, is to assume that we ourselves, and those who agree with us, are the judges of certainty, and judges without hearing the other side.[158]

On *the prospect of settled convictions*:

> As mankind improve, the number of doctrines which are no longer disputed or doubted will be constantly on the increase: and the well-being of mankind may

almost be measured by the number and gravity of the truths which have reached the point of being uncontested.[159]

On *the suspicion of the existentially static*:

> There is no reason that all human existence should be constructed on some one or some small number of patterns. If a person possesses any tolerable amount of common sense and experience, his own mode of laying out his existence is the best, not because it is the best in itself [which would be a disapproved-of intuition], but because it is his own mode. Human beings are not like sheep; and even sheep are not undistinguishably alike.[160]

Undeterred, Mill continued to juggle these three balls, throwing now one, now another, higher than the others.

Our task now is to probe a little further Mill's hostility to intuitionism, for on this his advocacy of utilitarianism, negatively, turns. Then, after some concluding remarks on Mill's libertarianism in relation to institutional religion, we shall be in a position to consider his desired alternative to all existing religions, the Religion of Humanity.

III

The motivation of Mill's anti-intuitionist campaign (it is not too much to call it that) is his disapproval of the way in which adherents of that philosophy unwarrantably claim certitude (however much they may differ from others who have different certitudes) and, all too frequently, seek to impose their allegedly assured truths upon others, thereby violating liberty of thought and discussion and threatening individuality. Intuitionism thereby becomes a tool in the hands of those who, for whatever reason, wish to maintain the status quo, whether social, political or ecclesiastical:

> The practical reformer has continually to demand that changes be made in things which are supported by powerful and widely spread feelings, or to question the apparent necessity and indefeasibleness of established facts ... There is therefore a natural hostility between him and a philosophy which discourages the explanation of feelings and moral facts by circumstances and association, and prefers to treat them as ultimate elements of human nature; as philosophy which is addicted to holding up favourite doctrines as intuitive truths, and deems intuition to be the voice of Nature and of God, speaking with an authority higher than that of our reason.[161]

In this quotation the words 'hostility' and 'addicted' are telling; they express something of Mill's abhorrence of any appeal to an authority 'higher than that of our reason'. It should, however, be pointed out that in less belligerent mood Mill could calmly accord intuition a place in the logical scheme of things:

> Truths are known to us in two ways: some are known directly, and of themselves; some through the medium of other truths. The former are the subject of intuition, or Consciousness; the latter, of inference. The truths known by intuition are the original premises from which all others are inferred … Examples of truths known to us by immediate consciousness, are our own bodily sensations and mental feelings.[162]

This qualification suggests that Mill's anti-intuitionist invective is reserved for those who abuse the deliverences of consciousness, and employ them in untoward ways:

> The notion that truths external to the mind may be known by intuition or consciousness, independently of observation and experiment, is, I am persuaded, in these times, the great intellectual support of false doctrines and bad institutions. By the aid of this theory, every inveterate belief and every intense feeling, of which the origin is not remembered, is enabled to dispense with the obligation of justifying itself by reason, and is erected into its own all-sufficient voucher and justification. There never was such an instrument devised for consecrating all deep seated prejudices.[163]

As early as 1842, Mill had expressed to Comte his opposition to what he called the 'ontological' school of thought, by which he meant the intuitionism of those in the wake of 'the German school', that is, Kant, Fichte, Hegel and their heirs. He thought it necessary to defeat this school since it 'alone is essentially theological and since its philosophy here presents itself as the national support of the old social order, and not only in terms of Christian, but even of Anglican ideas'.[164] In a letter of 1854, Mill did not leave his German correspondent, Theodor Gomperz, guessing as to his view of the source of the infection. He declared his opposition to

> the theory of innate principles so unfortunately patronized by the philosophers of your country, & which through their influence has become the prevailing philosophy throughout Europe. I consider that school of philosophy as the greatest speculative hindrance to the regeneration so urgently required, of man and society, which can never be effected under the influence of a philosophy which makes opinions their own proof, and feelings their own justification.[165]

In his opinion none in Britain had greeted the alien philosophy more enthusiastically than William Hamilton[166] and Henry Longueville Mansel, the latter of whom Mill represents as a disciple of the former – a representation which in general terms is sufficiently defensible. Mill pursued both of them relentlessly and not entirely fairly. As he confided to Bain, 'It almost goes against me to write so complete a demolition of a brother-philosopher after he is dead, not having done it while he was alive – & the more when I consider what a furious retort I shd infallibly have brought upon myself had he lived to make it.'[167]

Mill seems to have been particularly displeased with Hamilton because at first he had thought him an ally in maintaining the relativity of knowledge; and indeed, Hamilton did maintain that all our knowledge of mind and matter is relative, and that we know nothing of existence in itself.[168] But when Mill discovered that Hamilton's tying of knowledge to phenomena was with a view to admitting much else as belief, Mill swiftly cooled and protested. To Bain, for example, he described Hamilton's doctrine of the relativity of knowledge as 'little better than a play upon the word knowledge, since he maintains that a great mass of Belief, differing from Knowledge in the mode but not in the certainty of conviction, may philosophically & ought morally to be entertained respecting the attributes of the Unknowable'.[169]

At the heart of Mill's complaint is that Hamilton and those in his wake are too easily persuaded that, because they are psychologically compelling, certain convictions originate in intuition, whereas in fact they are inferred from experience. He does not deny that 'What we feel, we cannot doubt that we feel';[170] it is the presumed intuitive nature of many of these deliverances of consciousness that he queries. More precisely, he holds that the laws of association or, in the terms of another class of thinker, the categories of the understanding, 'are capable of creating, out of the data of consciousness which are uncontested, purely mental conceptions, which become so identified in thought with all our states of consciousness, that we seem, and cannot but seem, to receive them by direct intuition'.[171] It is difficult, Mill continues, to dispute that we have affirmations of consciousness; the dispute concerns whether these are original or acquired; and the question whether they are acquired is difficult and too infrequently tackled.

The plot thickens, from the point of view of religion, when Mill queries Hamilton's doctrine that these 'cognitions at first hand', 'as the essential conditions of our knowledge … *must* be accepted as true'. Otherwise we are in the position of supposing that 'God is a deceiver, and the root of our nature a lie.'[172] Here, just below the surface, is the appeal to authority to which Mill so stoutly objects. In reply, he urges that, by making the Creator's veracity the proof of the trustworthiness of our consciousness, Hamilton simply presses us to query the basis of the Creator's veracity. This, says Mill, can be known only by intuition or by evidence, but in either case these rest in the last resort on consciousness. Hence, 'Religion, thus itself resting on the evidence of consciousness, cannot be invoked to prove that consciousness ought to be believed.'[173] When this is overlooked, we find that, in practical religious terms, many who enjoy 'elevated feelings … either dislike or disparage all philosophy, or addict themselves with intolerant zeal to those forms of it in which intuition usurps the place of evidence, and internal feeling is made the test of objective truth'.[174]

The evils thus depicted are never closer at hand than in connection with the Unconditioned. It is at this point that Mill turns his attention to Mansel, whose 'peculiar doctrines were made the justification of a view of religion which I hold to be profoundly immoral – that it is our duty to bow down in worship before a Being whose moral attributes are affirmed to be unknowable by us, and to be perhaps extremely different from those which, when we are speaking of our fellow-creatures, we call by the same names'.[175]

With such Hamiltonian phrases as 'A God understood would be no God at all'[176] echoing in his mind, Mansel takes up the Scot's view that the Unconditioned is conceivable only as the negative of the Conditioned. It follows that reason cannot lead us to God: 'Of the Nature and Attributes of God in His Infinite Being, Philosophy can tell us nothing: of man's inability to apprehend that Nature, and why he is thus unable, she tells us all that we can know, and all that we need to know.'[177] Mansel does not deny that 'human reason is capable of attaining to some conception of a Supreme Being',[178] but reason's deliverances in this area are approximations only. In this field, therefore, reason is a coordinate authority only, not the primary authority. Even when philosophers through the ages have spoken of the Infinite and the Absolute, they have neglected the concept of personality; and 'The God demanded by our moral and religious consciousness must be a *Person*.'[179] We may believe in such a God, 'though we are unable, under our present conditions of thought, to *conceive the manner in which* the attributes of absoluteness and infinity coexist with those which constitute personality'.[180] The grounds of our belief lie in God's revelation in the Bible, and the deliverances of revelation take precedence over those of reason. This is not to say that our submission to the authority of revelation causes the evaporation of the antinomies with which reason leaves us: for example, that God is both the absolute being (and hence unrelated to anything else) and the cause of all things (and hence related to all else).[181] Nevertheless,

> an examination of the Limits of Religious Thought leads us ultimately to rest not on Reason but on Faith; appeals, not to our knowledge, but to our ignorance; and shews us that our intellectual trial in this life is analogous to our moral trial, that as there are real temptations to sin which nevertheless do not abrogate the duty of right conduct, so there are real temptations to doubt, which nevertheless do not abrogate the duty of belief.[182]

This is consistent with Mansel's exposition of the modes of religious intuition:

> These are the *Feeling of Dependence* and the *Conviction of Moral Obligation*. To these two facts of inner consciousness may be traced, as to their sources, the two great outward acts by which religion in various forms has been manifested among

men; *Prayer*, by which they seek to win God's blessing on the future; and *Expiation*, by which they strive to atone for the offences of the past.[183]

All of this was, to Mill, a capitulation to irrational authoritarianism. Mansel's book, he thunders is 'absolutely loathsome'.[184] Furthermore, it fosters an immoral view of God, for if we cannot use the moral terms we use of one another of God, because God is the Unconditioned and the divine goodness is utterly distinct from the human, then we are left with a God above morality who may be nothing more than a capricious tyrant. Because we do not know the ways of such a God, Mansel argues, we cannot rationally reconcile the infliction of suffering, for example, with infinite goodness; but we need not doubt that these things can be reconciled.[185] This prompted Mill's violent outburst:

> Whatever power such a being may have over me, there is one thing which he shall not do: he shall not compel me to worship him. I will call no being good, who is not what I mean when I apply that epithet to my fellow-creatures; and if such a being can sentence me to hell for not so calling him, to hell I will go.[186]

Mill notes a concession on Mansel's part. He does admit that such qualities as justice and goodness, as conceived by us, bear some likeness to God's justice and goodness. Mill retorts that this subverts his entire argument and fails to save him. For it raises the question whether this imperfect likeness, which is said to be distinct from God's qualities, agrees with what humans call goodness and justice. If it does, the rationalists are right; if it does not, the divine attribute is wrongly called goodness. For 'Unless there be some human conception which agrees with it, no human name can properly be applied to it; it is simply the unknown attribute of a thing unknown; it has no existence in relation to us, we can affirm nothing of it, and owe it no worship.'[187]

It is not necessary to pursue the Mill–Mansel dispute through all its thickets.[188] The general lines of the debate have been sufficiently indicated; but I do wish to underline its importance, and to make two concluding points. First, it would be quite wrong to suppose that Mill alone abhorred Mansel's views. On the contrary, his Anglican contemporary, F.D. Maurice, came out against him in the interest of reason as 'candle of the Lord' – a line of thought flowing down at least from the Cambridge Platonists, and in defence of the doctrine of the Incarnation, integral to which is the claim that in the Logos made flesh God has made himself known.[189] The two spoke past each other, Mansel making his epistemological case, and Maurice his religious response: 'The controversy resembles what one might imagine to have taken place had a discussion ever happened between Aristotle and one of the Minor Prophets, except that Mansel wrote much better than Aristotle and Maurice more copiously than any Minor Prophet.'[190] In more restrained tones James Martineau pointed out, against Mansel, that 'to a mind disqualified in its struggle for a "Philosophy of the Infinite", there can be made no Revelation of the Infinite … if natural religion be impossible, *through incapacity in the subject*, so is supernatural … Our author's logic, then, in mowing down its thistle-field, inconsiderately mows off its own legs.'[191] Others accused Mansel of legitimating agnosticism.[192] On the other hand, in our own time, some theologians have embraced a fideistic position and have thus placed themselves, consciously or otherwise, in Mansel's succession.[193]

Secondly (and this is more to our present purpose), Mill was by no means left unscathed by the theologians of his day. Thus an anonymous writer concludes an incisive tract by saying that Mansel

> has shown that if – as Mr. Mill declares – we have no immediate knowledge of God, it follows as an inevitable consequence that a so-called philosophy which presumes to dictate *à priori* conditions to which every divine Revelation must conform, and nonconformity to which proves any professed Revelation not to be divine, is unphilosophical. He has shown that if – as Mr. Mill declares – all our knowledge of God is relative, a so-called Rationalism which presumes to reject certain statements concerning Him – not as being unsupported by sufficient evidence, but simply as being inconsistent with some of our conceptions, is irrational. These were the two conclusions which Mansel sought to establish by his argument, and these he has established completely.[194]

With this we may leave this skirmish and pass to our concluding subject of enquiry in this chapter: Mill's view of the Church as an institution.

IV

Lest an account of Mill's views regarding religious institutions should appear as an intrusion into an otherwise philosophico-theological study, let it be remembered that Mill's overriding intentions were in the direction of practice, indeed, of the reform of current practice in many spheres, not least the ecclesiastical. Secondly, as we review a selection of his opinions we shall see the extent to which his positions on liberty and other topics close to his heart informed his ecclesiastical judgments. Thirdly, by rehearsing his conviction that sooner or later existing religious structures would be no more, we shall pave the way for a consideration of that better religion which he was sure would replace them.

As in other aspects of his thought, Mill's view of religion was subject to change. This is not surprising in view of his conviction, reinforced by the Saint-Simonians and Comte, that the age was one of transition, and that eventually new and more coordinated ideals would replace present ideals which, however much they lingered, were already redundant.

From Bentham and his own father, Mill had imbibed a strong lesson to the effect that religious institutions are reactionary. Bentham found the Church of England corrupt and attacked it forcefully in *The Church of Englandism and its Catechism Examined* (1819). For his part, James Mill

> held up to notice [the British constitution's] thoroughly aristocratic character: the nomination of the House of Commons by a few hundred families; the entire identification of the more independent portion, the county members, with the great landowners; the different classes whom this narrow oligarchy was induced, for convenience, to admit to a share of its power; and finally, what he called its two props, the Church and the legal profession.[195]

In this vein we find John Mill lamenting as early as 1823 that 'We are still subject to a constitution which is at best a shattered fragment of the feudal system; we are still subject to a priesthood who do whatever is yet in their power to excite a spirit of religious intolerance and to support the domination of a despotic aristocracy.' His hope lies in the spread of knowledge which 'has worked the downfall of much that is mischievous', and will not 'spare any institution the existence of which is pernicious to mankind'.[196] However, Mill was under no illusion that the end was yet in sight. While he himself believed that 'it is of the nature of the human mind to be progressive',[197] he well knew that the forces of reaction were strong, and nowhere stronger than in the Church of England. Hence his view, expressed five years later, that the established clergy 'by a sort of moral necessity must be, and at any rate always is, the bitter enemy' of education: 'When I say an established clergy I mean any clergy, which is paid on condition of teaching a particular creed, but more especially a clergy connected with the governing powers of the state, and bound by that connexion to the support of certain political tenets as well as religious ones.'[198]

The Church of England, Mill declares, compounds its inadequacy by being not only reactionary, but sectarian:

> The Establishment, in its present state, is no corrective, but the great promoter of sectarianism; being itself, both in the exclusiveness of its tenets, and in the spirit of the majority of its clergy, a thoroughly sectarian institution. Its very essence is subscription to articles, and the bond of union which holds its members together is a dead creed, not a living spirit.[199]

As for the Oxford Movement of Pusey and his friends – 'a new Catholic school without the Pope' – Mill informed Gustave D'Eichthal that its members 'reprobate the "right of private judgment" & consider *learning* rather than original thinking the proper attribut[ion] of a divine. They discourage the Methodistical view of religion which makes devotional feeling a state of *strong excitement*, & inculcate rather a spirit of humility and self-mortification ... It is one of the forms ... of the reaction of Anglicanism against Methodism, incredulity & rationalism.'[200]

All of this explains Mill's early adverse reaction to Coleridge's idea of the value of institutions, including religious ones, as conserving forces. The sad truth is that 'The people in general have not, nor ever had, any reason or motive for adhering to the established religion, except that it was the religion of their political superiors: and in the same ratio as their attachment to those superiors has declined, so has their adherence to the established church.'[201] As for the 'superiors', 'the fall of the Church will be the downfal [*sic*] of the aristocracy, as depositaries [*sic*] of political power. When all the privileged orders insist upon embarking in the same vessel, all must naturally perish in the same wreck'.[202]

Influenced both by his own observations, by his historical reflections[203] and by the teaching of Comte, Mill increasingly felt that the best way forward would be by the dissociation of the temporal and spiritual powers. He was 'thoroughly convinced of the great principle you [that is, Comte] alone among our contemporary philosophers have enunciated, that of the definitive separation of the temporal and spiritual powers. Incontestably, these two must develop in a totally distinct manner [from each other], a fact which to my view does incidentally not imply that it is impossible for the same individual to participate, up to a point, in both fields'.[204] By 1843, in a review of Michelet's *History of France*, Mill felt that he could even praise Hildebrand for the way in which he had strengthened the Church over against the state – a sentiment which set Mill apart from some of the more anti-clerical thinkers of the French Englightenment.

At the same time, Coleridge's continuing influence upon Mill, originally so important following his breakdown of 1826, is signified by a different strand of his thinking upon Church and state. Coleridge's distinction between the shadow and the substance of the established Church taught him that a radical rupture of the *status quo* might do more harm than good, not least because many within the Church of England were striving for its reform, and were in that respect akin to the Dissenting voluntaries.[205] After all,

> in all political societies which have had a durable existence, there has been some fixed point; something which men agreed in holding sacred; which, wherever freedom of discussion was a recognised principle, it was of course lawful to contest in theory, but which no one could either fear or hope to see shaken in practice.

Mill emphasizes the fact that he is not thinking in terms of narrow nationalisms, but of

> a principle of sympathy, not of hostility; of union, not of separation. We mean a feeling of common interest among those who live under the same government, and are contained within the same natural or historical boundaries.[206]

Not, indeed, that Mill had much confidence that the Church of England could serve effectively in a unifying capacity. He did not renege on his view of 1831:

> I certainly think it desirable that there should be a conservative branch of the legislature; and that there should be a national clergy or clerisy, like that of which Coleridge traces the outline … If therefore I thought that the present Peerage & Clergy would ever consent to become the peerage of a government constituted on anti-jobbing principles, & the clergy of a non-sectarian church, I should pray for their continuance. But they never will.[207]

To the end of his days Mill retained the opinion he expressed during the election of 1865, namely, that there ought to be no such thing as a State Church, 'but he did not think the time had yet come when it would be any use to try to abolish it'.[208]

Mill thus came to persuade himself that, whereas at first he had found the thought of it intolerable because the task of the clergy was to lead worship, not to teach, and the people, who are the Church, should not have teaching foisted upon them by those who are politically imposed upon them,[209] teaching given by representatives of the established Church in schools was permissible provided it were done with integrity. He praises Coleridge, however, for showing that, the principle apart, in practice the Church of England is in no fit state to act in this matter. He also applauds Coleridge's plea that there might be an 'endowed class, for the cultivation of learning, and for diffusing its results among the community'.[210] He much regrets that endowments, which might have been used in this way, never have been; and while he thinks it in order for the state to administer endowments, it is not the state's business to determine what those it supports financially should teach.

Mill argues that any public instruction in religion 'must be such as does not clash with the moral convictions of the majority of the educated classes'.[211] Since, in Christian countries, moral convictions are inextricably interwoven with religious ones, religious instruction cannot be excluded from the curriculum. But there must be no bigotry, whether of Pope or bibliolater. In this connection, as in others, he endorses Coleridge's view that the appeal to infallibility in either case is untenable.[212]

Not far below the surface of Mill's thinking upon all the topics currently under review is his conviction regarding the importance of religious liberty. He favours the admission of Jews to Parliament;[213] he supports moves to relieve Dissenters of legislation adverse to them regarding marriage, admission to the universities and the like;[214] he advocates liberty for the Puseyites within the Church of England;[215] and he speaks up for the laity who constitute the Church, over against its clergy in regard to public worship.[216]

Although he thinks that England's religious establishment will remain intact for the foreseeable future, Mill never loses his vision of a time when there will be a convergence of values and institutions. In the meantime both philosophers and religious believers have work to do:

> Whatever some religious people may think, philosophy will and must go on, ever seeking to understand what can be made understandable; and, whatever some philosophers may think, there is little prospect at present that philosophy will take the place of religion, or that any philosophy will be speedily received in this country, unless supposed not only to be consistent with, but even to yield collateral support to, Christianity. What is the use, then, of treating with contempt the idea of a religious philosophy? Religious philosophies are among the things to be looked for, and our main hope ought to be that they may be such as fulfil the conditions of a philosophy – the very foremost of which is, unrestricted freedom of thought.[217]

In the event Mill sought more than a religious philosophy compatible with Christianity. He advocated a religion which he was sure would, in time, replace Christianity. To his aspiration in this connection we must now turn.

Notes

1   Letter of Sidgwick to J.R. Mozley of 30 July 1881, in Arthur Sidgwick and Eleanor Mildred Sidgwick, *Henry Sidgwick: A Memoir*, London: Macmillan, 1906, p.357.
2   Ibid., p.358.
3   H.S. Solly, review of Mill's *Three Essays on Religion*, in *The Inquirer*, 28 November 1874, 774(c). For Solly (1848–1925) see *The Inquirer*, 4 April 1925, 213. He was trained at Manchester New College under James Martineau.
4   So Joseph Hamburger, *John Stuart Mill on Liberty and Control*, Princeton: Princeton University Press, 1999, p.71. Hamburger draws upon William Blackstone, *Commentaries on the Laws of England*, ed. Thomas A. Green, Chicago: University of Chicago Press, 1979, and also points out that as late as 1883, James Fitzjames Stephen, in his *A History of the Criminal Law of England*, London: Macmillan, 1883, declared that 'The unexpressed assumption on which all legislation and government from the conversion of the English from heathenism to our own days has proceeded, has been the truth of Christianity.'
5   J.S. Mill, *Autobiography*, CW, I, p.45. For Mill's reticence, see further J. Hamburger, op.cit., ch. 4. It is a running theme in Linda C. Raeder's *John Stuart Mill and the Religion of Humanity*, Columbia: University of Missouri Press, 2002.
6   As Eugene August put it, 'the superheated world of Victorian religious controversy was well avoided by any social reformer wishing to be heard on other topics with some degree of calmness'. See his *John Stuart Mill: A Mind at Large*, London: Vision, 1976, p.245.
7   Letter of Mill to Comte of 18 December 1841, in Oscar A. Haac (ed.), *The Correspondence of John Stuart Mill and Auguste Comte*, New Brunswick, NJ: Transaction Publishers, 1995, p.42.
8   Letter of Comte to Mill of 3 September 1846, ibid., p.381.
9   J.S. Mill, *Autobiography*, CW, I, p.45.
10   Idem, *On Liberty*, 1859, CW, XVIII, p.242.

11   Idem, *Auguste Comte and Positivism*, 1865, CW, X, p.332.

12   Idem, *Autobiography*, CW, I, p.274.

13   Letter of Mill to Charles Westerton of 21 June [1865], CW, XVI, p.1069. The context is Mill's critique of Mansel, to which we shall come shortly.

14   Letter of Mill to Bates of 9 November 1868, CW, XVI, p.1483. Mill admired the courage and lack of hypocrisy of Bradlaugh, who openly proclaimed views which he knew would be utterly repudiated by many. See Mill's letter to Thomas Dyke Acland of 1 December 1868, CW, XVI, p.1500, where he even draws an analogy between Bradlaugh and conscientious Ritualists and Dissenters who are willing to go to the stake for their beliefs. Cf. other letters of the same year, CW, XVI, pp.1478–9 (to Richard Marshall, 5 November 1868) and 1492 (to Mrs Elizabeth Lambert).

15   Idem, *Autobiography*, CW, I, p.47. Mill must surely mean '*necessarily* connected', since wicked unbelievers are not altogether unknown phenomena.

16   *Daily Free Press*, Aberdeen, 20 October 1874, 2.

17   B.V., *The National Reformer, Secular Advocate and Freethought Journal*, XXIV, no. 19, N.S., 8 November 1874, 291. This paper was edited by Bradlaugh. Thanks to the detective work of Graham Cranfield of The British Library I can divulge the information that 'B.V.' was the Scottish poet, James Thomson (1834–92), whose pseudonym, Bysshe Vanolis, indicates his affection for the writings of Percy Bysshe Shelley and Novalis.

18   J.S. Mill, 'Utility of Religion', CW, X, p.408. Mill could be quite off-target concerning the staying power of religion. It is ironic, for example, that in 1843 he could inform Comte of Bain's view that in Scotland 'minds are admirably prepared for the social triumph of positivism', for in that very year the 'ten years' conflict' over patronage, bound up as it was with the doughty assertion of evangelical views, came to a head, and Thomas Chalmers led the Disruption which led to the separate existence of the Free Church of Scotland, whose proponents judged that 'the Church came out'. Unlike those in the line of English Dissent these ministers and their followers were not opposed to the establishment principle, but did not wish to have non-evangelical ministers intruded upon congregations. They thought of themselves as 'the Church of Scotland (Free). Mill quotes Bain as saying in a letter, 'At a distance one can hardly believe, how very few points of every day human life are touched by theological views.' See Letter of Mill to Comte of 30 October 1843, in Oscar A. Haac (ed.), *The Correspondence of John Stuart Mill and Auguste Comte*, 205. The reality was that in parts of Scotland theological views were dividing families – something not altogether unrelated to 'every day human life.'

19   J.S. Mill, *On Liberty*, CW, XVIII, p.256.

20   Ibid., p.255.

21   Ibid.

22   Idem, 'Coleridge', 1840, CW, X, p.145.

23   Idem, 'Sedgwick's Discourse', 1830, p.70. This is a reply to the geologist Adam Sedgwick's *A Discourse on the Studies of the University*, London: Parker, 1834.

24   Idem, 'Blakey's History of Moral Science', CW, X, p.27.

25   Ibid.

26   Ibid., pp.27–8.

27   Ibid., pp.28–9.

28   Ibid., p.29.

29   'Utility of Religion', CW, X, p.417.

30   Letter of Mill to the Quaker, Robert Barclay Fox, of 23 December 1840, CW, XIII, pp.452–3.

31   I here touch upon a vast subject. See further, Alan P.F. Sell, *Dissenting Thought and the Life of the Churches. Studies in an English Tradition*, Lewiston, NY: Edwin Mellen Press, 1990, ch.7; idem, *Philosophy, Dissent and Nonconformity 1689–1920*, Cambridge: James Clarke, 2004, ch.3.

32   Letter of Mill to Fox, CW, XIII, p.453.

33   I have written an account of the atonement for ministers and laypersons in which the theme here touched upon is treated in more detail. See Alan P.F. Sell, *Christ Our Saviour*, Shippensburg, PA: Ragged Edge Press, 2000, chs3 and 4.

34   Letter of Mill to Walter Coulson of 22 November 1850, CW, XIV, p.53.

35   John Morley, 'Mr. Mill on religion', in his *Critical Miscellanies. Second Series*, London: Chapman and Hall, 1877, p.292.

36   J.S. Mill, 'Sedgwick's Discourse', CW, X, p.65.

37   Letter of Mill to Greene of 27 December 1861, CW, XV, p.758.

38   It is difficult to think of a more active period in post-Reformation Christian apologetics than the period 1850–1920. The theistic arguments and the internal 'evidences' of prophecy and miracle were still adverted to, albeit some writers struck out in new directions in the light of modern biblical criticism and evolutionary thought. For some examples, see Alan P.F. Sell, *Defending and Declaring the Faith. Some Scottish Examples 1860–1920*, Exeter: Paternoster and Colorado Springs: Helmers & Howard, 1987; *Philosophy, Dissent and Nonconformity*, ch.5; *Dissenting Thought and the Life of the Churches*, chs17, 19; Dale A. Johnson, *The Changing Shape of English Nonconformity, 1825–1925*, New York: OUP, 1999.

39   Letter of J.S. Mill to Thomas Dyke Acland of 1 December 1868, CW, XVI, p.1499.

40   Ibid.

41   Paul's classic statement of the predicament comes to mind: 'The good which I want to do, I fail to do; but what I do is the wrong which is against my will.' It is noticeable that he goes on to ask not, 'Will someone lend me an ethical textbook?' but 'Who is there to rescue me from this state of death?' (Romans 7: 19, 24).

42   Letter of Mill to Allen of 27 May 1867, CW, XVI, p.1274.

43   Psalm 14: 1; 53: 1. It is not inconceivable that Mill took an impish delight in facing the Archdeacon with an illustration in praise of a Dissenting cause.

44   J.S. Mill, 'Utility of religion', CW, X, p.406.

45   Ibid.

46   Linda C. Raeder concurs. See *John Stuart Mill and the Religion of Humanity*, 117.

47   J.S. Mill, unpublished letter to *The Reasoner and Herald of Progress*, the founder and editor of which was the secularist, George J. Holyoake, CW, XXIV, p.1084.

48   Idem, 'Utility of Religion', CW, X, pp.411–12.

49   Charles Douglas, *John Stuart Mill. A Study of his Philosophy*, Edinburgh: Blackwood, 1895, pp.253–4. For Douglas (1865–1924) see MR; A. Pyle, 'Introduction' to the reprint of Douglas's book, Bristol: Thoemmes Press, 1994.

50   Charles Douglas, *John Stuart Mill*, 1895, 252–5. Douglas quotes first 'Utility of Religion', CW, X, p.422, and then *An Examination of Sir William Hamilton's Philosophy*, CW, IX, p.36.

51   Charles Douglas, *John Stuart Mill*, 1895, 257.

52   J.S. Mill, *Auguste Comte and Positivism* (1862), CW, X, p.270.

53   Letter of Mill to Comte of 27 January 1845, *Correspondence*, p.288.

54   Idem, 'Utility of religion', CW, X, p.419.

55   Jeff Lipkes, *Politics, Religion and Classical Political Economy in Britain. John Stuart Mill and his Followers*, Basingstoke: Macmillan, 1999, p.39. Against G.H. Lewes's view that the nature of poetry is essentially religious Mill noted that this could be true only if we 'call every idea a religious idea which either grows out of or leads to, feelings of infinity & mysteriousness. If we do this, then religious ideas are the *most* poetical of all ... but surely not the *only* poetical' (Letter of Mill to Lewes of 1 March 1841, CW, XIII, p.466).

56   Letter of Mill to Thomas Dyke Acland of 1 December 1868, CW, XVI, p.1499.

57   Letter of Mill to John Pringle Nichol of 17 January [1834], CW, XII, p.210.

58   J.S. Mill, 'The universities [1]', CW, XXVI, p.349.

59   Idem, 'On genius', 1823, CW, I, p.337.

60   Idem, 'Utility of religion', CW, X, p.404.

61   Letter of Mill to Acland of 1 December 1868, CW, XVI, p.1500. Cf. Mill's article in the *Daily News*, 26 March 1849, on 'The attempt to exclude unbelievers from parliament', (CW, XXV, p.1137).

62   J.S. Mill, 'Inaugural Address delivered to the University of St. Andrews', 1867, CW, XXI, p.251.

63   C.B. Crane, 'John Stuart Mill and Christianity', *The Baptist Quarterly* (Philadelphia), VIII, 1874, 353.

64   J.S. Mill, *On Liberty*, CW, XVIII, p.265. This could almost have been written by the freethinker, B.V. He took exception to Mill's claim in 'Utility of Religion' that the immoral consequences of religion are separable from religion as such, and declares with respect to Christianity: 'I contend that the doctrines of the Fall of Man, Original Sin, of the Atonement, of Eternal Torments for unbelievers, are intensely immoral and mischievous, no less than intellectually absurd, and are of the very essence of the religion, so that in freeing itself from these it must become quite another religion, must cease to be in any honest sense Christianity at all.' See *The National Reformer*, 8 November 1874, 330.

65   J. Parker, *John Stuart Mill on Liberty. A Critique*, London: F. Pitman, 1865, pp.29–30.

66   Lying behind this sentence is a long story and a vast bibliography. But see, for example, Alan P.F. Sell, *The Great Debate. Calvinism, Arminianism and Salvation* (1982), reprinted Eugene, OR: Wipf & Stock, 1998, chs3–4; idem, *Confessing and Commending the Faith: Historic Witness and Apologetic Method*, Cardiff: University of Wales Press, 2002, pp.52–60.

67   W.G. Ward, *On Nature and Grace. A Theological Treatise. Book I. Philosophical Introduction*, London: Burns and Lambert, 1860, p.xliii.

68   J.S. Mill, *On Liberty*, CW, XVIII, p.244.

69   Idem, unpublished letter (of 1 February 1851) to the *Weekly Dispatch*, CW, XXV, p.1183.

70   Letter of Mill to James Martineau of 26 May 1835, CW, XII, p.265.

71   Letter of Mill to D'Eichthal of 10 January 1942, CW, XIII, p.497. For a brief account of 'The rise and reception of modern biblical criticism', see Alan P.F. Sell, *Theology in Turmoil: The Roots, Course and Significance of the Conservative-Liberal Debate in Modern Theology*' (1986), reprinted Eugene, OR: Wipf & Stock, 1998, ch.2.

72   Letter of Mill to Alexander Bain of 14 November 1859, CW, XV, p.646.

73   J.S. Mill, 'Diary', 7 February 1854, CW, XXVII, p.652.

74   C.L. Ten, 'Mill and liberty', *Journal of the History of Ideas*, XXX, 1969, 67; reprinted in C.L. Ten (ed.), *Mill's Moral, Political and Legal Philosophy*, Aldershot: Ashgate Publishing, 1999, pp.293–314.

75   Letter of Mill to Sterling of 20–22 October 1831, CW, XII, p.77.

76   Letter of Mill to Comte of 13 August 1846, *Correspondence*, p.377.

77   Letter of Mill to Bain of 6 August 1859, CW, XV, p.631.

78   Ibid.

79   Quoted by J.M. Robson, 'Textual Introduction' to Mill's *Utilitarianism*, CW, X, p.cxxviii.

80   J.S. Mill, *On Liberty*, CW, XVIII, p.250.

81   See further, Gertrude Himmelfarb, *On Liberty and Liberalism: The Case of John Stuart Mill*, San Francisco: ICS Press, 1990, pp.36–56. Cf. Mill's letter to Carlyle of 18 May 1833, CW, XII, p.153.

82   Anon., 'Christian ethics and John Stuart Mill', *Dublin University Magazine*, LIV, October 1859, 396.

83   John Morley, *Recollections*, London: Macmillan, 1917, I, p.60.

84   J.S. Mill, *On Liberty*, CW, XVIII, p.217.

85   Cf. Bernard Semmel, *John Stuart Mill and the Pursuit of Virtue*, New Haven: Yale University Press, 1984, p.165: 'The conflict between philosophical liberty and

necessity, between free will and determinism, was critical to the argument of *On Liberty*, in keeping with the central role it played in Mill's thought.'

86   J.S.Mill, *Autobiography*, CW, I, p.175.
87   Ibid., 177. For an account of some of those to whom Mill was intellectually indebted, see J.G. Rees, 'A phase in the development of Mill's ideas on liberty', *Political Studies*, VI, February 1958, 33–44.
88   Letter of Mill to Alexis de Tocqueville of 3 November 1843, CW, XIII, p.612.
89   See W. S. Jevons's criticism of Mill's thought in his *Pure Logic and Other Minor Works*, ed. Robert Adamson and Harriet Jevons, London: Macmillan, 1890, p.203.
90   J.S. Mill, *Diary* entry, 27 February 1854, CW, XXVII, p.657.
91   Idem, *A System of Logic Ratiocinative and Inductive*, 1843, CW, VIII, p.839.
92   Ibid., 841.
93   See, for example, C.B. Upton, 'Mill's Essays on Religion – II', *The Theological Review*, XII, 1875, 266.
94   James Drummond and C.B. Upton, *The Life and Letters of James Martineau*, London: Nisbet, 1902, II, p.277.
95   Ibid.
96   J. Martineau, *Types of Ethical Theory*, 3rd revised edn., Oxford: Clarendon Press, 1891, I, pp.xi–xiii.
97   C. Douglas, *John Stuart Mill*, 169, 170. Cf. Mill's *Logic*, CW, VIII, p.841. For his ideas on the development of character by individuals Mill was also indebted to the Unitarian minister (though CW, XIV, p.38 n.1 describes him only as 'author, journalist and public lecturer') William MacCall (1812–88), to whom he refers in his *Autobiography*, CW, I, p.152. See W. MacCall, *The Elements of Individualism. A Series of Lectures*, London: John Chapman, 1847, p.118. MacCall delivered his lectures at Crediton, where he was minister of the Presbyterian Church from 1841 to 1846 (so George Eyre Evans, *Vestiges of Protestant Dissent*, Liverpool: F. and E. Gibbons, 1897, p.61), between 9 March 1845 and 1 March 1846. For MacCall, see *The Inquirer*, 1888, 755, and *The Christian Life*, 1888, 557. I am grateful to Alan Ruston of the Unitarian Historical Society for these two references. By the end of the eighteenth century the majority of English Presbyterian churches had passed through 'Arianism' to Unitarianism. A number of chapels retained the name 'Presbyterian', even though the theology espoused by their members had changed. See Alan P.F. Sell, *Dissenting Thought and the Life of the Churches*, ch.5. See further, Valerie Wainwright, 'Discovering autonomy and authenticity in *North and South*: Elizabeth Gaskell, John Stuart Mill and the liberal ethic', CLIO, XXIII, no. 2, Winter 1994, 149–65.
98   K. Britton, *John Stuart Mill*, Harmondsworth: Penguin, 1953, p.186.
99   J.S. Mill, *On Liberty*, CW, XVIII, p.265.
100 Letter of Mill to Ward of 14 February 1867, CW, XVI, p.1241. Cf. *Logic*, CW, VIII, pp.836–67.
101 J.S. Mill, *An Examination of Sir William Hamilton's Philosophy*, CW, IX, p.469; cf. ibid., 440.
102 W. Cunningham, *The Reformers and the Theology of the Reformation*, 1862, reprinted London: The Banner of Truth Trust, 1967, 508–9. This careful paper sets out from a consideration of William Hamilton's views, and for that reason the comparison of Cunningham's conclusions with those of Mill is more than ordinarily interesting. Cf. J. Calvin, *Institutes of the Christian Religion*, 2 vols, trans. Ford Lewis Battles, ed. J.T. McNeil, Philadelphia: Westminster Press, 1961, II, ii.8–9; iii.13–14.
103 Cf. J.S. Mill, *Autobiography*, CW, I, p.260.
104 Ibid, 259.
105 Idem, *On Liberty*, CW, XVIII, pp.223–4.
106 Ibid., 224.
107 Ibid., 227.
108 Ibid., 233.

109   Ibid., 248.

110   Ibid.

111   Ibid.

112   Ibid., 250.

113   Ibid., 257.

114   See CW, XII, p.49 n.2.

115   J.S. Mill, *On Liberty*, CW, XVIII, p.261.

116   Ibid., 264.

117   Ibid., 283

118   Ibid., 289.

119   Idem, 'Law of libel and liberty of the press', 1825, CW, XXI, pp.13–14.

120   Ibid., 14. It is perhaps worth pointing out the distinction between toleration and tolerance. In the context of a paper on the law, toleration concerns the toleration of persons and groups under the law, and includes the right to free assembly, and the like – always having regard to civil safety. The majority of Dissenters were granted toleration in 1689, though the Unitarians had to wait until 1813 to be officially free in their worship and witness. The tolerance of views other than one's own implies a spirit of openness to others even where there is no agreement. It is possible to tolerate the views of those who have not been granted toleration under the law, and vice versa.

121   Idem, 'Persecution for religious principles', 1823, CW, XXII, p.47.

122   Idem, 'The Church',1828, CW, XXVI, p.419.

123   See further, Alan P.F. Sell, *John Locke and the Eighteenth-Century Divines*, Cardiff: University of Wales Press, 1997, ch.5. Locke, like many others, felt that atheists were not to be trusted, and that Roman Catholics owed allegiance to a foreign power and were therefore potentially dangerous.

124   See J. Priestley, *An Essay on the First Principles of Government, in The Theological and Miscellaneous Works of Joseph Priestley*, ed. J.T. Rutt, (1817–31), reprinted Bristol: Thoemmes Press, 1999, XXII, pp.64–5; Idem, *Various Observations relating to the Dissenters' application to Parliament for Relief from certain Penal Laws*, ibid., XXII, 478; cf. 68–76. Priestley argues that refusing toleration to atheists and Roman Catholics would foster hypocrisy and encourage the civil magistrate to become 'a vexatious inquisitor of opinions'.

125   See, for example, [Edward Lucas] in *The Dublin Review*, NS. XIII, 1869, reprinted in Andrew Pyle (ed.), *Liberty. Contemporary Responses to John Stuart Mill*, Bristol: Thoemmes Press, 1994, pp.268–9. [Lucas] contends that states must be either atheistical or the reverse. If they are religious then, since religion is the foundation of social order, they have a right to punish the publication of atheistic opinions which threaten such order. See further, J.C. Rees, *Mill and his Early Critics*, Leicester: University College Leicester, 1956.

126   See further, J. Hamburger, *John Stuart Mill on Liberty and Control*, 90.

127   [E. Lucas], 'Mill on liberty', in A. Pyle (ed.), *Liberty*, 256.

128   Ibid., 259.

129   See J. Parker, *John Stuart Mill on Liberty. A Critique*, 4–6.

130   Ibid., 9; Parker cites Mill as now at CW, XVIII, pp.224, 233.

131   J.F. Stephen, 'Mr. Mill on political liberty', *The Saturday Review*, 19 February 1859; reprinted in A. Pyle (ed.), *Liberty*, 16. Cf. R.H. Hutton in *The National Review*, and R.W. Church in *Bentley's Quarterly Review*, II, 1860, both in A. Pyle, op.cit., 81–4 and 243, respectively.

132   See Peter Nicholson, 'The reception and early reputation of Mill's political thought,' in J. Skorupski (ed.), *The Cambridge Companion to Mill*, Cambridge: CUP, 1998, pp.468–71. Nicholson cites Mill's *Autobiography*, I, 259–60.

133   The justice of this charge, or the degree to which it holds, has been widely debated. Jeff Lipkes has grouped some of the relevant authors under the classifications 'revisionist' and 'traditionalist' in *Politics, Religion and Classical Political Economy in Britain*.

John Stuart Mill and his Followers, 171. Supreme (according to some, extreme) among the former, for whom Mill is not as 'liberal' as is frequently supposed, is Maurice Cowling, *Mill and Liberalism*, Cambridge: CUP, 1963. Cf. J.C. Rees, 'The reaction to Cowling on Mill', *The Mill News Letter*, I, no. 2, Spring 1966, 2–11; idem, 'A phase in the development of Mill's ideas on liberty', 33–44. For an example of what may be termed the standard interpretation see C.L. Ten, 'Mill and liberty'.

134   J. Parker, *John Stuart Mill on Liberty*, 10. For the quotations, see CW, XVIII, pp.220, 226.

135   J. Orr, 'John Stuart Mill and Christianity', *Theological Monthly*, VI, 1891, 110. For Orr (1844–1913) see DNCBP, DSCHT, MR, ODNB; Alan P.F. Sell, *Defending and Declaring the Faith*, ch.7; Glenn G. Scorgie, *A Call for Continuity: The Theological Contribution of James Orr*, Macon, GA: Mercer University Press, 1988.

136   J.S. Mill, *On Liberty*, CW, XVIII, p.295. The writer in the *Dublin University Magazine* noticed the inconsistency between Mill's advocacy of rules and his denunciation elsewhere of Christianity as being a religion of 'Thou shalt nots'. See 'Christian ethics and John Stuart Mill', 401.

137   Idem, 'Utility of religion', CW, X, p.404.

138   J. Hamburger, *John Stuart Mill on Liberty and Control*, xvii. On p.15, Hamburger lists a number of Mill's assertions designed to exemplify Mill's commitment to the legitimacy of the morally coercive force of public opinion.

139   J. Plamenatz, *The English Utilitarians*, (1949), reprinted Oxford: Blackwell, 1966, p.126.

140   A.D. Lindsay, 'Introduction', xvii.

141   J. Hamburger, *John Stuart Mill on Liberty and Control*, xiv.

142   J.S. Mill, *On Liberty*, CW, XVIII, pp.268–9.

143   W.L. Courtney, *Life of John Stuart Mill*, London: Walter Scott, 1889, p.128. For Courtney (1850–1928) see DNCBP, MR, ODNB.

144   R.H. Hutton, in A. Pyle (ed.), *Liberty*, 90.

145   Ibid., 97.

146   Ibid., 100–01; cf.116–17.

147   H.S. Jones, 'John Stuart Mill as moralist', *Journal of the History of Ideas*, LIII, no. 2, April–June 1992, 305.

148   R.W. Church, in A. Pyle (ed.), *Liberty*, 234–5.

149   J.S. Mill, 'Coleridge', 1840, CW, X, pp.134–5.

150   Idem, 'Remarks on Bentham's philosophy', 1833, CW, X, p.9.

151   Idem, 'Ireland', CW, VI, p.62.

152   B. Semmel, *John Stuart Mill and the Pursuit of Virtue*, 14; cf. 166.

153   J.S. Mill, *On Liberty*, CW, XVIII, p.226.

154   N. Annan, 'John Stuart Mill', in H.S. Davies and G. Watson (eds), *The English Mind*, Cambridge: CUP, 1964, reprinted in J.B. Schneewind (ed.), *Mill. A Collection of Critical Essays*, London: Macmillan, 1968, p.40.

155   R. Vernon, 'J.S. Mill and the Religion of Humanity', in James E. Crimmins (ed.), *Religion, Secularization and Political Thought. Thomas Hobbes to J.S. Mill*, London: Routledge, 1989, p.176.

156   For the argument that Mill's liberalism fails because his view of progress is rooted in a false, Eurocentric, view of history, see John Gray, *Mill on Liberty: A Defence*, London: Routledge (1983), 2nd edn 1996, pp.130–58. That Mill himself was not averse to passing judgment on the philosophies of history of others is clear from his remarks in CW, XX, pp.260–61.

157   J.S. Mill, *On Liberty*, CW, XVIII, p.224.

158   Ibid., 233.

159   Ibid., 250.

160   Ibid., 270.

161   Idem, *Autobiography*, CW, I, pp.269–70.

162 Idem, *A System of Logic*, CW, VII, pp.6–7.

163 Idem, *Autobiography*, CW, I, p.233; cf. pp.269–70.

164 Letter of Mill to Comte of 11 July 1842, *Correspondence*, p.83.

165 Letter of Mill to Gomperz of 19 August 1854, CW, XIV, p.239.

166 See further Andy Hamilton, 'Mill, phenomenalism and the self', in J. Skorupski (ed.), *The Cambridge Companion to Mill*, Cambridge: CUP, 1998, pp.138–75. For William Hamilton (1788–1856) see DNCBP, ODNB; John Veitch, *Hamilton*, Edinburgh: Blackwood, 1882.

167 Letter of Mill to Bain of 22 November 1863, CW, XV, p.902.

168 See William Hamilton, *Lectures on Metaphysics and Logic*, Boston: Gould and Lincoln, 1860, I, pp.96–97.

169 Letter of Mill to Bain of January 1863, CW, XV, p.816.

170 J.S. Mill, *An Examination of Sir William Hamilton's Philosophy*, CW, IX, p.128; cf. 130.

171 Ibid., 140.

172 W. Hamilton, quoted by Mill, ibid., 132.

173 Ibid.

174 J.S. Mill, 'Utility of Religion', CW, X, p.404.

175 Idem, *Autobiography*, CW, I, p.270. For Mansel (1820–71) see DNCBP, ODNB.

176 Hamilton quotes this declaration of 'a pious philosophy' with approval. See his *Discussions on Philosophy and Literature, Education and University Reform*, London: Longman, Brown, Green and Longmans, 2nd enlarged edn, 1853, 15n.

177 H.L. Mansel, *The Limits of Religious Thought Examined in Eight [Bampton] Lectures* (1858), 5th edn, London: John Murray, 1870, p.185.

178 Ibid., vii.

179 Ibid., ix.

180 Ibid., xi.

181 For Mill's response to this point, see his *Examination*, CW, IX, p.92.

182 H.L. Mansel, *The Limits of Religious Thought Examined*, xix.

183 Ibid., 78.

184 Letter of Mill to Bain of 7 January 1863, CW, XV, p.817.

185 Mill quotes Mansel to this effect: *Examination*, CW, IX, p.101.

186 Idem, *Examination*, CW, IX, p.103; cf. pp.106–7.

187 Ibid., 107. Among divines who supported Mill on this matter was W.H. Lyttelton (1820–84), who became Canon of Gloucester. See Mill's letter to him of 21 July 1865, CW, XVI, pp.1080–81.

188 Mansel replied to Mill in his *The Philosophy of the Conditioned*, London: Alexander Strahan, 1866, and, in the edition of his *Examination* used in CW, Mill replies to this as well as to Mansel's original statement of his argument.

189 See F.D. Maurice, *What is Revelation?* Cambridge: Macmillan, 1859; and idem, *Sequel to the Inquiry, What is Revelation?* Macmillan, Cambridge, 1860. Of Maurice, Mill wrote, in a splendid example of praising with faint damns: 'I have always thought that there was more intellectual power wasted in Maurice than in any other of my contemporaries. Few of them certainly have had so much to waste' (*Autobiography*, CW, I, p.161).

190 W.R. Matthews, *The Religious Philosophy of Dean Mansel*, (Friends of Dr. Williams's Library, 10th Lecture, 1956), London: OUP, 1956, p.18.

191 J. Martineau, 'Mansel's Limits of Religious Thought', in idem, *Essays Philosophical and Theological* (1866), reprinted New York: Henry Holt, 1879, I, pp, 231–232, 223.

192 In his book, *The Philosophy of the Infinite* (1854), for example, Henry Calderwood (1830–97) sought to rescue Scottish common sense realism from the clutches of agnosticism into which he felt William Hamilton had betrayed it. For Calderwood, see ODNB, DNCBP; W.L. Calderwood and David Woodside, *The Life of Henry*

Calderwood, LLD, FRSE, London: Hodder and Stoughton, 1900. The *Life* includes a chapter on Calderwood's philosophy by A.S. Pringle-Pattison.

193   Alan Ryan's verdict is shared by many writers: 'Mansel thought it an aid to Christian belief to show that the sceptic could not attack its doctrines on rational grounds; but the way in which he rescued them from the sceptic was by making them too elusive to disbelieve. Inevitably the price he paid was making them too elusive to be believed either.' See his 'Introduction' to Mill's *Examination* of Hamilton, CW, IX, p.xxxvi. I suspect that more may be said on Mansel's behalf, and I hope in due course to pursue this matter further.

194   Anon., *Is Theism Immoral? An Examination of Mr. J. S. Mill's Arguments against Mansel's View of Religion*, Swansea: E.E. Rowse, 1877, p.58.

195   J.S. Mill, *Autobiography*, CW, I, p.95. Mill refers to James Mill, 'Periodical literature: *Edinburgh Review*', *Westminster Review*, I, January 1824, 206–9.

196   J.S. Mill, 'Speech on the utility of knowledge,' delivered to the Mutual Improvement Society, 1823, CW, XXVI, p.261.

197   Idem, 'Speech on the Church', delivered to the London Debating Society, 15 February 1828, CW, XXVI, p.424.

198   Ibid., 425.

199   Idem, 'Lord Brougham's defence of the Church establishment', 13 May, 1834, CW, VI, pp.229–30.

200   Letter of Mill to D'Eichthal of 27 December 1839, CW, XIII, pp415–16.

201   Idem, 'The spirit of the age', CW, XXII, p.313.

202   'Lord Melbourne's reason for his religion', 1834, CW, VI, p.287.

203   See, for example, his review of George Brodie's *A History of the British Empire*, 1822, in CW, p.VI.

204   Letter of Mill to Comte of 25 February 1842, *Correspondence*, p.51.

205   Idem, 'Reorganization of the Reform Party', CW, VI, pp.490–92. Not, indeed, that Mill thought that reform movements from within the Church would be successful. He thought it more likely that the Church would be 'pulled down from without'. See his Letter to Carlyle of 28 April 1834, CW, XII, p.225. For all his distaste for Whately's intuitionism, Mill, in 1831, was able to welcome his appointment as Archbishop of Dublin, for his works display 'an enlarged and liberal interpretation of religion, remote from the narrow and exclusive spirit of a sect [and unlike] the modern ascetics, who have inherited the worst qualities both of the Churchmen and the Puritans of former times, without the redeeming virtues of either'. See CW, XXIII, p.356.

206   Idem, 'Coleridge', 1840, CW, X, pp.134, 135.

207   Letter of Mill to John Sterling of 20–22 October 1831, CW, XII, pp.75–6. For further praise from Mill for Coleridge's idea of a clerisy, see CW, IV, pp.220–21.

208   Idem, as reported in CW, XXVIII, p.38.

209   See idem, CW, VI, pp.226, 245.

210   Idem, 'Coleridge', CW, X, p.150.

211   Idem, CW, VI, p.227.

212   Idem, 'Coleridge', CW, X, pp.161–2.

213   See CW, VI, p.251.

214   Ibid., 193–6.

215   See CW, XXIV, pp.816–20.

216   See CW, XXVIII, p.38.

217   J.S. Mill, 'Coleridge', CW, X, p.160.

Chapter 3

Mill's Substitute Religion

Although, as Mill famously said, 'I am ... one of the very few examples, in this country, of one who has, not thrown off religious belief, but never had it',[1] religion was never far from his mature thoughts. Indeed, to treat of Mill's philosophy in abstraction from his religious ideas may be to falsify the former. In further attempting to justify this claim I shall first consider in general terms the religion which Mill wished to substitute for all other varieties of religion (deemed abortive); I shall then discuss his creed, his underlying doctrine of humanity and his mission (I use the familiar religious terms advisedly).

I

Mill owes much of his religion to the writings of Auguste Comte,[2] though with the proviso that, in this matter as in others, Mill is nobody's clone; indeed, we may already be feeling that the further he strays from his mentors in taking account of facts which he considers they have unjustifiably neglected, the less rigorously consistent his own position becomes.

It was in 1829, three years after his breakdown, that Mill met Gustave D'Eichthal, a Saint-Simonian. Through him Mill first learned of Comte's views and, as he later wrote to Comte, this encounter assisted him in breaking from strict Benthamism.[3]

Comte's positivism grew in soil which was fertilized by the general Romantic interest in humanity: this in place of older systems of religious thought, whether Calvinist, Catholic or deistic, all of which were deemed barren in the wake of the onslaught against natural theology conducted by Hume and others. Contemporary with this was the ever-intensifying critique of doctrinal positions on predestination, providence and the like, which were branded immoral by critics ranging from the hostile to the regretful. A further impetus to fresh thinking was provided by biological science which, even before Darwin's *Origin of Species* (1859), was construing nature as an organism characterized by progress and development.

As to the analysis of 'positivism', the distinguished apologist Robert Flint judged that

> Positivism is a hopelessly ambiguous term, and has been claimed by and applied to diverse and dissimilar theories. Some consider themselves positivists because

they are positive that matter is the only reality; others because they are positive
that sensation is the source and measure of all knowledge; others because they
are positive that there is no God, no soul, and no future life; others because they
are positive that there is nothing positively certain; and others for other reasons.[4]

Among the 'other reasons' operative in Flint's own day we may mention the
attraction to a select few of the Religion of Humanity,[5] and a strain of
activism which prompted some of the metaphysically disinclined, Mill
among them, to deal with the realities of life as they were, and to attempt the
improvement of the lot of their fellows in respect of everything from diet to
drains. As grandchildren and great-grandchildren of nineteenth-century
positivism we may note in passing the logical positivism of the 1920s and
1930s, which wielded a theory of verification in such a way as to rule out
much of the most interesting discourse in which human beings have engaged
– ethical, aesthetic and religious – as, strictly, meaningless;[6] and present-day
scientism (the doctrine that scientific method alone yields truth) as
propounded in strangely unsophisticated ways by prejudiced media pundits,
clever in their own disciplines, but insufficiently wise to think it worthwhile
countering opposing views, or even carefully studying them, and this in
defiance of the way they would treat rival hypotheses in their own fields of
enquiry.[7]

Owing to the diversity of meanings which the term acquired, not to
mention the idiosyncracies of some of its prophets, positivism proved
remarkably productive of sectarianism, not least among English followers of
the Religion of Humanity, whose liturgical disagreements and personality
clashes of 1877–8 resulted in a schism. According to one report, the devotees
arrived at the crucial meeting in one cab, and left in two. But let us return to
the fountain-head.

Comte was born at Montpellier in 1798, and was married in 1825.
Temperamentally edgy to the point of violence, and somewhat less than a
'team player', he lost his position at the École Polytechnique. Mill, Grote
and others provided financial support for about one year, but when the
funding ceased Comte, who seems to have expected that others would be
honoured to lend indefinite support to such an eminent thinker as himself,
objected bitterly. On another occasion, in a mood of despair he threw himself
into the Seine, from which he was rescued by a passing soldier. He separated
from his wife in 1842, and in 1845 met Clothilde de Vaux, who was
separated from her husband. She was (at least) his Mrs Taylor, so to speak.
She became the object of his adulation:

> Irrevocably incorporated into the true Supreme Being, her tender image supplies
> me, in the eyes of all, with its best impersonation. In each of my three daily
> prayers, the adoration of the two condenses all my wishes for inward perfection
> in the admirable form in which the sublimest of the Mystics foreshadowed in his
> own way the moral motto of Positivism – (*Live for Others*).[8]

After Clothilde's death a year later, Comte visited her grave weekly and prayed to her daily. Not even his founding of the Positivist Society of Paris in 1848 assuaged his grief, and he continued disconsolate until his death in 1857.

Comte's *System of Positive Philosophy* was published in six volumes between 1830 and 1842, and his *Positive Polity* appeared between 1851 and 1854. That this latter work owed much to Clothilde is clear from the Preface, in which Comte informs us that from her he learned that the affective life takes precedence over the intellectual. In the Preface to *The Catechism of Positive Religion*, Comte confided – or, rather, proclaimed – that having already pursued 'the career of Aristotle', he was now equipped to embark upon 'that of St. Paul'. His 'great passion' for Clothilde, declared John Tulloch, 'marks the transition in M. Comte's life from the Philosopher to the Pontiff ... [H]enceforth he takes up the position of a new Priest of Humanity, the Legislator of a new religion, which, amidst the decay of theistic no less than polytheistic belief, is to preside over the future development of the human race.'[9] We may already have gathered enough to suspect that Flint was not wide of the mark in writing that Comte was 'a man of remarkable intellectual power, but also of immoderate intellectual self-conceit and arrogance'.[10]

To Comte's religion we shall return in due course, but first a brief account of the main lines of his philosophy is called for. Comte repudiates Rousseau's extreme individualism and, influenced by the socialist Henri de Saint Simon (1760–1825), replaces it with his quasi-biological motif that society is an organism of which each person is a part and, moreover, a part charged to serve the whole. It is as they are constituents of the organism that people have significance: 'the individual' is an abstraction.

With a view to explaining how this understanding of things has come about, Comte first takes a long run at history. Prompted by Condorcet's progressivism, he explains human history in terms of three successive stages. There was first the theological stage which proceeded from fetishism (that is, animism) through polytheism to monotheism. Under the impact of moral difficulties deriving from such claims as that God is good while Nature is cruel, the metaphysical stage ensued, during which previously held religious convictions were cashed in terms of abstractions, not least, 'Nature'. With the birth and spread of modern science we are on the threshold of the positivistic stage of human history. Unlike our forebears who were held in thrall by theology and metaphysics, we now see that to seek the causes of things is to embark upon a fool's errand (at which point Comte acknowledges a debt to Hume). All we can do, and it is enough, is to observe sequences and study phenomena and the laws by which they operate, and this in order to benefit humanity. Society as such is the subject matter of the new science of sociology, and in the emerging industrial order our leaders will be not metaphysicians or jurists, but scientists. By a good deal of this Mill was considerably impressed, as we shall see.

Secondly, Comte turns his attention to the classification of the sciences. He distinguishes between an abstract science such as chemistry, and a concrete science such as zoology. The laws governing the former apply to a wide field, while the latter is concerned with a delimited range of phenomena. The Positive Philosophy is concerned with the former only, for these yield widely-applicable knowledge. Comte proceeds to arrange the abstract sciences in descending order of preference, thus: mathematics, astronomy, physics, chemistry and physiology. Comte does not deny that human beings comprise Nature's highest creations, but since, epistemologically, he is limited to the consideration of phenomena, he cannot discuss human beings in terms of a mind–body distinction. For this reason (to Mill's dismay), he does not admit psychology to the ranks of the sciences. To him mental activity can be only a topic within physiology – indeed, he thinks of it in terms of phrenology.

In all of this Comte's ultimate objective is to show that now that we are on the verge of the final stage of human history we must learn all that the sciences have to teach us concerning humanity; society as such is now the subject of positive science. We must diligently learn our lessons so that we may live in the service of our fellows ('altruism' is his term) and rightly worship that Humanity which is logically prior to us all. In this worship women have a special part to play, for their sex is characterized by sympathy (the Marian – Comte was raised in the Roman Church – and/or the Clothilde factor?), and they are thus fitted to mediate between Humanity and men.

Not least because, as we shall see, Mill retained some of the theory of the Religion of Humanity whilst stoutly rejecting the religious practices enjoined by its founder, it is important for us to recognize that to Comte himself his thought was all of a piece, and that his religion was inseparable from the theoretical container from which it emerged. This is in keeping both with his Clothilde-inspired discovery of the importance of the feelings relative to the intellect, and with his conviction that knowledge is with a view to action on behalf of others. As G.H. Lewes remarked,

> Nothing can be more evident than that from the first Comte's aim was to construct a polity on the basis of science … A doctrine which furnished an explanation of the world, of man, and of society, which renovated education and organised social relations, above all, which established a spiritual power, was in all its chief functions identical with a religion.[11]

We shall return to Comte's religion in due course. For the present let us consider a selection of adverse criticisms which were levelled against Comte's general position (without at all implying that the authors to be cited found nothing valuable in his thought). Against the background of these, Mill's ambivalent and selective response to Comte's ideas will be seen more clearly in perspective.

First, some writers took issue with the law of sociology enunciated by Comte in terms of his successive historical epochs. To James M'Cosh, trained in the intuitionalist tradition of Scottish Common Sense realism and writing in 1866, this law 'is about as rash a generalization as was ever made by a Presocratic physiologist, a medieval schoolman, or a modern German speculator'.[12] He argues that far from one epoch's being succeeded by another there is an easily traceable line of philosophers from ancient times to the present day – from the Ionian philosophers through the Middle Ages to Locke, Kant, Hegel and the Scottish School – who have been at pains to show that their views support, are consistent with, or at least are not destructive of, religion. Accordingly,

It is surely an ominous circumstance, that in this the nineteenth century there should arise a system of philosophy, supported by very able men, and with very extensive ramifications and applications, especially in social science, but which contains within it no argument for the Divine existence, or sanctions to religion.[13]

One decade on, Flint, in his Baird Lecture of 1877, argued:

Theology, metaphysics and positive science, instead of following only after one another, each constituting an epoch, have each pervaded all epochs – have co-existed from the earliest times to the present day ... [W]hile each has been advancing and evolving within its proper sphere and in due relationship to the others ... they are distinguishable but not divisible.[14]

On this point Mill comes to Comte's defence. Comte, he declares, expressly states that the three stages have always coexisted and continue to do so. His point is that the theological and metaphysical residues are indefensible intellectual relics. They concern 'imaginary entities', belief in whose objective reality has now been destroyed. However, 'that belief has left behind it vicious tendencies of the human mind, which are still far enough from being extinguished'.[15]

Comte's phenomenalism came under attack from many quarters. Flint was among those who regretted Comte's limitation of phenomena to things material: 'We have a direct and immediate knowledge of thinking, feeling, and willing, and simply as phenomena these are markedly distinct from the phenomena called material.'[16] Indeed, it is the individual's mental experience alone which constitutes the final bulwark against absolute scepticism. The evidence of such experience is stronger than that supplied by the senses. Hence

The so-called positivism ... which affirms that the objects of sense are the only phenomena apprehended, instead of keeping close to facts, as it pretends to do, contradicts the facts which the experience of every moment of conscious existence testifies to in the most direct and decisive manner.[17]

Flint proceeds to challenge Comte's assumption that material phenomena are the only known existences, that upon them science properly rests, and that we know phenomena only through the senses. For if the senses are our sole means to knowledge, counters Flint, the only things we really know are sensations; but 'sensations are states of consciousness – phenomena of mind, not of matter'.[18] Hence 'The materialistic positivism of Comte is bound to abdicate in favour of the idealistic positivism of Mill, which, no less unsatisfactorily, confines all our knowledge to mental phenomena.'[19] A similar point was made by the Unitarian James Martineau. He maintains that, since all knowledge is knowledge of relations, to profess to know phenomena only is to concern ourselves with one only of a related pair: 'To forbid our thought to pass behind the screen of phenomena is to put out the very light that shows them.'[20]

In the view of many Comte's phenomenalism was not only limited, it was internally inconsistent. In Flint's opinion Comte's position was essentially materialistic; but in so far as it was this, it was not positivistic. For materialism regards matter as both substance and cause, while Comte will have no truck with causation, seeing only successions of events. *A fortiori*, Comte repudiates the final cause, reserving special animosity for the God of theism. But he does so inconsistently on the basis of the spurious argument that

> We cannot *see* causality, and therefore we cannot *know* causes … [The positivists'] entire argumentation proceeds on a superficial hypothesis as to the nature of knowledge – one which fails to note that the mind itself is the most important factor in knowledge, and that the simplest and directest experience presupposes a constitution in thought as well as in things.[21]

Furthermore, Comte illegitimately assumes belief in final causes when arguing that things fulfil their purposes inadequately and might succeed better than they do.[22] Above all, where God as final cause is in question Comte's agnosticism is shown to be inconsistent. For the only way of demonstrating the unknowability of God would be by invoking those very rational–metaphysical procedures which positivism rules out *ab initio*.[23]

A further line of adverse criticism concerns Comte's discounting of the moral consciousness. Robert Mackintosh reviewed Comte's biological–social model and pronounced upon it thus:

> Religion, at least in its historic forms, has been deposed; Christianity has been scouted; intuition has been laughed down; philosophy has been told to vanish with the ghosts before the noontide of science. Yes, but how are you going to bring men under authority when so many authorities have been sent packing? It is very convenient if you can assert the claim, the moral claim, of the community in the parable of body and members! … Yet this doctrine of the social organism is no pronouncement in the name of facts; it is a moral dictum, picturesquely stated in terms of popular science.[24]

Against the possible retort that, rather than appealing to a biological parable Comte is actually adverting to facts which demonstrate that human beings are dependent upon society and that selfishness breeds unhappiness whereas altruism conduces to happiness, Mackintosh points out that this is to introduce hedonistic considerations to which, with his aversion to individualism, a consistent Comtian positivist would be immune.[25] Indeed, it is a further charge against Comte that when setting his face against egoism he wrongly equates Christianity with it.[26] He seems fixated upon the notion that Christians are so concerned with their future state as individuals that they quite overlook that disinterested service of others which he considers to be of vital importance.[27] 'The immediate effect of putting personal salvation in the foremost place,' Comte declares, 'was to create an unparalleled selfishness, a selfishness regarding all social influences nugatory, and thus tending to dissolve public life.'[28] Any Christians who have been guilty as charged by Comte have missed a large part of the meaning of their faith – just as Comte has overlooked many New Testament exhortations which elevate altruism above selfishness. In characteristically Victorian tones Edward Caird sought to redress the balance:

> In the life of its Founder, the Christian Church has always had before it an individual type of that harmony of the spiritual and natural life, which it is its ideal to realize in all the wider social relations of man; nor, till that ideal is reached, can it be said that the Christian idea is exhausted, or that the place is vacant for a new religion, – great as may be the changes of form and expression through which Christianity must pass under the changed contitions of modern life.[29]

The implication of the above charges is that, under the impact of a sensationalism inherited from the eighteenth century, Comte too quickly banished theology and metaphysics from his purview. Indeed, according to Edward Caird, it can 'easily' be shown that his own theory 'involves a metaphysic, and ends in a theology; and that he only succeeds in concealing this from himself, because he is unconscious of the presuppositions he makes'.[30] Thus, having repudiated metaphysics because it treats universals as if they were real entities, he announced that the family, the state and humanity – universals all – are objectively real.[31] He is, says Caird, thrown by his failure to realize that his view (in oppositon to earlier varieties of individualism), that society is organic and progressive, is a further idea and not, as he seems to think, a statement of fact.[32] He did not see that his positivism was not simply a negation of earlier theology and metaphysics, but was 'essentially a new reading of experience, which implied, therefore, a new form of metaphysics and theology'.[33] Caird's former pupil, Robert Mackintosh, illustrates his similar conclusion by reference to Comte's hierarchy of the sciences:

It is a somewhat remarkable development of phenomenalism, this arrangement of
the sciences, not merely in sequence, but on a rising scale. It recalls to mind the
great Idealistic systems of Germany, so like, and so unlike, Comte's philosophy
… In spite of the prejudices of phenomenalism, a scale of values *will* assert itself
as we deal with the different branches of human knowledge. Of course Comte has
his own explanation of the origin of this scale of values. It is purely subjective, a
matter of human convenience … [But] how comes it that our subjective synthesis
does not distort the knowledge which phenomena afford, but rather brings out its
inner meaning? Comte is in a curious half-way position between phenomenalism,
to which one fact is as good as another, and idealism, to which knowledge is a
thing that objectively and really grades itself. It is a thin disguise of intellectual
helplessness when Comte asserts that we have such a grouping of phenomena in
our knowledge, but that the grouping is due merely to man's capricious regard for
the interests of his own species.[34]

We shall shortly have cause to observe the incongruity of the appeal to
phenomena and the worship of Humanity, but first we must discover how
Mill stands in relation to Comte's general philosophical approach and the
representative adverse criticisms of it which we have presented.[35]

In a letter to Comte of 15 December 1842, Mill writes,

Having had the rather rare fate in my country of never having believed in God,
even as a child, I always saw in the creation of a true social philosophy the only
possible base for the general regeneration of human morality, and in the idea of
Humanity the only one capable of replacing that of God. But there is still a long
way from this speculation and belief to the manifest feeling I experience today –
that it is fully valid and that the inevitable substitution [of Humanity for God] is
at hand.[36]

Mill's explicit precociousness may be queried; the euphoria was soon to be
tempered; the time scale for the introduction of the replacement religion was
lengthened, but the expectation that the day would come never left him.

If only because of the ambiguity of 'positivist' it is not easy to deny that
Mill was significantly influenced by positivism; but a careful sifting of the
evidence reveals that he was never a fully paid-up Comtian, and that the
older he grew the less in sympathy with Comtism he became. This shows
itself, for example, in the toning down of the eulogistic references to Comte
in later editions of Mill's *System of Logic*, first published in 1843, when
Mill's correspondence with Comte, which continued from 1841 to 1847, was
well under way.

Mill emphasizes the fact that Comte was not the originator of positivism,
nor did he claim to be:

M. Comte claims no originality for [his] conception of human knowledge … The
philosophy of Positivism is not a recent invention of M. Comte, but a simple
adherence to the traditions of all the great scientific minds whose discoveries
have made the human race what it is.[37]

Comte was the man of the hour in the sense that on the basis of intellectual demolitions and developments the time was ripe for his account of the way in which the three stages of history, overlaps notwithstanding, had succeeded one another. Of Comte's original exposition of the three stages, *Système de politique positive* (1822), Mill later wrote,

> This doctrine harmonized well with my existing notions, to which it seemed to give a scientific shape. I already regarded the methods of physical science as the proper models for politics. But the chief benefit which I derived at this time from the trains of thought suggested by the St. Simonians and by Comte, was, that I obtained a clearer conception than ever before of the peculiarities of an era of transition in opinion, and ceased to mistake the moral and intellectual characteristics of such an era, for the normal attributes of humanity.[38]

Although Mill's agreement with Comte on the three stages never faltered,[39] he was, as early as 1829, aware of the danger of mistaking 'the perfect coherence and logical consistency of his system, for truth'.[40] He nevertheless commended Comte's account of the stages of historical development to his friend Alexander Bain and others. Later, however, he qualified his endorsement thus:

> Instead of the Theological we should prefer to speak of the Personal, or Volitional explanation of facts; instead of Metaphysical, the Abstractional or Ontological: and the meaning of Positive would be less ambiguously expressed in the objective aspect by Phaenomenal, in the subjective by Experiential.[41]

Again, Mill was convinced, and remained so, that in arranging the hierarchy of sciences as he did Comte had made an intellectually creative advance. Indeed, so eager was he to benefit from Comte's views in this connection that he did not complete his *Logic* (1843) until the sixth volume of Comte's *Cours* was to hand, and, when it was, he revised his sixth Book in the light of it. His enthusiasm somewhat abated with the passage of time, not least because of his breach with Comte. This was a complicated matter involving the cessation of financial contributions to Comte from Mill and his friends, and Mill's declining an invitation from Comte to contribute to a positivist journal on the ground that British public opinion precluded the open discussion of anti-Christian themes. As we saw earlier, Comte construed Mill's reticence as weakness. The two also disagreed significantly over the status of women, for whom Mill sought equality. In the event Mill managed to persuade himself that

> In a merely logical point of view, the only leading conception for which I am indebted to him is that of the Inverse Deductive Method, as the one chiefly applicable to the complicated subjects of History and Statistics: a process differing from the more common form of the Deductive Method in this, that instead of arriving at its conclusions by general reasoning and verifying them by

specific experience … it obtains its generalizations by a collation of specific experience, and verifies them by ascertaining whether they are such as would follow from known general principles. This was an idea entirely new to me when I found it in Comte: and but for him I might not soon (if ever) have arrived at it.[42]

But not even during his first flush of excitement did Mill swallow Comte whole. He noted Comte's omission of logic and political economy from his list of sciences, but above all, Mill, standing as he did in a line of associationists descending from Locke through Hartley and his father to himself, could not acquiesce in Comte's exclusion of psychology from the ranks of the sciences.[43] He regretted in particular the lowly place accorded to introspection.[44] Comte

> claims the scientific cognizance of moral and intellectual phenomena exclusively for physiologists; and not only denies to Psychology, or Mental Philosophy properly so called, the character of a science, but places it, in the chimerical nature of its objects and pretensions, almost on a par with astrology.[45]

Mill, more ironically, reiterated his concern 21 years later:

> [Comte] gives no place in his series to the science of Psychology, and always speaks of it with contempt. The study of mental phaenomena, or, as he expresses it, of moral and intellectual functions [Vol. III, p.530], has a place in his scheme, under the head of Biology, but only as a branch of physiology. Our knowledge of the human mind must, he thinks, be acquired by observing other people. How we are to observe other people's mental operations, or how interpret the signs of them without having learnt what the signs mean by knowledge of ourselves, he does not state. But it is clear to him that we can learn very little about our feelings, and nothing at all about the intellect, by self-observation. Our intelligence can observe all other things, but not itself: we cannot observe ourselves observing, or observe ourselves reasoning: and if we could, attention to this reflex operation would annihilate its object, by stopping the process observed.[46]

In writing thus (as he informs us a further decade on when in autobiographical mode), Mill was attempting 'the task of sifting what is good from what is bad in M. Comte's speculations'. He felt under a particular obligation in this matter because 'I had contributed more than anyone else to make [Comte's] speculations known in England.'[47]

Mill's disquiet concerning the place and importance of psychology surfaces on other occasions in his writings. One further example will suffice. It occurs in his *An Examination of Sir William Hamilton's Philosophy*, published a year after his essay on Comte. He here declares that

> a true Psychology is the indispensable basis of Morals, of Politics, of the science and art of Education; that the difficulties of Metaphysics lie at the root of all science; that those difficulties can only be quieted by being resolved, and that

until they are resolved, positively wherever possible, but at any rate negatively, we are never assured that any human knowledge, even physical, stands on solid foundations.[48]

On this admission, W.L. Courtney remarked, 'No clearer or franker avowal could be made by one who is often, though inaccurately, called an English Positivist.'[49] Charles Douglas agreed that his assertion of the importance of psychology places Mill 'in direct opposition to the positive philosophy of Comte'.[50]

Further suggestions that Mill has not banished metaphysics as firmly as Comte said he himself had done recur in Mill's writings, nowhere more clearly than in his examination of Hamilton. With regard to the material world, Mill does not hesitate to declare that while mind is 'in a philosophical point of view the only reality of which we have any evidence',[51] matter is but 'a Permanent Possiblity of Sensation'.[52] He thereby prompts Flint's rebuttal:

> If we know only what is phenomenal, we cannot know what is possible as distinct from and explanatory of the phenomenal ... [M]atter cannot be a possiblity of producing sensations in the view of a consistent positivism which refuses to recognise causation, efficiency. A consistent positivism must be a purely idealistic positivism. Even the dim ghost of matter which Mr Mill would retain must be discarded.[53]

Mill proceeds to argue that mind is 'nothing but the series of our sensations (to which must ... be added our internal feelings)',[54] but here, as he admits, difficulties 'which it seems to me beyond the power of metaphysical analysis to remove'[55] arise for his position. The problem is that 'The thread of consciousness which composes the mind's phaenomenal life' comprises not only present sensations, but memories and expectations, and each of these 'involves a belief in more than its own present existence'.[56] The upshot is that

> If ... we speak of the Mind as a series of feelings, we are obliged to complete the statement by calling it a series of feelings which is aware of itself as past and future; and we are reduced to the alternative of believing that the Mind, or Ego,[57] is something different from any series or feelings, or possibilities of them, or of accepting the paradox, that something which *ex hypothesi* is but a series of feelings, can be aware of itself as a series.
>
> The truth is, that we are here face to face with that final inexplicability, at which, as Sir W. Hamilton observes, we inevitably arrive when we reach ultimate facts.[58]

Hence Thomas Whittaker's judgment that Mill 'remains in the end nearer to Berkeley than to Hume ... Mind is for him ultimately more real than matter'.[59] Certainly it is difficult to square the foregoing with Mill's characterization of Comte's positivism as teaching that 'We have no knowledge of anything but Phaenomena; and our knowledge of phaenomena is relative, not absolute.'[60] It is even clearer that his view that 'The Positive mode of thought is not necessarily a denial of the supernatural'[61] places Mill at a considerable distance from Comte, of whom, indeed, Mill declares that 'It is one of M. Comte's mistakes that he never allows of open questions.'[62]

A further consideration will return us to Comte's three stages of history. While Mill agrees with Comte that, as he had earlier learned from Coleridge, there were patterns of thought, shared ideals and common interests which characterized both the theological and the metaphysical stages, he also notes that untoward authoritarianism can arise, and had in the Catholic Church done so, in such a way as to threaten the individual's liberty – something of which Comte, not least in his anti-Protestant strictures, had taken insufficient account.[63] In this connection Mill concludes that Comte and the liberals or revolutionaries have each got hold of half of the truth. Comte understands that in any society most people normally receive their opinions from those competent to express them, but it does not follow that a formally constituted and centralized moral authority such as Comte desires is necessary. Mill is appalled that Comte can contemplate a body which would not only inculcate moral values in general, but also presume to prescribe the individual person's duties.[64] As he afterwards reflected,

> I had fully agreed with [Comte] when he maintained that the mass of mankind, including even their rulers in all the practical departments of life, must, from the necessity of the case, accept most of their opinions on social and political matters, as they do non physical, from the authority of those who have bestowed more study on those subjects than they generally have it in their power to do … I agreed with him that the moral and intellectual ascendency, once exercised by priests, must in time pass into the hands of philosophers, and will naturally do so when they become sufficiently unanimous, and in other respects worthy to possess it. But when he exaggerated this line of thought into a practical system, in which philosophers were to be organized into a kind of corporate hierarchy, invested with almost the same spiritual supremacy (though without any secular power) once possessed by the Catholic Church; when I found him relying on this spiritual authority as the only security for good government, the sole bulwark against practical oppression, and expecting that by it a system of despotism in the state and despotism in the family would be rendered innocuous and beneficial; it is not surprising, that while as logicians we were nearly at one, as sociologists we could travel together no further.[65]

In Comte's *Système de Politique Positive*, Mill continues, we have

> the completest system of spiritual and temporal despotism which ever yet emanated from a human brain, unless possibly that of Ignatius Loyola … The book stands a monumental warning to thinkers on society and politics, of what happens when once men lose sight, in their speculations, of the value of Liberty and of Individuality.[66]

Yet just as he inconsistently clung to phenomenalism, so, despite Comte's quasi-papal pretensions, Mill advocated the Religion of Humanity to the end of his days. It behoves us now to examine this religion with a view to seeing what purposes Mill thought it might serve. We shall in passing, and subsequently, advert to the barrage of criticism which the idea attracted from a disparate array of writers.

I deliberately said that we should ask what purposes Mill thought the Religion of Humanity might serve, rather than what truth it might contain, because here as elsewhere Mill's interests are primarily practical. It is not without significance that he regrets 'the quietist tendencies in the metaphysics of Schelling and Hegel,'[67] or that a primary source of Mill's opinion on this subject is his essay, written between 1850 and 1858, on 'The *Utility* of Religion'.[68] As Alan Ryan has pointed out, 'Mill was very much in the European mainstream in devoting so much thought not simply to the truth of religion, but to its social meaning, and to its social usefulness.'[69] It was in the wake of the Revolution of 1848, and of what may not unkindly be called his 'somewhat-sentimental-softening-up' under the influence of Clothilde, that Comte embarked upon what he called his 'second career' as Grand Pontiff of Humanity. The fear of anarchy was not the least of the motives which urged positivists to seek to fill the void left by traditional religion.[70] We might also note that, just as Comte cannot be called the founder of positivism, so he cannot be called the founder of the Religion of Humanity, for, as T.R. Wright reminds us, the roots of the worship of Humanity go back to the French Revolution: 'Comte's rituals ... grew from the revolutionary cults of Reason and the Supreme Being. As early as 1794 there were official festivals to celebrate Humanity and her benefactors.'[71]

In his 'Utility' essay Mill sets out from the recognition that, whereas the truth of religion has traditionally been uppermost in people's minds, now that so many of the old certainties have been shaken, the question of religion's utility is increasingly raised. Mill admits that, as a ground for justifying religion, utility is less than ideal, but he points out that the sceptical denial of religion is problematic also, for

> When the only truth ascertainable is that nothing can be known, we do not, by this knowledge, gain any new fact by which to guide ourselves; we are, at best, only disabused of our trust in some former guide-mark ... It is, in short, perfectly conceivable that religion may be morally useful without being intellectually sustainable.[72]

Following his breakdown of 1826, Mill had learned from Coleridge, Wordsworth and others that the spiritual aspirations and sensitivities of human beings are not to be discounted, and he sought a non-theistic way of satisfying these. It is, he says, the 'craving for higher things' which causes human nature to require a religion.[73] While welcoming, with Comte, the Enlightenment's destruction of the traditional foundations of religious belief,

Mill sees that it is not enough to sweep away the redundant: something new will have to be introduced if the exit from an intellectually transitional period is to be accomplished without engendering social anarchy. He further fears that 'the passing away of supernatural religion might drain away the emotional resources required for the pursuit of worthwhile ends.'[74] None of which inhibits him from declaring with all the enthusiasm of a soap salesman:

> The essence of religion is the strong and earnest direction of the emotions and desires towards an ideal object, recognized as of the highest excellence, and as rightfully paramount over all selfish objects of desire. This condition is fulfilled by the Religion of Humanity in an eminent degree, and in as high a sense, as by the supernatural religions even in their best manifestations, and far more so than in any of their others.[75]

He underlines the point with his claim that to live in accordance with one's 'highest feelings and convictions' is more than morality, it is 'real religion'.[76] But religion is one thing, theology another. Mill makes it clear that Comte and those of the positivist church espouse a 'religion without a God'; and of the supporters of the Religion of Humanity he writes,

> Though conscious of being in an extremely small minority, we venture to think that a religion may exist without belief in a God, and that a religion without a God may be, even to Christians, an instructive and profitable object of contemplation.[77]

This passage calls to mind the mock lament of the scientist T.H. Huxley concerning Comte:

> Great ... was my perplexity, not to say disappointment, as I followed the progress of this 'mighty son of earth', in his work of reconstruction. Undoubtedly 'Dieu' disappeared, but the 'Nouveau Grand-être Suprême', a gigantic fetish, turned out bran-new by M. Comte's own hands, reigned in his stead.[78]

Mill explains that the focus of the new religion is not simply the aggregate of human beings living at any one time. It is an abstraction comprising those only 'who, in every age and variety of position, have played their part worthily in life. It is only as thus restricted that the aggregate of our species becomes an object deserving our veneration.'[79] We may note in passing that this was too much for John Tulloch. While welcoming the way in which Comte 'speaks with enthusiasm of the manner in which the smallest tribe, and even family, may come to look upon themselves as the essential stock of humanity', he regrets that Comte also refers disparagingly to those who 'are "born upon the earth merely to manure it" ... "mere digesting machines," "forming no real part of humanity."' 'Here,' Tulloch concludes, 'the essential exclusiveness – the aristocratic narrowness – of all merely human religion comes out: how different from the human ideal of the Gospel, which is "preached to the poor," and which came "to save that which was lost"!'[80]

Among the considerable advantages of the Religion of Humanity, in Mill's opinion, is that it is not encumbered with the need to justify the ways of an allegedly loving God to human beings with regard either to the evil in the world or in connection with predestinarian doctrine. To Mill, indeed, it is a great attraction of the Religion of Humanity that it is radically opposed to both theological and metaphysical standpoints.[81] No doubt the supernatural religions offer the prospect of life after death, but the idea of self-interest, coupled with that of postmortem rewards which motivates the behaviour of religious believers, is 'a radical inferiority in the best supernatural religions, compared with the Religion of Humanity'.[82] Furthermore, if the Religion of Humanity were as sedulously cultivated as the supernatural religions are, 'It seems to me not only possible but probable, that in a higher, and, above all, a happier condition of human life, not annihilation but immortality may be the burdensome idea' because the latter entails being 'chained through eternity to a conscious existence which [human nature] cannot be assured that it will always wish to preserve'.[83] 'To a conclusion so lame and impotent as this,' declared Noah Porter from the lofty height of the president's chair at Yale, 'is the author reduced in order to sustain his position that supernatural religion is no longer useful for the moral elevation or the happiness of man.'[84]

In Mill's view a religion needs a creed 'deliberately adopted, respecting human destiny and duty, to which the believer inwardly acknowledges that all his actions ought to be subordinate'. The set of beliefs should be matched by a sentiment 'sufficiently powerful to give it in fact, the authority over human conduct to which it lays claim in theory'.[85] Comte 'refers the obligations of duty, as well as all sentiments of devotion, to a concrete object, at once ideal and real; the Human Race, conceived as a continuous whole, including the past, the present, and the future'.[86] The golden rule of morality in the Religion of Humanity is altruism, though Mill dissents from Comte's refusal to acknowledge the place of proper self love. This lapse on Comte's part originates, he thinks, in the Frenchman's preoccupation with a unity which finds it hard to respect differences: 'That all perfection consists in unity, he apparently considers to be a maxim which no sane man thinks of questioning.'[87] Hence Comte's passion for undue systematization and Mill's fear for individual liberty:

> [Comte] aims at establishing (though by moral more than by legal appliances) a despotism of society over the individual, surpassing anything contemplated in the political ideal of the most rigid disciplinarian among the ancient philosophers.[88]

Turning to the cultus which Comte establishes on the basis of his theory, Mill says that 'Here we approach the ludicrous side of the subject.'[89] He reminds us that Comte enjoins prayer, though not to the Grand Être, collective

Humanity (albeit he occasionally refers to this as a goddess). Corporate prayer is an outpouring of feeling, while private prayer may be addressed to our guardian angels, 'the mother, the wife, and the daughter, representing severally the past, the present, and the future, and calling into active exercise the three social sentiments, veneration, attachment, and kindness'.[90] Comte provides for philosopher–priests, seven secular sacraments, 84 festival days, and much else besides. He reintroduces fetishism, justifying this on the ground that fetishism is a religion of feelings, not of the intellect, and in poetic fashion he invokes Space and the Earth as objects of adoration.[91] In which connection Edward Caird endorses the remark that this amounts to 'spiritual book-keeping by double entry', for by it the 'imagination is allowed to revive, for practical purposes, the fictions which science has destroyed'.[92] For his part, James Orr avers,

> There is the smell of the lamp in all this, which betrays too obviously the character of Comtism as an artificial or 'manufactured' religion; but if it receives this name, it is because there is an application of Divine attributes to objects which, however unworthy of having Divine honours paid to them, are still worshipped as substitutes for God, and so form an inverted testimony to the need which the soul feels for God.[93]

Mill proceeds to advert to others of Comte's earlier ideas which their propagator modifies for the worse, and at last Mill gasps, 'We cannot go on any longer with this.'[94] Less impatiently, to Richard Congreve, one of England's prominent practitioners of the Religion of Humanity, Mill wrote, 'It is M. Comte himself who … has thrown ridicule on his own philosophy by the extravagances of his later writings.'[95] But for all his disquiet regarding Comte's specifications of the Religion of Humanity, he is, as we saw, convinced that that religion will serve its purpose far better than any supernaturalist religion; and in 'Theism', his celebrated essay withheld from publication until after his death, he has no hesitation in proclaiming that it is destined to be 'the religion of the Future'.[96]

   It remains briefly to gather a selection of further reactions to the Religion of Humanity. First, Robert Flint complained that Comte and those who followed him had simply annexed the term 'religion' and applied it to something that was not a religion at all. Flint reaches this conclusion by specifying belief in God as of the essence of all religion. Hence 'A religion which is independent of a belief in God is a conception of the same kind as a circle whose radii are not all equal.'[97] Flint does not deny that the Religion of Humanity corresponds in some measure to a system of morality, and in this respect it is akin to Buddhism. Otherwise, 'it has scarcely the most distant resemblance to religion'.[98] Taking a broader view, the twentieth-century philosopher W.G. De Burgh opined:

The history of the last two centuries, especially in France and Russia, abundantly illustrates how the ideal of humanity, when divorced from the religious context in which it had its origin, degenerates into an empty abstraction, proving either an object for ridicule, as in its apotheosis by Comte, or a menace to the liberty of mankind.[99]

Again, while not denying that much in humanity is worthy of reverence, John Laird argued that 'mankind cannot be worshipped *as divine* for the simple and sufficient reason that neither individual men and women, nor humanity collectively, are effective agents on a cosmic scale'.[100] With this criticism we may couple the observation of Pringle-Pattison that 'Comte's religious philosophy remains to the end, what he explicitly designates it, a "subjective synthesis" – a synthesis of humanity, that is to say, which leaves the rest of the universe out of account.'[101] Pringle-Pattison acknowledges that in his later writings Comte 'goes so far in retracting the dualism of nature and man as to add Space and the Earth to Humanity as objects of worship ... But, with Comte's presuppositions, this can be no more than a conscious appeal to poetry to cover with its flowers the cold reality of the situation'.[102]

Secondly, if some were concerned by what they perceived as the positivistic abuse of the term 'religion', others queried the ambiguous way in which Comte speaks of Humanity. Thus G.D. Hicks observes that on occasion Comte understands 'collective being' by 'humanity', whereas at other times 'Humanity' stands for 'an organic unity with a life and consciousness of its own'. In either case there are difficulties:

> A totality of minds presupposes the existence of individual minds composing the totality ... over and above their thinking and feeling and willing, there can be no thinking and feeling and willing on the part of the whole as such. On the other hand, if Humanity be an organic unity ... while individual minds are mere abstractions, then, doubtless, this existent Mind may be said to think and feel and will, but there will be no thinking and feeling and willing on the part of individual minds. It will not be they that think and feel and will, but the organic unity that thinks and feels and wills in them.[103]

Thirdly, some, like Mill himself, though for different reasons, found Comte's ethical ideal, altruism, deficient. Flint, for example, contrasted Comte's law with the Christian Gospel, thus:

> unlike the Gospel, although it enjoins love to one another with the urgency which is due, it unseals no fresh source and brings to light no new motives of love. A mere doctrinal inculcation of the duty of active and affectionate beneficence, under the barbarous name of altruism, is its highest service as a system of religion, what is added thereto being worse than useless, because tending to render even 'the royal law' of love itself ridiculous.[104]

Karl Britton wondered how non-theistic altruism can be justified:

> If the theological arguments are rejected, is there any reason for saying that the meaning of my life is to serve my fellow men? Since 'my' refers to any speaker, presumably those whom I serve may find the point of their lives in serving me and others. Or they may not.[105]

Finally, to come full circle, many writers found it impossible to square the positivistic recourse to phenomena alone with the worship of Humanity (personified and dignified by a capital letter). Caird put the point in a nutshell: 'the peculiarity of Comte's position is that he admits the principle on which [the] Agnostic view is based, and yet at the same time rejects the conclusions which are usually drawn from it'.[106] James Seth illustrates the point in the following way. Comte, he says, sets up 'on the throne vacated by the fictitious deity of metaphysical abstraction, a new fiction, the latest product of hypostatisation, the last relic of scholastic Realism, a "great being" which derives its greatness and worshipfulness from the elimination of those characteristics which alone make it real and actual'. He drily concludes, 'A touch of logic, or, at any rate, of that metaphysic which we are supposed to have outgrown, but whch we cannot afford to outgrow, is enough to reveal the unreality and ghostliness of the Positivist's *Grand Être*.'[107] For a final example of this line of criticism, and in view of Comte's own practice, I do not scruple to have recourse to a Unitarian minister in poetic vein:

> Upon the subject of any new Positivist Religion little needs to be said. So far as it is not a matter of mere words and sentiment, as it evidently was to some extent with Mr. Mill, it may be regarded as an attempt to bind under the yoke of phenomenal law, and for mundane ends, the most unmanageable of human feelings, the feeling of religion, the powerful protest of universal experience against earth-bound limitations of the experience-philosophy, – making a tram-road for the chariot of the sun.[108]

II

Mill, as we saw, understood that a religion has a creed, a system of belief. What then was his? On his own testimony, it was utilitarianism. Unlike Bertrand Russell who, on being converted to Hegelianism in 1894, exclaimed 'Great Scott, the ontological argument is sound',[109] Mill did not elatedly thrown a tin of tobacco in the air on making his discovery of the value of utilitarianism; neither did he subsequently forsake his new-found conviction as did Russell. But the sense of excitement and relief at having found a belief to which he could conscientiously commit himself shines through in Mill's *Autobiography*:

The 'principle of utility', understood as Bentham understood it [that is to say, as divorced from the sanctions of supernatural religion insisted upon by, for example, the Anglican divine William Paley[110]] ... fell exactly into its place as the keystone which held together the detached and fragmentary component parts of my knowledge and beliefs. It gave unity to my conceptions of things. I now had opinions; a creed, a doctrine, a philosophy; in one among the best senses of the word, a religion; the inculcation and diffusion of which could be made the principal outward purpose of a life. And I had a grand conception laid before me of changes to be made in the condition of mankind through that doctrine.[111]

Indeed, as he later informs us, from the time he first read Bentham in 1821 Mill 'had what might truly be called an objective in life; to be a reformer of the world'.[112] Thus Mill's creed and mission. He stated and re-stated his creed on numerous occasions, but never more succinctly than in *Utilitarianism*:

The creed which accepts as the foundation of morals, Utility, or the Greatest Happiness Principle, holds that actions are right in proportion as they tend to promote happiness, wrong as they tend to promote the reverse of happiness. By happiness is intended pleasure, and the absence of pain; by unhappiness, pain, and the privation of pleasure.[113]

Mill was doggedly opposed to the supernaturalism and postmorten rewards of Christianity as he understood it. For this reason he denied Adam Sedgwick's claim that William Paley was a utilitarian, for while Paley undoubtedly elevated happiness into the criterion of moral judgment and action, he 'does not consider utility as itself the source of moral obligation, but as a mere index to the will of God, which he regards as the ultimate groundwork of all morality, and the origin of its binding force'.[114] For all that, Mill was nevertheless eager to annexe as much of Christianity's good reputation (not to mention its God) as he could: '*If* it be a true belief that God desires, above all things, the happiness of creatures, and that this was his purpose in their creation, utility is not only not a godless doctrine, but more profoundly religious than any other.'[115] Again, 'In the golden rule of Jesus of Nazareth, we read the complete spirit of the ethics of utility.'[116] Underlying such annexations is Mill's declared method of 'fairness' to those of a religious persuasion.[117] 'We ought,' he recommends, 'to suppose religion to have accepted the best human morality which reason and goodness can work out, from philosophical, christian, or any other elements.'[118] But this, of course, begs the question of the religious person's actual convictions regarding the source of morality. It is, however, a useful supposition to one who, like Mill, wishes to argue that 'a religion may be morally useful without being intellectually sustainable'[119] – a bifurcation of creed and life which puzzled Leslie Stephen, among others.

It goes without saying that Mill's utilitarianism has been widely discussed down to our own time. D.P. Dryer goes so far as to say that 'The majority of

Mill on God

serious students of ethics today are utilitarians, and those who are not see utilitarianism as the chief position in need of amendment. John Stuart Mill's writings on ethics, and especially on utilitarianism, are thus of vital contemporary interest and importance.'[120] What is equally clear, however, is the justice of Dale Miller's remark:

> Among contemporary philosophers, Mill's views on moral theory are perhaps the most frequently discussed aspect of his thought. Nevertheless, no confident consensus has emerged concerning the content of his views. Of course, no one hesitates to describe Mill as a utilitarian, yet is is virtually impossible to say anything more specific than this without finding oneself contradicted by other interpreters. Commentators disagree, for example, over whether Mill subscribes to act utilitarianism, to some form of rule utilitarianism, or to some more exotic position; there are passages in *Utilitarianism* and Mill's other discussions of morality that apparently lend support to each of these possible readings.[121]

Mill's elusiveness as here reported is but one instance of a certain fluctuating tendency which characterizes his writing on many topics. While we are not here concerned to pursue present-day discussions concerning the reception of, and proposed adjustments to, utilitarianism, we shall do well to bear in mind Miller's judgment that Mill's legacy was an oscillating or ambiguous one. We might also note the grain of truth in the cadences of an older writer, William Davidson:

> Justice has rarely been done to [Mill's utilitarianism] by opponents, because they have failed to see (a) that it is not a treatise of pure abstract reasoning, but one written out of the living conviction of a man who loved his fellow-men; (b) that it is practical in its object, and not merely theoretical; and (c) that, although it sets forth pleasure or happiness as the standard and test of human conduct, it makes supreme the conception of man as a social being and conditions all by the conception of the general welfare.[122]

The first point here recalls Martineau's opinion that owing to his practical interests Mill did not probe philosophical first principles to any great degree. This seems generally to be the case. However, we should misunderstand Mill's advocacy of utilitarianism if we did not take due account of his concern to root out intuitionism wherever he found it. As we have seen, this desire fuelled his critique of Hamilton and Mansel in the context of epistemology; it equally fuelled his critique of William Whewell in the context of ethics. For Whewell insisted that 'there must be *reasons* why actions are right and good', and these reasons are found in self-evident principles.[123] This, of course, ran directly counter to Mill's insistence that inductive methods may be applied to conduct no less than to all other phenomena. The general point to emerge from Davidson's remarks is that, for Mill, the utilitarian creed was the inspiration of the mission, but the mission was the primary concern.

Mill, like Bentham himself, was well aware that 'the generalities of [Bentham's] philosophy have little or no novelty'.[124] Bentham himself acknowledged Helvetius as among his sources, and Shaftesbury and Thomas Brown were among other harbingers of utilitarianism. We may also recall with Karl Britton that Bentham derived his consequentialist view from Joseph Priestley, and his equation of good with pleasure from Locke and Hume.[125] Bentham, however, 'more than anyone else, provided [utilitarianism] with its secular character, and ... this was a radical departure from the then prevailing version of utilitarian theory in Britain'.[126] But although he remained ever grateful for Bentham's stimulus, and ever-admiring of the 'rare union' in him of 'self-reliance and moral sensibility',[127] Mill could not rest content with what he perceived as a narrowness in Bentham's doctrine.[128] To put the point in their own homely language, whereas to Bentham, if push-pin and poetry afforded equal pleasure they were equally valuable, to Mill it was 'better to be a human being dissatisfied than a pig satisfied; better to be Socrates dissatisfied than a fool satisfied'.[129] But with this introduction of a scale of values as evidenced by the fact that some people act according to 'higher faculties', while others act more sensually, Mill embarks upon what most commentators regard as a serious departure from his mentor.[130] In the opinion of T.H. Green, for example,

> on the principle that pleasure is the only thing good ultimately or in its own right ... one man can be better than another, one faculty higher than another, only as a more serviceable instrument for the production of pleasure ... it is altogether against Utilitarian principles that a pleasure should be of more value because the man who pursues it is better. They only entitle us to argue back from the amount of pleasure to the worth of the man who acts so as to produce it.[131]

A.D. Lindsay's perceptive comment is to the point. Of Mill he writes that 'He is afraid of an *à priori* which would do without experience or an intuition which would save the trouble of thinking; but his own position, if its implications are properly understood, affirms a moral experience involving ultimate principles for which in the end he claims intuitive assent.'[132]

Undeterred, Mill declares that 'It is quite compatible with the principle of utility to recognise the fact, that some *kinds* of pleasure are more desirable and more valuable than others.'[133] For this he was rebuked by W.L. Courtney, among many others:

> a distinction in quality between pleasures *can* be made if our standard of estimation be something other than feeling, but *can not* be made if we remain true to the psychological theory of Bentham. In this instance, as in many others, Mill has included in his scheme a distinction which his ground-plan does not admit of.[134]

It is not difficult to trace the course of Mill's qualification of his original Benthamism. Thus, looking back on the aftermath of his breakdown of 1826, Mill reflected thus:

> I never, indeed, wavered in the conviction that happiness is the test of all rules of conduct, and the end of life. But I now thought that this end was only to be attained by not making it the direct end. Those only are happy (I thought) who have their minds fixed on some object other than their own happiness ... The cultivation of the feelings became one of the cardinal points in my ethical and philosophical creed.[135]

W.H. Mallock was unimpressed:

> Now what does Mill gain by this ...? For the question still remains unsettled, what kind of happiness for others is it, that it will be worth our while to promote? We are really thus removing the matter to a little distance, in the hopes of gaining a clearer view of it.[136]

The result of Mill's move, as R.J. Halliday remarked, was that 'by a drastic act of surgery, Mill had detached utilitarianism from its basis in hedonism; the ethics of utility now claimed to be disinterested, and expediency was a thing of the past'.[137] Again, in 1834, we find Mill informing Carlyle that he is likely to remain a utilitarian, 'though not one of "the people called utilitarians"...'.[138] Nevertheless, 'Mill remained a utilitarian: for he held (1) that where there is a conflict of moral principles an appeal must be made to the Happiness Principle; and (2) that moral principles are reached through experience and rational reflection and are therefore liable to revision in the light of new experience or reflection.'[139]

Even so, with more than a hint of indebtedness to the Romantics, Mill came to conceive of a more affectively sensitive utilitarianism and, in the wake of his father's death, he sought to soften the 'harder & sterner' features of radicalism and utilitarianism. He now favours

> a utilitarianism which takes into account the whole of human nature,, not the ratiocinative faculty only – the utilitarianism which never makes any peculiar figure as such, nor would ever constitute its followers a sect or school ... & which holds in the highest reverence all which the vulgar notion of utilitarians represents them to despise – which holds Feeling at least as valuable as Thought, & Poetry not only on a par with, but the necessary condition of, any true and comprehensive Philosophy.[140]

As Karl Britton observed, there is enough here to 'place Mill fairly and squarely outside the sectarian creed of rationalistic hedonism'.[141] By 1838 we find Mill concluding that Bentham's empiricism was that of an emotionally stunted individual:

He had neither internal experience nor external; the quiet, even tenor of his life, and his healthiness of mind, conspired to exclude him from both ... Knowing so little of human feelings, he knew still less of the influences by which those feelings are formed ...[142]

Having picked over Mill's position in some detail, John Plamenatz concluded that

There is not much left of Benthamite utilitarianism when John Stuart Mill has completed his defence of it. What is left is, strictly speaking, not utilitarianism at all, but a kind of naturalistic ethics that it would be misleading to call a variety of hedonism.[143]

I find Plamenatz's branding of Mill's ethics as 'naturalistic' somewhat implausible. It is true, on the one hand, that Mill finds the source of moral obligation within the world. It is the 'firm foundation' of 'the social feelings of mankind; the desire to be in unity with our fellow creatures'.[144] But on the other hand, having regard to the intellectual–affective influences at work upon Mill there is, I suspect, at least as much to be said in favour of Charles Douglas's view that in complaining that Benthamism

'will do nothing ... for the spiritual interests of society', [Mill] betrays a consciousness of an ideal which is not expressed in his hedonism. The mere summation of pleasures has become in a high degree irrelevant. Mill is thinking of moral life in terms of an idea of character, to which no justice is done when it is criticised merely as a means to the production of pleasant feeling.[145]

Be that as it may, Mill affirms his commitment to a scale of values in his tract on *Utilitarianism*, wherein he problematically has recourse to those competent to make the necessary judgments of value: 'Of two pleasures, if there be one to which all or almost all who have experience of both give a decided preference, irrespective of any feeling of moral obligation to prefer it, that is the more desirable pleasure.'[146] As Karl Britton pointed out, the likes or dislikes of competent judges cannot be decisive; they may 'incline us to a decision: but they do not enable us to *infer* what the "correct" decision is'.[147] F.H. Bradley was more trenchant: 'Not only has moral obligation nothing in Mr. Mill's theory to which it can attach itself save the likes or dislikes of one or more individuals, but in the end it *is* itself nothing more than a similar feeling.'[148] In a word, Mill pays scant attention to the inherent morality of the choices which people actually make. This point was seized upon by T.H. Green in the course of his critique of the 'Hedonists': 'We cannot think of an object as good, *i.e.* such as will satisfy desire, without thinking of it as in consequence such as will yield pleasure; but its pleasantness depends on its goodness, not its goodness upon the pleasure it coveys.'[149] J. Radford Thomson specified the underlying metaphysical distinction thus: 'The radical difference between Mr. Green and Mr. Mill is that, according to the former, man is not a part of nature, but is a subject in which the eternal consciousness reproduces itself, and as a knowing subject is a free cause.'[150]

The plot thickens when Mill further proposes that one may properly sacrifice a greater pleasure for a lesser; but, as A.C. Ewing retorted, 'If pleasure is the only good, the more pleasure always the better.'[151] Again, with reference to Mill's phrase suggesting that of two pleasures the more desirable one is that which commends itself to majority opinion 'irrespective of any moral obligation to prefer it', Alexander Bain cautioned,

> Apart from moral attributes and consequences, I do not see a difference of quality at all; and, when these are taken into account, the difference is sufficient to call forth any amount of admiring preference. A man's actions are noble if they arrest misery or diffuse happiness around him; they are not noble if they are not directly or indirectly altruistic; they are essentially of the swinish type.[152]

But the underlying point of interest here is that by one of Mill's oscillations we seem to be returned from a tentative idealism to a species of utilitarian calculus.153 However, it is not a pristine Benthamite calculus, for Mill is clearly concerned with quality as well as quantity of pleasure, whereas Bentham had regard to the latter alone. Mill is quite clear: 'It would be absurd that while, in estimating all other things, quality is considered as well as quantity, the estimation of pleasures should be supposed to depend on quantity alone.'[154] But the fact that he proposes a quasi-empirical test of what are presented as two normative properties of goodness would seem to place him at a remove from his more idealistic-sounding intuitions. Yet these latter are still implied in his procedure for, as F.H. Bradley saw, 'the theory which begins with the most intense democracy, wide enough to take in all life that feels pleasure and pain, ends in a no less intense Platonic aristocracy'[155] in that those most competent to make the necessary value judgments are the few. For his part, W.D. Ross argued that Mill's logic is flawed: Mill 'silently assumes' but does not seek to prove the premiss which lies behind his contention that pleasure and freedom from pain are the only desirable ends, namely, that the 'productivity of what is desirable as an end is the sole ground of rightness'. This in turn rests upon 'the non-naturalistic premiss that only pleasure is good, but this in turn rests on the naturalistic premiss that only pleasure is desired + the non-naturalistic premiss that the only thing that is desired is the only thing that is desirable'.[156]

There would thus seem much to be said for the verdict of W.L. Courtney. He specifies 'the cardinal characteristic of Mill, as a thinker' thus:

> the desire to engraft on the older stock of Benthamism the blossoms of an alien growth. While the old foundation remains it is sometimes dangerous to add the width of the superstructure; in philosophy, at all events, such lateral extension of dogmas only confuses the issue, and ends by discrediting that ground-plan which it was intended to justify.[157]

However it may be with the internal consistency of his position, we must not overlook the fact that to Mill himself his mission was the priority. While, as we have seen, he rebuked Comte for supposing that no individual ought to seek his or her own happiness, on the ground that this placed persons at the mercy of the social machine,[158] his teleology nevertheless was of the happiness of all persons together as the ultimate good. He clarified his position on this matter to Henry Jones:

> when I said that the general happiness is a good to the aggregate of all persons I did not mean that every human being's happiness is a good to every other human being; though I think, in a good state of society & education it would be so. I merely meant ... to argue that since A's happiness is a good, B's is a good, C's is a good, &c., the sum of all these goods must be a good.[159]

Not all were satisfied, however, and, against Mill's assertion that as 'each person's happiness is a good to that person' so 'the general happiness ... is a good to the aggregate of all persons',[160] J.S. Mackenzie brought the charge that this exemplifies the fallacy of composition:

> It is inferred that because my pleasures are a good to me, yours to you, his to him, and so on, therefore my pleasures + your pleasures + his pleasures are a good to me + you + him. It is forgotten that neither the pleasures nor the persons are capable of being made into an aggregate. It is as if we should argue that because each one of a hundred soldiers is six feet high, therefore the whole company is six hundred feet high. The answer is that this would be the case if the soldiers stood on one another's heads. And similarly Mill's argument would hold good if the minds of all human beings were to be rolled into one, so as to form an aggregate. But as it is, 'the aggregate of all persons' is nobody, and consequently cannot be a good to him. A good must be a good for somebody.[161]

In this connection we may recall Henry Sidgwick's reluctant conclusion that the only way of resolving the individualism/altruism discrepancy was to have recourse to an ethical intuition of the kind which Mill himself had striven to avoid.[162] Not, indeed, that Mill's strivings were entirely successful, for as early as 1833 Mill, in countering Bentham's hedonism, had declared that 'no one who had thought deeply and systematically enough to be entitled to the name of a philosopher, ever supposed that his *own* private sentiments of approbation and disapprobation must necessarily be well-founded, and needed not to be compared with any external standard'.[163] There is, in his mind, a place and a role for 'certain general laws of morality'.[164] Again, as Plamenatz points out, whereas Bentham and James Mill were solely concerned with the happiness or otherwise of individuals, Mill declared that 'It really is of importance not only what men do, but also what manner of men they are that do it.'[165] He thus brought a wider range of considerations than Bentham into his ethical calculations. He can even say that 'conduct is *sometimes* determined by an *interest*, that is, by a deliberate and conscious aim; and sometimes by an *impulse*, that is, by a feeling (call it an association if you think fit) which has no ulterior end, the act or forbearance becoming an end in itself'.[166] Moreover, 'Nothing could be less utilitarian than the spirit of [Mill's] question', 'what more or better can be said of any condition of human affairs, than that it brings human beings themselves nearer to the best thing they can be?'[167]

But this last phrase recalls the goal of Mill the social reformer, and in one telling sentence Douglas brings together that Mill and Mill the moral philosopher: 'When [Mill] insists that "the greatest happiness of the greatest number" is the criterion of morality, he is the spokesman of those to whom life brings too much pain.'[168] In fact Mill has a wider view still: one which embraces 'all sentient beings'[169] under the rubric that 'the promotion of happiness is the ultimate principle of Teleology'.[170] He immediately proceeds to grant that while happiness is the supremely good end the promotion of happiness is not the end of all actions or all rules of action. There are occasions when pleasure must be sacrificed, but if this is done from noble intentions, the eventual outcome will be an increase of happiness, and this is the justification of such selfless actions.[171] It would therefore seem that Douglas construes Mill's teleology too individualistically when he charges that the sacrificial denial of immediate happiness is 'a surrender of the doctrine that only happiness can be desired'.[172] So, too, does James Martineau when he remarks,

> Most persons would be affected with some surprise and amusement on being told that in their friendships, their family affections, their public spirit, their admiration for noble character, their religious trust, they had a single eye to their own interests, and were only *using* their fellows, their children, their country, their heroes, their God, as instruments of their personal pleasure.[173]

No doubt they would; but to impute such a position to Mill is to descend into caricature. In fact Mill went to some trouble to distance himself from the view that one's own happiness should be one's immediate objective:

> Ask yourself whether you are happy, and you cease to be so. The only chance is to treat, not happiness, but some end external to it, as the purpose of life. Let your self-consciousness, your scrutiny, your self-interrogation, exhaust themselves on that; and if otherwise fortunately circumstanced you will inhale happiness with the air you breathe ... This theory now became the basis of my philosophy of life. And I still hold to it as the best theory for those who have a moderate degree of sensibility and of capacity for enjoyment, that is, for the great majority of mankind.[174]

This elicited a whimsical response from R.H. Hutton:

> That the true end of life should be always in the position of the old gentleman's macaroons, which he hid amongst his papers and books, because he said he

enjoyed them so much more when he came upon them unawares, than he did if
he went to the cupboard avowedly for them, is surely a very odd compliment to
the end of life.[175]

III

There can be little question that Mill's utilitarian creed presupposes a
doctrine of humanity: 'the ultimate appeal on all ethical questions,' he
affirms, must be 'grounded in the permanent interests of man as a
progressive being'.[176] Let us, then, enquire more closely into who are they
who are bidden to strive for the greatest possible happiness of the greatest
possible number. We recall that Mill concurred with Comte in holding that
the Humanity which is to be the object of veneration is not the aggregate of
all human beings of all time, but of the worthiest of them. For this he was
charged with aristocratic elitism, a charge the force of which his further
claim that 'the unworthy members of [our species] are best dismissed from
our habitual thoughts'[177] did nothing to reduce. What interests us now is the
apparent incongruity of the elevation of 'Humanity' as an ideal projection
conceivable only through the bracketing of selected real people – the
unworthy ones – who are known to us. By a logical sleight of hand
'humanity' is redefined in such a way that it denotes only an abstraction; it
is a term reserved to actual humanity's noblest examples, with the
implication that what one might call the '*humanly* non-elect' are somehow
sub-human. That a social reformer should set out from this premise is
distinctly odd, and the possibility that one might through social improvement
raise individuals to an acceptable level of humanness is distinctly
patronizing: indeed, it is at least faintly totalitarian; it is tantamount to doing
what might be called, in circles other than the coterie of devotees of the
godless religion of Humanity, playing God.

   All of which raises the question of human nature. Mill appears to have no
difficulty in specifying the constituents of human nature. He does this in the
context of chiding Comte for omitting them from his 'Springs of Action': the
desire for perfection, the accusing or approving conscience, the sense of
honour and dignity, the love of beauty, order, power as an instrument of
good, and the love of action.[178] More problematic is what seems to be an
ambivalence in Mill's thought. His individualism prompts him to contend
that even in society, 'Men ... are still men; their actions and passions are
obedient to the laws of individual human nature.'[179] These laws, he further
explains, combine with the laws governing the circumstances in which
people are placed to form their characters.[180] The inherent determinism in
his psychology, however, is difficult to square with his ethical libertarianism,
according to which we are free to follow nature, or not. It is even more
difficult to accommodate Mill's idea, that since the self is not a unity but is
rather an aggregate of independent impressions and emotions, a stream of

feelings, it could be purposeful at all.[181] This seems to be the rock upon which associationism founders, and Mill was more than somewhat aware of this:

> If ... we speak of the Mind as a series of feelings, we are obliged to complete the statement by calling it a series of feelings which is aware of itself as a past and future; and we are reduced to the alternative of believing that the Mind, or Ego, is something different from any series of feelings or possibilities of them, or of accepting the paradox that something which *ex hypothesi* is but a series of feelings can be aware of itself as a series.[182]

On which pronouncement Scott Lidgett remarked,

> As a matter of fact, the existence of a permanent self is the original datum of faith upon which the whole possibility of perception, thought, and purpose is based. It is the initial postulate of all human life, and cannot be explained in terms of anything to the explanation of which it is itself essential.[183]

More dramatically, the Baptist theologian, Cephas Bennett Crane, opined,

> One would think that [Mill] would now give up his theory. Not so. Standing serene on the scaffold, with the rope around his neck, he quietly observes that the fault is not in the theory, but in the facts; wriggles out of the noose, jumps from the scaffold, shoulders his theory, leaps over the contradictory facts, and moves on briskly. Evidently, he has discovered a philosophical doctrine of justification by faith by the efficacy of which he and his theory with him are delivered from the law of death. This theory can bear a load of difficulties under which the back of Christianity would be hopelessly broken.[184]

A further puzzle arises when we attempt to square Mill's psychological determinism with his strong conviction that human nature is improvable – indeed, educable into better things.[185] There can be character growth: indeed Mill contemplated, but never produced, an ethology – a science of character. Individuals are free to make the choices which will improve their characters, conceived as 'dispositions, and habits of mind and heart'.[186] But this, he argues, is compatible with determinism construed not as 'Asiatic' fate but as having causes in a person's character. He even thinks that there may be a place for prayer in all of this. The philosopher Henry Jones had written to Mill concerning a number of religious matters which were troubling him. In the course of his reply Mill says,

> I think you have omitted to mention one effect that prayer may reasonably be said to have on the mind, & which may be granted to it by those who doubt as well as by those who admit divine interposition in answer to it: I mean the effect produced on the mind of the person praying, not by the belief that it will be granted but by the elevating influence of an endeavour to commune & to become in harmony with the highest spiritual ideal that he is capable in elevated moments

of conceiving. This effect may be very powerful in clearing the moral perceptions & intensifying the moral earnestness ... I know of no proof sufficient to entitle psychologists to assert it as *certain* that the whole of this influence is reducible to the known elements of human nature, however highly probable they may think it.[187]

Utilitarian, anthropocentric and, from a Christian point of view, reductionist this understanding of prayer may be; but it is more than Mill is strictly entitled to from the standpoint of his own philosophy. It is characteristic of him, however, to take an instrumentalist view of anything which will advance his utilitarian cause.

Incongruities apart, Mill had a very high view of the individual's sanctity and potential. Indeed some writers, with hindsight stimulated by more settled evolutionary views, felt that 'In Mill, as in Comte, there is a theoretical opposition of man to the cosmos which seems to make of him a kind of miracle in nature. Evolution in its larger aspects restores a wholeness that both were sometimes too willing to renounce.'[188] Be that as it may, when discussing duty to country, for example, Mill relates this directly to the individual's

> absolute obligation towards the universal good. A morality grounded on large and wise views of the good of the whole, neither sacrificing the individual to the aggregate nor the aggregate to the individual, but giving to duty on the one hand and to freedom and spontaneity on the other their proper province, would derive its power in the superior natures from sympathy and benevolence and the passion for ideal excellence: in the inferior, from the same feelings cultivated up to the measure of their capacity, with the superadded force of shame. This exalted morality would not depend for its ascendency on any hope of reward; but the reward which might be looked for, and the thought of which would be a consolation in suffering, and a support in moments of weakness, would not be a problematical future existence, but the approbation, in this, of those whom we respect, and ideally of all those, dead or living, whom we admire or venerate.[189]

We may here note, once again, the elitist slant given to the realistic notion that some individuals make a better fist of morality than others, but that the latter may be prone to having their worthier feelings cultivated – an echo here of Wordsworth's influence upon Mill, elsewhere more specifically reiterated: 'Religion and poetry ... both supply ... ideal conceptions grander and more beautiful than we see realized in the prose of human life.'[190] We also note further evidence of Mill's departure from Bentham's and his father's intellectualism. Bentham, he thought, had 'limited insight into the formation of character, and knowledge of the internal workings of human nature'.[191] In particular, 'Nothing is more curious than the absence of recognition in any of his writings of the existence of conscience, as a thing distinct from philanthropy, from affection for God or man, and from self-interest in this world or in the next.'[192] Not, indeed, that Mill's own view of

conscience was immune to attack. 'Unfortunately,' declared Richard Holt
Hutton, 'this "ideal conception of a perfect Being" is not a *power* on which
human nature can lean. It is merely its own best thought of itself; so that it
dwindles when the mind and heart contract, and vanishes just when there is
most need of help',[193] a point which Hutton illustrates from Mill's own
crisis of 1826.

From the time of his early speeches to the London Debating Society Mill
espoused a generally optimistic view of human nature. In his 'Speech on
perfectibility' of 2 May 1828 he declares that 'so far from its being a mark
of wisdom to despair of human improvement there is no more certain
indication of narrow views and a limited understanding, and that the wisest
men of all political and religious opinions, from Condorcet to Mr. Coleridge,
have been something nearly approaching to perfectibilians'.[194] In the same
year, and to the same body, he argued that 'it is of the nature of the human
mind to be progressive',[195] and the burden of his message was that the
Church of England was an impediment to progress.

Not surprisingly, a number of Christian commentators faulted Mill for
undue optimism. True, he enumerated those factors which preclude human
happiness: 'indigence, disease, and the unkindness, worthlessness, or
premature loss of objects of affection';[196] but (not surprisingly in one who
has no belief in God) he tends to overlook humanity's sinful propensities.
Thus to W.G. Ward he writes,

> I recognise two kinds of imperfections: those which come independently of our
> will & which our will could not prevent, & for these we are not accountable; &
> those which our will has either positively or negatively assisted in producing &
> for which we *are* accountable ... You ride over this ... perfectly definite
> distinction by the ambiguous word *sin*, under which a third class of defects of
> character finds entrance which is supposed to unite both attributes – to be
> culpable & extra-culpable *although* the person thus morally guilty cannot help it.
> This seems to me to exemplify the unmeaningness of the word sin which if it is
> anything other than the theological synonym of 'morally wrong' is a name for
> something which I do not admit to exist.[197]

Mill thus evacuates from the concept of sin anything concerning the flouting
of a holy God, the very emphasis upon which James M'Cosh wished to
insist: 'Sin is quite as much a fact of consciousness and of our moral nature
as even virtue'; and while Mill speaks of self-reproach as a restraining force,
he does not consider when it is justifiable and, hence, 'Not knowing what to
make of sin, the system provides no place for repentance. The boundary line
between moral good and evil is drawn so uncertainly, that persons will ever
be tempted to cross it without allowing that they have done so, – the more
so that they are not told what they should do when they have crossed it.'[198]
To the Baptist C.B. Crane it was desperately important that Mill be answered
on this point because 'Your barber will appeal to him while he holds your
nose between his finger and thumb. Your tailor will prattle of him while he

takes your measure for a waistcoat. Your college student will pause, in his unsuccessful scanning of Horace, to laud him.'[199] Crane stoutly testifies,

> Given the facts of man's moral being and man's sin, together with a redemption unmistakably accomplishing, the problem of evil seems always possible of a solution which will not involve a denial of the wisdom and goodness of God. This old Boethius, fourteen hundred years ago, clearly apprehended and generously acknowledged.[200]

All the sadder, therefore, that Mill does not take the trouble to examine the defenses of Christianity supplied by its best advocates, and that his 'principal objection against Christianity [namely, the incongruity in believing in a God of love who permits such a world as we experience] is one which you may hear urged any day by ignorant striplings about whose chins the brown beard has not yet begun to curl'.[201] Indeed, 'It is difficult to suppress one's indignation against this superb Alcibiades, who treated Christianity with a neglect so horribly unscientific and contemptuous.'[202] We may yet return to Crane's delightful huffings and puffings.

It must in fairness be admitted that if Crane could preach, so could Mill. Indeed, there is something to be said for the view that his optimism concerning human possibilities of moral progress comes to the fore when he is urging societal reform. Elsewhere he takes a gloomier view of human nature – Mill is no Romantic sentimentalist. Indeed, so gloomy is his view at times, that the *Edinburgh* reviewer felt able to perpetrate a *tu quoque* argument against him. Thus, having 'sneered' at most Christian denominations for holding that 'man is by nature wicked',[203] Mill himself contends that 'there is hardly a single point of excellence belonging to human character, which is not decidedly repugnant to the untutored feelings of human nature'.[204] 'That,' concludes the reviewer, 'seems to us very much like saying that man is by nature wicked, and much more akin to the teaching of the Genevese theologian Calvin than to that of the Genevese philosopher Rousseau.'[205]

Certainly the Manichaean dualism inherited from his father, according to which there is a battle between the forces of good and evil, never entirely left him; on the contrary, it probably fuelled his ethics and his reforming zeal alike, especially from 1850 onwards. In that year he came to the conclusion that he could no longer expect much by way of human betterment through purely economic and political means 'by reason of the low intellectual & moral state of all classes: of the rich as much as of the poorer classes'.[206] Moral renovation was required. As he somewhat dolefully notes in his *Autobiography*, change of character in 'the uncultivated herd' and their employers, and the growth of interest in the common good develop only slowly over time, 'not because it can never be otherwise, but because the mind is not accustomed to dwell on it as it dwells from morning till night on things which tend only to personal advantage'.[207]

All of which does rather call into question the short, and even the long-term utility of Mill's ultimate moral sanction, 'the conscientious feelings of mankind'. As if aware of this Mill immediately, and lamely, adds, 'Undoubtedly this sanction has no binding efficacy on those who do not possess the feelings it appeals to; but neither will these persons be more obedient to any other moral principles than to the utilitarian one.'[208] It also raises the issue of a further ambiguity in Mill's corpus, for while he extols individualism in *On Liberty*, in *Utilitarianism*, written during the same period, he considers that the selfish egoism of those who are 'devoid of any feeling or care apart from those which centre in [their] own miserable individuality'[209] is something to be overcome. As undeterred by the inconsistencies of his position as by the inadequacies of humanity at large, Mill never forsook the hope that his religious aspiration would, in however distant a future, be achieved through education, which topic he addressed with missionary zeal.

IV

In his 'Inaugural Address delivered to the University of St. Andrews' (1867) Mill proposed a broad view of education: 'Whatever helps to shape the human being; to make the individual what he is, or hinder him from being what he is not – is part of his education.'[210] This much he might have learned from Bentham. But Mill went further in his focus on the education of society as a whole, feeling as he did that Bentham's philosophy was weak in relation to 'the greater social questions'.[211] In this latter connection, and almost three decades earlier, he had not been slow to praise those whom he variously called 'philosophers of the reactionary school' and the 'Germano-Coleridgian school' for comprehensively and deeply enquiring into 'the inductive laws of the existence and growth of human society', and for producing a 'philosophy of society'.[212] Mill's idea of the growth of society accords closely with his anthropology which, as we have seen, to a considerable extent turns upon the conviction that man is a progressive being. The engine of progress is education: 'The power of education is almost boundless: there is not one natural inclination, which it is not strong enough to coerce, and, if needful, to destroy by disuse.'[213] This is consistent with Mill's 'Romantic' critique of the Enlightenment and with his belief in the progress of the human race. The *philosophes*, he thought, had overestimated the invariability of moral sentiments and played down the societal: 'They thought [moral feelings were] the natural and spontaneous growth of the human heart; so firmly fixed in it, that they would subsist unimpaired, nay invigorated, when the whole system of opinions and observances with which they were habitually intertwined was violently torn away.'[214] In fact, however, the moral sentiments are socially influenced, and require to be educated.

For all his belief in human progress, Mill's view of actual human beings is sufficiently doleful for him to declare that the English public are not only undiscerning where political economy is concerned, they are

> still further from having acquired better habits of thought and feeling, or being in any way better fortified against error, on subjects of a more elevated nature. For, though they have thrown off certain errors, the general discipline of their minds, intellectually and morally, is not altered. I am now convinced, that no great improvements in the lot of mankind are possible, until a great change takes place in the fundamental constitution of their modes of thought. The old opinions in religion, morals, and politics, are so much discredited in the more intellectual minds as to have lost the greater part of their efficacy for good, while they have still life enough in them to be a powerful obstacle to the growing up of any better opinions on those subjects.[215]

Statements of this kind prompted Joseph Parker, the blunt and quizzical Congregational minister of London's City Temple, gently to wonder how likely it was that 'a community of fools' could 'rear a generation of philosophers'.[216] Another Congregational minister J. Radford Thomson, professor at New College, London, noting Mill's hope that 'a regard for the happiness of others may by careful education acquire the force of a religion', drily remarked, 'For those persons in whose mind no such association has been established, Mr. Mill does not seem to have any special sanction provided.'[217] Undeterred by such considerations, Mill pressed on with his case, summoning Christ to his aid, as we shall see.

Because of humanity's predicament as thus described, Mill clearly sees that sociomoral progress in desirable directions requires careful nurture. Thus, for example, against W.G. Ward's view that children have 'a natural idea of right and duty' he (aristocratically) contends that 'I am satisfied that all such ideas in children are the result of inculcation & that were it not for inculcation they would not exist at all except probably in a few persons of pre-eminent genius & feeling.'[218] Although he understands that the utilitarian parousia will be a long time coming, Mill is buoyed by the optimism that educators will in fact be able to mould the moral sense of their charges:

> by the improvement of education, the feeling of unity with our fellow creatures shall be (what it cannot be doubted that Christ intended it to be) as deeply rooted in our character, and to our own consciousness as completely a part of our nature, as the horror of crime is in an ordinarily well-brought up young person.[219]

For this to happen, as Mill confided to his diary on 18 February 1854, what is needed is 'the reconstruction of the human intellect *ab imo*'.[220] There would seem to be a certain tension between the required 'inculcation' by educators, with its concomitant of 'rigid discipline', and 'liability to punishment' as 'indispensable means',[221] and Mill's elsewhere expressed view that it is by *self*-improvement that we become truly free, and that it is not 'the object of instruction to inculcate opinions'.[222] In this connection Mill's lauding of Sparta's success in forming morally aware citizens (and doing so without benefit of religion) is instructive;[223] and with regard to Mill's propensity for knowing what is best for everyone, Hamburger's judgment is ominous: 'When one considers the accumulated effects of education, public opinion, and the trained conscience that internalizes the morality of the Religion of Humanity, one is left with an individual that was indoctrinated, socially pressured, and internally restrained.'[224]

Be that as it may, Mill argues that

> If you take an average human mind while still young, before the objects it has chosen in life have given it a turn in any bad direction, you will generally find it desiring what is good, right, and for the benefit of all; and if that season is properly used to implant the knowledge and give the training which shall render rectitude of judgment more habitual than sophistry, a serious barrier will have been erected against the inroads of selfishness and falsehood. Still, it is a very imperfect education which trains the intelligence only, but not the will.[225]

Mill had a good deal to say concerning the curriculum, and this need not detain us here, except to note that in his estimation rigour ought to characterize all education:

> It is, no doubt, a very laudable effort, in modern teaching, to render as much as possible of what the young are required to learn, easy and interesting to them. But when this principle is pushed to the length of not requiring them to learn anything *but* what has been made easy and interesting, one of the chief objects of education is sacrificed. I rejoice in the decline of the old brutal and tyrannical system of teaching, which however did succeed in enforcing habits of application; but the new, as it seems to me, is training up a race of men who will be incapable of doing anything which is disagreeable to them.[226]

Indeed, if reliance may be placed upon Mill's strictures against Oxford and Cambridge universities, too many were doing nothing at all to do with education. Thus, at the time when the question of the possibility of opening the ancient universities to Dissenters was under discussion, Mill asked,

> What is it that the Dissenters want? Is it education? Or is it that their sons should herd with lords' sons? If the former, they ought to know … that Cambridge and Oxford are among the last places where any person wishing for education, and knowing what it is, would go to seek it.[227]

More positively, Mill insists upon the importance of the home in the education of children: 'It is the home, the family, which gives us the moral or religious education we really receive; and this is completed, and modified, sometimes for the better, often for the worse, by society, and the opinions and feelings with which we are there surrounded.'[228] Negatively, if education were made the business of the state individuality could be at risk, and a dominant power of any kind would possess a ready tool of oppression and control. He recommends that the state should take a hand only if society is so backward that otherwise there would be no educational provision at all.[229]

As to the objectives of education, these are both personal and social. First, of great importance to Mill is the moral education of the feelings. Individuals need both to discern and to desire the virtuous, and to exalt 'to the highest pitch the desire of right conduct and the aversion to wrong'.[230] In particular, altruism is to be cultivated: 'It is as much a part of our scheme as of M. Comte's, that the direct cultivation of altruism, and the subordination of egoism to it, far beyond the point of absolute moral duty, should be one of the chief aims of education, both individual and collective.'[231] Secondly, it is necessary that people become 'effective combatants in the great fight which never ceases to rage between Good and Evil, and more equal to coping with the ever new problems which the changing course of human nature and human society present to be resolved'.[232] Moreover, this enterprise should be engaged in without regard to reward, albeit 'there is one reward which will not fail you ... the deeper and more varied interest you will feel in life'.[233] Above all, education is to be the driving force in the spread of the utilitarian creed:

> education and opinion, which have so vast a power over human character, should so use that power as to establish in the mind of every individual an indissoluble association between his own happiness and the good of the whole ... so that not only he may be unable to conceive the possibility of happiness to himself, consistently with conduct opposed to the general good, but also that a direct impulse to promote the general good may be in every individual one of the habitual motives of action.[234]

Underlying Mill's constructive views of education are one fear, one hearty dislike, and one unrealistic piece of musing. As to the fear: in the context of some remarks on the French Revolution he declared that the 'higher classes ... had more to fear from the poor when uneducated, than when educated'.[235] As to the hearty dislike: this returns us to Mill's abhorrence of the inculcation of supernaturalistic religious doctrines, and especially to the claim, in his opinion false, that religious belief was the *sine qua non* of moral living.[236] As to the unrealistic musing, it is this:

> If it were possible to blot out entirely the whole of German metaphysics, the whole of Christian theology, and the whole of the Roman and English systems of technical jurisprudence, and to direct all the minds that expand their faculties in these three pursuits to useful speculation or practice, there would be talent enough set at liberty to change the face of the world.[237]

Of James Mill, John wrote,

> In psychology, his fundamental doctrine was the formation of all human
> character by circumstances, through the universal Principle of Association, and
> the consequent unlimited possibility of improving the moral and intellectual
> condition of mankind by education. Of all his doctrines none was more important
> than this, or needs more to be insisted on.[238]

In this connection, more perhaps than in any other, Mill, despite his
qualifications of the doctrine, remained his father's son.

V

Mill's substitute religion has now been examined in sufficient detail. I have
sought to show that he derived the theory of his Religion of Humanity from
Comte, while making such amendments to it as he thought fit, and entirely
repudiating Comte's religious practices and rubrics. I have examined his
utilitarian creed, his underlying doctrine of humanity, and his quasi-
missionary advocacy of education. All of this has been done with an eye to
his critics, contemporary and subsequent. It remains to offer some general
reflections on what Mill's substitute religion amounts to from the
perspective of Christian orthodoxy. Three points will suffice.

First, we have seen that in advancing his own views Mill is less than fully
consistent. He oscillates between positions, sometimes within the same text.
It has graciously been suggested that this may in part be explained by the
practical rather than analytical interests which dominated his life. It may also
be that with the passage of time he felt more able to articulate his true
religious feelings than was the case in earlier years when, rightly or wrongly,
he felt constricted by a public opinion which he felt would throw out
positivism lock stock and barrel if it were presented as overtly hostile to
Christianity. But quite apart from argumentative inconsistency there is the
question of his argumentative strategy, and here he cannot receive full
marks. Whether for rhetorical purposes, or because of his self-confessed lack
of close knowledge of Christian theology and writings, he is very much the
'barrack-room lawyer' in setting up allegedly Christian Aunt Sallies with a
view to knocking them down. Where the issues discussed in this chapter are
concerned, his (and Comte's) accusation that Christianity is a reward-
obsessed, selfish religion which is short on altruism exemplifies the point.
Selectively, and without any recourse to Christian authors, he puts the most
unfavourable interpretation on Christian teaching, and this is simply not
good philosophical practice. To say that the New Testament is replete with
exhortations to altruism and denunciations of selfishness; and that, properly
conceived, the eternal reward is a divine gift consequent upon godly living
but not the motive of it, is to utter commonplaces which cannot easily be

denied.[239] It is logically possible that all Christians who think along these lines are misguided, but that is not the point at issue here. The point is that Christians are in no way bound to accept Mill's account of their attitudes and beliefs. Moreover, it is not unfair of Christians to ask Mill questions about the motive force of his creed. As W.G. De Burgh insisted,

> The religious motive alters the whole scale. For morality, man is the measure ... for religion, the measure is God ... This is where Christianity parts company with Stoicism. It was a fatal misapprehension that led John Stuart Mill, after declaring that self-respect was one of the noblest incentives to a life of virtue, to claim, almost in the same breath, that his utilitarianism was wholly in accord with the teaching of the Founder of Christianity ... It is clear that the new motive, the love of God, involves a transformation that is radical and all-pervasive.[240]

Secondly, in the line of many of Mill's critics, Christians will clearly not be able to accept humanity (however idealized) as an adequate object of worship. Some of his Christian critics were quick to accuse him of idolatry but, as we have seen, his idol was intangible to the point of extreme elusiveness. As for actual human beings, Mill's attitude is frequently but not consistently unwholesomely aristocratic in that he can contemplate leaving on one side the masses in favour of the 'Gnostic' few whose feelings are cultivated sufficently for them to grasp the principles of the Religion of Humanity and subscribe to its creed. On other occasions Mill appears to think that the Religion of Humanity is capable of reaching much further: 'If we suppose cultivated to the highest point the sentiments of fraternity with all our fellow beings ... universal moral education making the happiness and dignity of this collective body the central point to which all things are to tend and by which all are to be estimated, instead of the pleasure of an unseen and imaginary Power ... there is no worthy office of a religion which this system of cultivation does not seem adequate to fulfil ... Now this is merely supposing that the religion of humanity obtained as firm a hold on mankind ... as other religions have in many cases possessed.'[241] But the

> 'merely' in the last sentence here is enormous. Confronted by such expansive evangelical optimism we cannot but be brought up short by the wag who described the Fetter Lane Comtian worship of Richard Congreve, E.S. Beesly and Frederic Harrison as the worship of 'three persons and no God'.[242]

In opposition to unrealistic assessments of the human condition such as those espoused by Mill, traditional Christianity invokes the concepts of grace, sin[243] and redemption as referring to the realities of humanity's creation, situation and final end. From many examples I select the words of one of the more thoughtful and less polemical nineteenth-century Christian tractarians:

Those who take the spiritual view of human nature and morality differ, no doubt among themselves. But all agree that man is spiritual, that the voice of Duty speaks from above, that Right is to be sought in what is higher and more authoritative than feeling, – whether the sensations of the body of the emotions of the soul.[244]

Does Christianity take a less noble view than Positivism of human nature, as created by God, and as re-created in Christ by the Spirit of God? On the contrary, the Scriptures assure us that 'God created man *in His own image*', and 'made him *but little lower than God*' [Revised Version], that 'there is a spirit in man, and the breath of the Almighty giveth them understanding'. Christianity confers upon our nature the highest honour, for its central truth is that the eternal Word became '*the Son of Man*,' that He might redeem and save the nature which He deigned to share.[245]

These points are underscored and supplemented by Sydney Cave, Thomson's successor at New College:

To a facile optimism, which believes that men need only to be organized aright and all will be well, the Christian estimate of man opposes the recognition of our human sinfulness and the need of a divine Redeemer ... Yet the Christian estimate of man is no less opposed to the cynicism and pessimism which are often the aftermath of idealism ... We cannot hold low views of man when we remember that the Divine took our manhood upon Himself. And the Cross, which is the gravest exposure of human sin, is at the same time the symbol of how God counts men dear ...
> *Quaerens me sedisti lassus*
> *Redemisti crucem passus,*
> *Tantus labor non sit cassus ...*
These ancient words express the abiding source of the Christian hope for man.[246]

This is not the place to defend the doctrine to which these witnesses hold. It suffices to observe the profound difference between the Christian estimate of man and Mill's, and to regret that Mill, far from countering or even noticing such views, resorts to caricature when referring to the Christian position. Ironically, he writes that the success of those who seek to understand human nature and human life 'will be proportional to two things: the degree in which his own nature and circumstances furnish him with a correct and complete picture of man's nature and circumstances; and his capacity of deriving light from other minds'.[247] As to the first, Mill's nature and circumstances (especially his early training) were not such as to furnish him with a 'complete picture of man's nature and circumstances'; as to the second, where the Christian doctrine of humanity is concerned Mill's myopia is as disturbing as it is disabling, and his very next sentence, 'Bentham failed in deriving light from other minds' constitutes as splendid an example as one could wish for of the pot calling the kettle black.

Thirdly, Christians cannot concur with Mill that happiness in any mundane sense is the ultimate value. Even on his own terms, as we saw, he has to make room for self-sacrifice – albeit with a view to the ultimate greater happiness of all, but the issue is deeper than that. With reference to God's saving activity at the Cross, Christians hold that in Christian ethics love, not 'the greatest amount of happiness altogether',[248] is the criterion, and gratitude the motive. In Christian teleology the end is beatitude: 'Man's chief end is to glorify God and to enjoy him for ever.'[249] The means to the end is, on the ground of the Son's saving work, a reconciled life of praise and service enabled by the sanctifying grace of God the Holy Spirit. To put it otherwise, it is a matter of the restoration of the defaced, but not obliterated, *imago dei*. But, to repeat, Mill cannot take this line (and does not counter it either, except obliquely with his anti-supernaturalism), for he does not believe in God as Christians do. The question how far he believes in God at all will occupy us in the next chapter. For the present, and for the reasons given, we must respectfully decline to espouse the Religion of Humanity.

Notes

1 J.S. Mill, *Autobiography*, CW, I, p.45.
2 For a helpful introduction to Comte's thought see Gertrude Lenzer, *Auguste Comte and Positivism: The Essential Writings*, New York: Harper, 1975. For a wide-ranging account of the influence of positivism upon nineteenth century theology see Charles D. Cashdollar, *The Transformation of Theology, 1830–1890. Positivism and Protestant Thought in Britain and America*, Princeton: Princeton University Press, 1989.
3 Letter of Mill to Comte of 8 November 1841, CW, XIII, p.489. In this letter Mill records 1828 as the year of his first acquaintance with Comte's ideas, but other letters show that this was a mistake on his part.
4 R. Flint, *Anti-Theistic Theories*, Edinburgh: Blackwood, 6th edn, 1899, p.505. For Flint (1838–1910) see DNCBP, ODNB; Alan P.F. Sell, *Defending and Declaring the Faith: Some Scottish Examples 1860–1920*, Exeter: Paternoster Press and Colorado Springs: Helmers & Howard, 1987, ch.3.
5 For an engaging account of this, see T.R. Wright, *The Religion of Humanity. The Impact of Comtian Positivism on Victorian Britain*, Cambridge: CUP, 1986.
6 For a brief attemted justification of this bold claim, see Alan P.F. Sell, *Confessing and Commending the Faith: Historic Witness and Apologetic Method*, Cardiff: University of Wales Press, 2002, pp.99–106.
7 Since it would take me too far afield to adduce evidence for this claim here (though see ibid., 305–7, 448–9) I ought, perhaps, to apologize for this uncharacteristically hoity-toity observation. (But some of them *are* a pain!)
8 A. Comte, 'Preface' *The Catechism of Positive Religion*, trans. Richard Congreve, 2nd edn, London: Trübner, 1883, p.25. The Congregational minister J. Radford Thomson mused, 'It would be interesting to know whether any habitual votaries of Clothilde de Vaux are to be found in the select circle of our English Positivists.' See his *Auguste Comte and 'The Religion of Humanity'*, London: The Religious Tract Society (bound in *Present Day Tracts*, VIII, no. 47, 1887), p.15. For Thomson (d.1918) see DNCBP.
9 J. Tulloch, *Modern Theories in Philosophy and Religion*, Edinburgh: Blackwood, 1884, p.25.
10 R. Flint, *Anti-Theistic Theories*, 177.

11   G.H. Lewes, *The History of Philosophy from Thales to Comte*, London: Longmans Green, 1867, II, p.637. Cf. J.H. Bridges, *The Unity of Comte's Life and Doctrine*, London: Trübner, 1866.

12   J. M'Cosh, *An Examination of Mr. J. S. Mill's Philosophy. Being a Defence of Fundamental Truth*, London: Macmillan, 1866, p.389. For M'Cosh (1811–94) see DNCBP, DSCHT; James D. Hoeveler, Jr., *James M'Cosh and the Scottish Intellectual Tradition*, Princeton: Princeton University Press, 1981.

13   J. M'Cosh, *An Examination of Mr J.S. Mills's Philosophy. Being a Defence of Fundamental Truth*, 395.

14   R. Flint, *Anti-Theistic Theories*, 192–3.

15   J.S. Mill, *Auguste Comte and Positivism*, CW, X, p.279.

16   R. Flint, *Anti-Theistic Theories*, 181.

17   Ibid., 183.

18   Ibid., 184. Cf. the remark of B.M.G. Reardon, *Religious Thought in the Nineteenth Century*, Cambridge: CUP, 1966, p.25: 'contrary to its own principles [positivism] reintroduced metaphysics in the shape of naturalism'.

19   R. Flint, *Anti-Theistic Theories*, 184–5. Robert C. Scharff has more recently attributed the differing emphases of Comte and Mill *vis-à-vis* positivism and the philosophy of science to the fact that Comte, standing at the threshold of the era of science, felt a need to justify the positivist approach, whereas Mill could more easily take it for granted. See his 'Positivism, philosophy of science and self-understanding in Comte and Mill', *American Philosophical Quarterly*, XXVI, 1989, 253–68, reprinted in Víctor Sánchez-Valencia (ed.), *The General Philosophy of John Stuart Mill*, 155–70.

20   J. Martineau, *Types of Ethical Theory*, Oxford: Clarendon Press, 3rd revised edn, 1891, I, p.456.

21   R. Flint, *Anti-Theistic Theories*, 195.

22   Ibid., 196–7.

23   Ibid., 189.

24   R. Mackintosh, *From Comte to Benjamin Kidd. The Appeal to Biology or Evolution for Human Guidance*, London: Macmillan, 1899, p.29. For Mackintosh (1858–1932) see DNCBP, ODNB; Alan P.F. Sell, *Robert Mackintosh: Theologian of Integrity*, Berne: Peter Lang, 1977.

25   R. Mackintosh, *From Compte to Benjamin Kidd*, 30.

26   See *The Positive Philosophy of Auguste Comte*, freely translated and condensed by Harriet Martineau, London, J. Chapman, 1853, II, p.288.

27   The charge is found in his *Catechism* and elsewhere.

28   A. Comte, *System of Positive Polity*, trans. J. H. Bridges *et al.*, London: Longmans, 1875–7, III, p.383.

29   E. Caird, *The Social Philosophy and Religion of Comte*, Glasgow: Maclehose, 1893, pp.190–91. For Caird (1835–1908) see DNCBP, DSCHI, ODNB; Alan P.F. Sell, *Philosophical Idealism and Christian Belief*, Cardiff: University of Wales Press and New York: St. Martin's Press, 1995.

30   E. Caird, *The Social Philosophy and Religion of Comte*, 53–4.

31   Ibid., 66.

32   Ibid., 67.

33   Ibid., 78.

34   R. Mackintosh, *From Comte to Benjamin Kidd*, 23–4.

35   See further Iris Wessel Mueller, *John Stuart Mill and French Thought*, Urbana: University of Illinois Press, 1956.

36   Oscar A. Haac (ed.), *The Correspondence of John Stuart Mill and Auguste Comte*, New Brunswick, NJ: Transaction Publishers, 1995, pp.118–19.

37   J.S. Mill, *Auguste Comte and Positivism*, CW, X, pp.266, 267.

38   Idem, *Autobiography*, CW, I, p.173.

39 Cf. A. Bain, *John Stuart Mill. A Criticism: With Personal Recollections*, London: Longmans, Green, 1882, p.72: 'Mill, it will be seen from the *Logic* (Book VI., chap. X), accepted the Three Stages as an essential part of Comte's Historical Method, which method he also adopts and expounds as the completion of the Logic of Sociology.' For his part, Flint wondered how Mill could suppose himself a follower of Comte as regards the three stages, while at the same time allowing that the fixed order which phenomena are said to obey *may* have been instituted by God. See *Anti-Theistic Theories*, 190–91.

40 Letter of Mill to Gustave D'Eichthal of 8 October 1829, CW, XII, p.35.

41 J.S. Mill, *Auguste Comte and Positivism*, CW, X, pp.267–8.

42 J.S. Mill, *Autobiography*, CW, I, p.219.

43 W.L. Courtney was not alone in detecting an incongruity in the thought of those who wished both to espouse both sensationalism and associationism. See, for example, his T*he Metaphysics of John Stuart Mill*, (1879), Bristol: Thoemmes Press, 1990, p.62: 'If Realism be accepted, then Sensations can be associated, because they may be conceived as already existing in a certain objective order: but if Sensationalism be accepted, then Sensations cannot be associated at all, for there must first be a mental process (not "feeling") to bring them into relations with one another, in order that they may be associated. So little is it true that Association explains Thought, that the reverse is the case. It is Thought which explains the possibility of Association.' R. Scharff argues that the underlying difference here is that 'the empirical and introspectionist psychology Mill defends is not the old-fashioned "rational" psychology Comte rejects'. See 'Positivism, philosophy and science', 259 (reprint, 161). See further, Thomas Heyd, 'Mill on Comte and psychology', *Journal of the History of the Behavioural Sciences*, XXV, 1989, 125–38; Fred Wilson, 'Mill and Comte on the method of introspection', ibid., XXVII, 1991, 107–29; both reprinted in V. Sánchez-Valencia (ed.), *The General Philosophy of John Stuart Mill*.

44 For the argument that Mill and Comte spoke past one another on this issue see Robert C. Sharff, 'Mill's misreading of Comte on "interior observation"', *Journal of the History of Philosophy*, XXVII no.4, October 1989, 559–72. Scharff's point is that, whereas Mill took Comte to be attacking the empirical procedure of introspection, Comte was denying a metaphysical possibility. We need not adjudicate this matter; it suffices us to know that, rightly or wrongly, Mill was at odds with Comte over introspection.

45 J.S. Mill, *A System of Logic, Ratiocinative and Inductive*,CW, VIII, pp.850–51.

46 Idem, *Auguste Comte and Positivism*, CW, X, p.296.

47 Idem, *Autobiography*, CW, I, p.271.

48 Op.cit, CW, IX, 2.

49 W.L. Courtney, *The Metaphysics of John Stuart Mill* (1879), 45.

50 C. Douglas, *John Stuart Mill. A Study of His Philosophy*, Edinburgh: Blackwood, 1895, p.119. Douglas proceeds to express his opinion that, while Comte's positivism is a Catholic one, Mill's, with its elevation of the individual, is a Protestant one.

51 J.S. Mill, 'Theism', CW, X, p.463.

52 Idem, *Hamilton*, CW, IX, p.183.

53 R. Flint, *Anti-Theistic Theories*, 185–6.

54 J.S. Mill, *Hamilton*, 189.

55 Ibid., 193.

56 Ibid., 194.

57 This was the point which James M'Cosh pressed against Mill. See his *Examination of Mr. J.S. Mill's Philosophy*, 80–83. See further, J. David Hoeveler, Jr., *James McCosh and the Scottish Intellectual Tradition*, ch.4.

58 J.S. Mill, *Hamilton*, 194.

59 T. Whittaker, *Comte and Mill* (1908), reprinted Bristol: Thoemmes Press, 1993, p.44.

60 J.S. Mill, *Auguste Comte and Positivism*, CW, X, p.265. Concerning one of Mill's important linguistic oscillations, we should be warned by W.L. Courtney, *The*

Metaphysics of John Stuart Mill, 79: 'Mill as an Inductive Logician supposes that phenomena (objective facts) are immediately cognised by us, while Mill as a Psychologist, a critic of Hamilton, and a metaphysician, supposes that phenomena, the facts immediately cognised by us, are mere subjective presentations.'

61   J.S. Mill, *Auguste Compte and Positivism*, CW, X, 270.
62   Ibid.
63   Cf. ibid., 310.
64   Ibid., 313–14.
65   Idem, *Autobiography*, CW, I, pp.219, 221.
66   Ibid., 221. Cf. John Morley, *Critical Miscellanies*, London: Macmillan, 1898, p.74: 'Comte ... presumed ... to draw up a minute plan of social reconstruction, which contains some ideas of great beauty and power, some of extreme absurdity, and some which would be very mischievous if there were the smallest chance of their ever being realised.'
67   Letter of Mill to Comte of 31 December 1844, *Correspondence*, p.278.
68   My italics. This tract was published posthumously as one of his *Three Essays on Religion*, 1874. As Whittaker correctly pointed out, Mill's first *published* endorsement of the Religion of Humanity (though not by name) is in his *Utilitarianism*, which appeared in *Fraser's Magazine* in 1861, and was separately pubished in 1863. See T. Whittaker, *Comte and Mill*, 70; cf. Mill, CW, X, p.232: Comte 'has super-abundantly shown the possibility of giving to the service of humanity, even without the aid of a belief in Providence, both the psychical power and the social efficacy of a religion'.
69   A. Ryan, *J.S. Mill*, London: Routledge & Kegan Paul, 1974, p.219. Cf. Charles D. Cashdollar, *The Transformation of Theology, 1830–1890*, 161: 'the ideas that [Mill] said Comte advanced – a religious faith tested by its fruits, a commitment to living for others, the solidarity of the human race – proved especially suggestive to those intent on restructuring theology'.
70   Cf. Robert Carr, 'The religious thought of John Stuart Mill: a study in reluctant scepticism', *Journal of the History of Ideas*, XXIII, 1962, 485; reprinted in Victor Sánchez-Valencia (ed.), *The General Philosophy of John Stuart Mill*, 432.
71   T.R. Wright, *The Religion of Humanity*, 9.
72   J.S. Mill, 'Utility of Religion', CW, X, p.405. The possibility articulated in the latter sentence here is urged by some present-day Church of England dignitaries as a ground for the building of more Church schools.
73   Ibid., 419.
74   Alan Millar, 'Mill on religion', in John Skorupski (ed.), *The Cambridge Companion to Mill*, Cambridge: CUP, 1998, p.197.
75   J.S. Mill, 'Utility of Religion', CW, X, p.422.
76   Ibid.
77   Idem, *Auguste Comte and Positivism*, CW, X, p.332.
78   T.H. Huxley, *Lay Sermons, Addresses and Reviews*, London: Macmillan, 1883, p.148.
79   J.S. Mill, *Auguste Comte and Positivism*, CW, X, p.334.
80   J. Tulloch, *Modern Theories in Philosophy and Religion*, 76 n.
81   See Letter of Mill to Comte of 1 May 1844, *Correspondence*, p.232. It is testimony to the pervasiveness in his writings of Mill's desire to replace old religion with new that he reports to Comte his belief that his *Logic* will ease the transition from 'the metaphysical to the positive spirit', while through his *Political Economy* the spirit of positivism will penetrate political discussion. See his letters of 12 December 1842 and 6 February 1844, *Correspondence*, pp.120, 228, respectively.
82   Idem, 'Utility', CW, p.423.
83   Ibid., 428.
84   Noah Porter, 'John Stuart Mill as a religious philosopher', *Dickinson's Theological Quarterly*, 1875, 503. For Porter (1811–92) see DAB, MR.
85   J.S. Mill, *Auguste Comte and Positivism*, CW, X, p.332.

86   Ibid., 333.
87   Ibid., 337.
88   Idem, *On Liberty*, CW, XVIII, p.227.
89   Idem, *Auguste Comte and Positivism*, CW, X, p.341.
90   Ibid., 341–2. The emblem of Comte's Religion of Humanity is a woman of 30 carrying a child. Comte ordained that a statue of mother and child should be placed in every temple of humanity, and that the pair should appear on processional banners.
91   Ibid., 364.
92   E. Caird, *The Social Philosophy and Religion of Comte*, 136.
93   J. Orr, *The Christian View of God and the World*, 4th edn, Edinburgh: Andrew Elliot, 1897, p.385.
94   J.S. Mill, *Auguste Comte and Positivism*, CW, X, p365.
95   Letter of Mill to Congreve of 8 August 1865, CW, XVI, p.1085.
96   Idem, 'Theism,' CW, X, p.489. Cf. his letters to Comte of 15 December 1842, *Correspondence*, p.118; and 18 December 1841, CW, XII, p.491; and his diary entry of 24 January 1854, CW, XXVII, p.646
97   R. Flint, *Anti-Theistic Theories*, 198–9.
98   Ibid., 201.
99   W.G. De Burgh, *From Morality to Religion*, London: MacDonald & Evans, 1938, pp.104–5.
100   J. Laird, *Theism and Cosmology*, London: Allen and Unwin, 1940, p.61.
101   A.S. Pringle-Pattison, *The Idea of God in the Light of Recent Philosophy*, 2nd revised edn, New York: OUP, 1920, p.133; cf. p.146.
102   Ibid., 149.
103   G.D. Hicks, *The Philosophical Bases of Theism*, London: Allen and Unwin, 1937, pp.83–4.
104   R. Flint, *Anti-Theistic Theories*, 209.
105   K. Britton, *Philosophy and the Meaning of Life*, Cambridge: CUP, 1969, p.93.
106   E. Caird, *The Social Philosophy and Religion of Comte*, xiv.
107   J. Seth, *A Study of Ethical Principles*, 5th edn, Edinburgh: Blackwood, 1899, pp.403–4.
108   Henry Ireson, 'The religious views of John Stuart Mill', *The Unitarian Review and Religious Magazine*, I, no. 2, April 1874, 105–6. For Ireson (1819–1892) see *The Inquirer*, 3 September 1892, 573–4; 10 September 1892, 591–2; 5 November 1892, 712; 12 November 1892, 729.
109   See B. Russell, 'My mental development', in P.A. Schlipp (ed.), *The Philosophy of Bertrand Russell*, Evanston and Chicago: Northwestern University Press, 1944, p.10.
110   See W. Paley, *Principles of Moral and Political Philosophy*, 1st edn, (1785), reprinted London: J. Faulder, *et al.*, 19th edn, (1811). For a brief account of utilitarianism's eighteenth-century harbingers see James E. Crimmins, *Utilitarians and Religion*, Bristol: Thoemmes Press, 1998, pp.3–25.
111   J.S. Mill, *Autobiography*, CW, I, p.69. In apparent contradiction of Mill's own testimony, H.S. Jones argues that 'if Mill had a single fundamental commitment that permeated all his major works, it was neither to utilitarianism nor to liberty as such but to what might be termed – if we may be excused a striking paradox – a conception of virtue or the good life, and that the basic constituent of that conception was an ideal or rationality.' Unlike the person whose ethic is grounded in instinct or an innate moral sense, a good person is one who can provide a rational defence of an ethical stance. See 'John Stuart Mill as moralist', *Journal of the History of Ideas*, LIII, no. 2, April–June 1992, 288. It would be interesting to know what Jones makes of the view of D.D. Raphael, who understands Mill as locating virtue within the category of aesthetics rather than of morality: 'It is a species of the "beautiful or noble", and is commended as noble rather than prescribed as obligatory.' See 'Fallacies in and about Mill's *Utilitarianism*', *Philosophy*, XXX, October 1955, 346 n.
112   J.S. Mill, *Autobiography*, CW, I, 137.

113   Idem, *Utilitarianism*, CW, X, p.210.

114   Idem, 'Sedgwick's discourse', 1835, CW, X, p.53. Cf. Mill's paper, 'Whewell on moral philosophy', 1852, CW, X, p.173. The former is a reply to Adam Sedgwick's *A Discourse on the Studies of the University*, 1833, 3rd edn, reprinted London: Parker, 1834. James E. Crimmins's remark that Sedgwick's *Discourse* 'provoked a sympathetic response from J.S. Mill' is puzzling (see his *Utilitarians and Religion*, Bristol: Thoemmes Press, 1998, p.24), the more so because he immediately quotes Mill's concurrence with his father and others who were indignant at Sedgwick's 'intemperate assault on analytic psychology and utilitarian ethics' via an 'attack' on the views of Locke and Paley. See Mill's *Autobiography*, CW, I, p.209. For Paley see M.L. Clarke, *Paley: Evidences for the Man*, Toronto: University of Toronto Press, 1974, esp. pp.59–62.

115   J.S. Mill, *Utilitarianism*, CW, X, p.222. My italics. Just as Mill, however hypothetically, summons the God in whom he does not believe to enlist in his cause, so he can elsewhere show to his own satisfaction that the doctrine of innate ideas, to which he does not subscribe, hypothetically bears witness to the truth of utilitarianism. See ibid., 230.

116   Ibid., 218. What we actually read there is Jesus's summary of the Decalogue, the Jewish Law. The quintessence of *Christian* ethics, as T.W. Manson observed, is 'Love as I have loved you.' See T.W. Manson, *Ethics and the Gospel*, London: SCM Press, 1960, pp.60–62. In 'Utility of Religion' (CW, X, p.416) Mill does refer to 'the new commandment to love one another', and he cites John 13: 34. But he omits the very words which make it new: 'as I have loved you'.

117   See L. Stephen, *The English Utilitarians*, London: Duckworth, 1900, III, p.447. Cf. W.L. Courtney, *Life of John Stuart Mill*, London: Walter Scott, 1889, 173.

118   J. S. Mill, 'Utility of Religion', CW, X, p.406.

119   Ibid., 405.

120   D.P. Dryer, 'Mill's utilitarianism', in CW, X, p.lxiii.

121   D.E. Miller, 'Mill, John Stuart', in W.J. Mander and Alan P.F. Sell (eds), *Dictionary of Nineteenth-Century British Philosophers*, Bristol: Thoemmes Press, 2002, p.795. For contrasting papers which have by now attained classic status see, for example, J.O. Urmson, 'The interpretation of the philosophy of J.S. Mill', *The Philosophical Quarterly*, III, 1953, reprinted in J.B. Schneewind (ed.), *Mill. A Collection of Critical Essays*, London: Macmillan, 1968, pp.179–189; J.D. Mabbott, 'Interpretation of Mill's utilitarianism', *The Philosophical Quarterly*, VI, 1956, reprinted in J.B. Schneewind, op.cit., pp.190–98; D. Daiches Raphael, 'Fallacies in and about Mill's *Utilitarianism*'; R.F. Atkinson, 'J.S. Mill's "proof" of the principle of utility', *Philosophy*, XXXII, April 1957, pp.158–67.

122   W.L. Davidson, 'Mill, James and John Stuart', *Encyclopaedia of Religion and Ethics*, ed. James Hastings, Edinburgh: T. & T. Clark, VII, 1915, pp.640–41. Davidson (1848–1929) was professor of logic and metaphysics at the University of Aberdeen. See DNCBP.

123   W. Whewell, 'Preface', *The Elements of Morality Including Polity*, London: John W. Parker, 1845, p.3. See further, Charles Douglas, *The Ethics of John Stuart Mill*, Edinburgh: Blackwood, 1897.

124   J.S. Mill, 'Bentham', CW, X, p.86.

125   K. Britton, *John Stuart Mill*, Harmondsworth: Penguin, 1953, p.9.

126   James E. Crimmins, *Utilitarians and Religion*, 271.

127   J.S. Mill, 'Bentham', CW, X, p.81.

128   Mill later questioned the wisdom of publishing his criticisms of Bentham when he did, on the ground that Bentham's philosophy had been 'to some extent discredited before it had done its work, and that to lend a hand towards lowering its reputation was doing more harm than service to improvement'. See his *Autobiography*, CW, I, p.227.

129   J.S. Mill, *Utilitarianism*, CW, X, p.212.

130 Linda C. Raeder, *John Stuart Mill and the Religion of Humanity*, 347, queries how great a departure this really was, since both Bentham and James Mill ranked intellectual above sensual pleasures: 'Mill's differentiation of pleasures did not represent a dramatic departure from Benthamism but seems to have been a rhetorical strategy intended to defeat various popular objections to Benthamite utilitarianism.' This simply means that Bentham and James Mill were as untrue to strict 'Benthamism' as John Stuart Mill later became. The impression remains that, however inconsistently, Mill built his 'departure' more firmly into his position than did his predecessors.

131 T.H. Green, *Prolegomena to Ethics*, 4th edn, Oxford: Clarendon Press, 1899, p.192.

132 A.D. Lindsay, 'Introduction' to Mill's *Utilitarianism, Liberty, and Representative Government*, London; Dent, n.d., p.xv.

133 J.S. Mill, *Utilitarianism*, CW, X, p.211.

134 W.L. Courtney, *Life of John Stuart Mill*, p.134.

135 J.S. Mill, *Autobiography*, CW, I, pp.145, 147.

136 W.H. Mallock, 'Is life worth living?' *The Nineteenth Century*, II, 1877, 269.

137 R.J. Halliday, *John Stuart Mill*, London: Allen & Unwin, 1976, p.56.

138 Letter of Mill to Carlyle of 12 January 1834, CW, XII, p.207.

139 K. Britton, 'Utilitarianism: the appeal to a first principle,' *Proceedings of the Aristotelian Society*, NS, LX, 1959–60, p.144.

140 Letter of 23 November 1836 to Edward Lytton Bulwer, CW, XII, p.312.

141 K. Britton, *John Stuart Mill*, 22. Later Britton writes, 'Mill's method turns out to be very much the same as that which Coleridge had applied to history; a personal, intuitive, morally discriminating method, a method of direct observation, but not the method of the experimental sciences' (Ibid., 74).

142 J.S. Mill, 'Bentham', CW, X, pp.92, 93.

143 J. Plamenatz, *The English Utilitarians*, 2nd edn, Oxford: Blackwell, 1966, p.144.

144 J.S. Mill, *Utilitarianism*, CW, X, p.231.

145 C. Douglas, John Stuart Mill. A Study of his Philosophy, Edinburgh: Blackwood, 1895, p.204. Douglas quotes from Mill's *Dissertations and Discussions*, I, p.363.

146 J.S. Mill, *Utilitarianism*, CW, X, p.211.

147 K. Britton, *John Stuart Mill*, 54.

148 F.H. Bradley, *Ethical Studies*, (1876), reprinted London: OUP, 1962, p.123.

149 T.H. Green, *Prolegomena to Ethics*, 201. Cf. Peter Nicholson, *The Political Philosophy of the British Idealists: Selected Studies*, Cambridge: CUP, 1990. For a variety of contemporary responses to Green see Alan P.F. Sell, *Philosophical Idealism and Christian Belief*, 147–53.

150 J. Radford Thomson, *A Dictionary of Philosophy in the Words of the Philosophers*, London: R.D. Dickinson, 1887, p.xl.

151 A.C. Ewing, *Ethics*, London: English Universities Press, 1953, p.43. Cf. James Seth, *A Study of Ethical Principles*, 124.

152 A. Bain, *John Stuart Mill. A Criticism*, London: Longmans, Green, 1882, p.113.

153 For discussions of Mill's notion of higher and lower values see Robert W. Hoag, 'Mill's conception of happiness as an inclusive end', *Journal of the History of Philosophy*, XXV, 1987, 417–31; and David O. Brink, 'Mill's deliberative utilitarianism', *Philosophy and Public Affairs*, XXI, 1992, 67–103, both of which are reprinted in C.L. Ten (ed.), *Mill's Moral, Political and Legal Philosophy*.

154 J. S. Mill, *Utilitarianism*, CW, X, p.211. This point is developed by Wendy Donner, 'Utilitarianism', in John Skorupski (ed.), *The Cambridge Companion to Mill*, ch. 7.

155 F.H. Bradley, *Ethical Studies*, 122 n.

156 W.D. Ross, *Foundations of Ethics*, Oxford: Clarendon Press, 1939, p.66.

157 W.L. Courtney, *Life of John Stuart Mill*, 132.

158 See *Auguste Comte and Positivism*, CW, X, pp.335–8.

159 Letter to H. Jones, CW, XVI, p.1414. Mill was pleased to note that, for all his ethical deontologism, Coleridge could declare that 'the *outward* object of virtue' is 'the

greatest producible sum of happiness of all men'. See his 'Coleridge', CW, X, p.159. F.H. Bradley charged Mill with according more than one sense to 'happiness'. See *Ethical Studies*, 120, n.

160 J.S. Mill, *Utilitarianism*, CW, X, p.234.
161 J.S. Mackenzie, *A Manual of Ethics*, 6th edn, London: University Tutorial Press, 1929, p.174.
162 See H. Sidgwick, *The Methods of Ethics*, London: Macmillan, 1930, *passim*.
163 J.S. Mill, 'Remarks on Bentham's philosophy', CW, X, 6. Cf. 'Bentham', ibid., 95–6.
164 Ibid.
165 Idem, *On Liberty*, CW, XVIII, p.263. Cf. J. Plamenatz, *The English Utilitarians*, 129.
166 J.S. Mill, 'Remarks on Bentham's philosophy', CW, X, p.13.
167 J. Plamenatz, *The English Utilitarians*, 129, citing *On Liberty*, CW, XVIII, p.267.
168 C. Douglas, *John Stuart Mill*, 196.
169 As is well known, Thomas Carlyle fumed that utilitarianism was an ethical position for non-human sentient beings only. The pleasure-seeking theory would have us expostulate, 'Not on Morality, but on Cookery, let us build our stronghold: there brandishing our frying-pan, as censer, let us offer sweet incense to the Devil, and live at ease on the fat things *he* has provided for his Elect!' See his *Sartor Resartus*, London: Chapman and Hall, 1858, II, pp.vii, 99.
170 J.S. Mill, *A System of Logic*, CW, VIII, p.951.
171 Cf. idem, *Utilitarianism*, CW, X, p.218. Unlike his friend Carlyle, Mill did not approve of self-renunciation for its own sake, and was critical of those versions of Christianity which advocated this.
172 C. Douglas, *John Stuart Mill*, 189.
173 J. Martineau, *Types of Ethical Theory*, 3rd revised edn, Oxford: Clarendon Press, 1891, II, p.309.
174 J.S. Mill, *Autobiography*, CW, I, p.147.
175 Richard Holt Hutton, 'John Stuart Mill's philosophy as tested in his life', in his *Criticisms on Contemporary Thought and Thinkers Selected from The Spectator*, London: Macmillan, 1894, I, p.185.
176 J.S. Mill, *On Liberty*, CW, XVIII, p.224.
177 Idem, *Auguste Comte and Positivism*, CW, X, p.334.
178 Ibid., 295–6.
179 Idem, *A System of Logic*, CW, VIII, p.879.
180 Ibid., 913–15.
181 See idem, *An Examination of Sir William Hamilton's Philosophy*, CW, IX, pp.206–8.
182 Ibid., 194.
183 J. Scott Lidgett, *The Christian Religion its Meaning and Proof*, London: Robert Culley [1907], p.368. For Lidgett (1854–1953) see DMBI, DNCBP, ODNB.
184 C.B. Crane, 'John Stuart Mill and Christianity', *The Baptist Quarterly* (Philadelphia), VIII, 1874, 356.
185 Cf. John Skorupski, *John Stuart Mill*, London: Routledge, 1989, 23. Cf. my remarks on Mill's view of progress in Chapter 2.
186 J.S. Mill, *Remarks on Bentham's Philosophy*, CW, X, p.7.
187 Letter of Mill to Jones of 13 June 1868, CW, XVI, p.1414.
188 T. Whittaker, *Comte and Mill*, 90–91.
189 'Utility of Religion', CW, X, p.421.
190 Ibid., 419.
191 'Remarks on Bentham's philosophy', CW, X, p.8.
192 'Bentham', Ibid., 95.
193 R.H. Hutton, *Criticisms on Contemporary Thought and Thinkers selected from The Spectator*, 174–5.
194 J.S. Mill, CW, XXVI, 429–30.
195 Idem, 'The Church', 15 February 1828, 424.

196   Idem, *Utilitarianism*, CW, X, p.216.
197   Letter of Mill to William G. Ward of [Spring, 1849], CW, XIV, p.26.
198   J. M'Cosh, *An Examination of Mr. J.S. Mill's Philosophy. Being a Defence of Fundamental Truth*, 376–7.
199   C.B. Crane, 'John Stuart Mill and Christianity', 349. One hundred and thirty years on, one has some reason to suspect that the supply of barbers and tailors is more plentiful than hitherto, whereas that of college student scanners of Horace, whether unsuccessful or successful, has diminished significantly.
200   Ibid., 358.
201   Ibid., 359.
202   Ibid.
203   'Nature,' CW, X, p.376.
204   Ibid., 393.
205   [Henry Reeve] *The Edinburgh Review*, CCLXXXVII, January 1875, 13. For Reeve see MR.
206   Mill to Edward Herford, 22 January 1850, CW, XIV, p.45.
207   J.S. Mill, *Autobiography*, CW, I, pp.239, 241.
208   Idem, *Utilitarianism*, CW, X, p.229.
209   Ibid., 216.
210   Idem, 'Inaugural Address', CW, XXI, p.217. It is interesting to note that in specifying the role of universities Mill advocates a view from which many in our pragmatic–materialistic time would strongly dissent: the university 'is not a place of professional education. Universities are not intended to teach the knowledge required to fit men for some special mode of gaining their livelihood'. Such things should be attended to elsewhere; universities are to produce 'capable and cultivated human beings' (ibid., 218). Again, 'Unless we are to become a nation of mere tradesmen … There must be places where those kinds of knowledge and culture, which have no obvious tendency to better the fortunes of the possessor, but solely to enlarge and exalt his moral and intellectual nature, shall be, as Dr. Chalmers expresses it, *obtruded* upon the public.' See 'Debate on the Universities Admission Bill', CW, VI, p.259. Mill refers to Chalmers, *Considerations on the System of Parochial Schools in Scotland, and on the Advantage of Establishing Them*, Glasgow: James Hedderwick, 1819, p.6. The context of Chalmers's phrase is his argument that free schooling is undesirable, for 'What is gotten for no value, is rated at no value.'
211   Idem, 'Remarks on Bentham's philosophy', CW, X, p.9.
212   Idem, 'Coleridge', 1840, CW, X, pp.138–9.
213   Idem, 'Utility of religion', CW, X, p.409.
214   Idem, 'Coleridge', CW, X, p.131.
215   Idem, *Autobiography*, CW, I, pp.245, 247. Cf. *On Liberty*, CW, XVIII, p.271; and Mill's reflection on his father in his *Autobiography*, CW, I, p.51: 'He would sometimes say, that if life were made what it might be, by good government and good education, it would be worth having: but he never spoke with anything like enthusiasm even of that possibility.'
216   J. Parker, *John Stuart Mill on Liberty. A Critique*, London, 1865, pp.18–19.
217   J.R. Thomson, *Utilitarianism: An Illogical and Irreligious Theory of Morals*, London: The Religious Tract Society (*Present Day Tracts*, VII, no. 40, 1886), 41.
218   Letter of Mill to Ward of [Spring, 1849], CW, XIV, p.30.
219   J.S. Mill, *Utilitarianism*, CW, X, p.227.
220   Idem, CW, XXVII, p.655.
221   Idem, *Autobiography* (Early Draft), CW, X, p.52. This draft was completed in 1854, the year in which *On Liberty* was planned. See Joseph Hamburger, *John Stuart Mill on Liberty and Control*, Princeton: Princeton University Press, 1999, p,14, n.33.
222   J.S. Mill, 'Notes on the newspapers', CW, VI, p.228. Cf, for example, *On Liberty*, CW, XVIII, pp.262–4, 266, etc. If at this point Mill recalled the parental regime under which

he himself had been educated, it is a little surprising that the apostle of liberty did not add, 'nor to censor opinions' – his father's educational policy where Christian doctrine was concerned.

223   J.S. Mill, 'Utility of religion', CW, X, p.409.
224   J. Hamburger, 'Religion and *On Liberty*', in Michael Laine (ed.), *A Cultivated Mind. Essays on J. S. Mill Presented to John M. Robson*, Toronto: University of Toronto Press, 1991, p.166.
225   J.S. Mill, 'Inaugural Address', CW, XXI, p.247.
226   Idem, *Autobiography*, CW, X, pp.53, 55.
227   Idem, 'Notes on the newspapers', CW, VI, p.259.
228   Idem, *Autobiography*, CW, I, p.248. Cf. 'Utility of religion', CW, X, pp.408–9.
229   See idem, *On Liberty*, CW, XVIII, p.302. Twenty years earlier he had argued that, while instruction was the business of the state, education was the responsibility of the family. See 'Notes on the newspapers', CW, VI, p.227.
230   Idem, *An Examination of Sir William Hamilton's Philosophy*, CW, IX, p.453.
231   Idem, *Auguste Comte and Positivism*, CW, X, p.339. In 'Get some service in!' mood Mill adds, 'Something has been lost as well as gained by no longer giving to every citizen the training necessary for a soldier.'
232   Idem, 'Inaugural Address', CW, XXI, p.256.
233   Ibid., 257.
234   Idem, *Utilitarianism*, CW, X, p.218.
235   Idem, *Autobiography*, CW, I, p.179.
236   See *On Liberty*, ch. 4; Letter to Richard Marshall of 5 November 1868, CW, XVI, pp.1478–9.
237   Mill's *Diary*, 7 February 1854, CW, XXVII, p.652.
238   J.S. Mill, *Autobiography*, CW, I, pp.109, 111.
239   The fact that Mill could so easily think of Christainity as inculcating selfishness and as being non-altruistic is the more surprising when one remembers that he was writing at a time when the modern missionary movement was in full swing. While it is fashionable in some quarters today to lambast early missionaries for their imperialism – a charge which, as a good deal of evidence suggests, may more properly be levelled against Western commercial and political interests than against missionaries, many of whom, at great personal cost (even martyrdom and death through disease) sought to carry the Gospel to the ends of the earth. No doubt they made many mistakes, but their concern for the souls, the education and the health of those amongst whom they went was nothing if not altruistic. Closer to home, this was the age when many Christians were in the van of prison reform, opposed to the slave trade, self-sacrificial in the establishment and maintenance of orphanages, urgent in seeking justice for industrial workers: so one could go on. All in all, Mill overlooks a good deal of evidence of altruism in Christian circles, thereby cheapening his argument.
240   W.G. De Burgh, *From Morality to Religion*, pp.237, 239.
241   Mill's *Diary*, 24 January 1854, CW, XXVII, p.646.
242   Recounted by R.F. Horton, *An Autobiography*, London: Allen and Unwin, 1917, p.31.
243   It is interesting to observe how frequently Mill's language seems at first sight to be analogous to Christian ways of speaking. Thus, for example, he informs us that 'nearly every respectable attribute of humanity is the result not of instinct, but of victory over instinct.' See 'Nature', CW, X, p.393. Would Christians be true to Mill's meaning if they were to substitute 'sin' for 'instinct'? Hardly, for the Christian concept of sin derives its meaning from the Christian concepts of grace and divine holiness. Similarly, when Mill speaks of the need to 'reconstruct the human intellect *ab imo*', he is a long way from the apostle Paul's idea of the renewing of the mind. Cf. CW, XXVII, p.655; Ephesians 4: 23.
244   J. Radford Thomson, *Auguste Comte and Positivism*, 5.
245   Idem, *Utilitarianism*, p.62.

246 S. Cave, *The Christian Estimate of Man*, London: Duckworth, 1944, pp.228–9. For Cave (1883–1953) see DHT; *Congregational Year Book*, 1954, 506–7; Ronald Bocking, 'Sydney Cave (1883–1953), missionary, principal, theologian', *Journal of the United Reformed Church History Society*, VII, no. 1, October 2002, 28–35.

247 J.S. Mill, 'Bentham', CW, X, p.90.

248 Idem, *Utilitarianism*, CW, X, p.213.

249 *Westminster Shorter Catechism*, answer to question one: 'What is the chief end of man?'

Chapter 4

Theism, Theology and Christ

From his teenage years to his late essay on 'Theism', John Stuart Mill was fairly regularly occupied with the question of God's existence and character. In 1822, at the age of sixteen, he had, on his father's instruction, written a reply to Paley's *Natural Theology*.[1] But what is noteworthy to the point of astounding is his admission to Carlyle in 1833 that it is not the case that 'the ordinary *difficulties* as they are called, as the origin of evil, & such like, are any serious obstacles to me;'[2] it is rather than he is constitutionally unable to believe. It is not clear why Mill should have written in these terms. If his remark concerning obstacles to belief was honest at the time, it certainly does not represent his general position, in which he appears very much as his father's son. James Mill, he informs us, was not a dogmatic atheist – a position he regarded as absurd. Rather, as we saw in Chapter 1,

> my father's rejection of all that is called religious belief, was not, as many might suppose, primarily a matter of logic and evidence: the grounds of it were moral, still more than intellectual. He found it impossible to believe that a world so full of evil was the work of an Author combining infinite power with perfect goodness and righteousness. His intellect spurned the subtleties by which men attempt to blind themselves to this open contradiction.[3]

This general attitude informed Mill's views on theism, which recur in many of his writings. His inductive method ruled out many of the conclusions of classical theism, as did his crusade against Hamilton's intuitionism. In his more-than-formal *Logic* he appeared as a humanist Valiant for Truth, propagating his method of inference with a view to the accurate estimation of what he regarded as genuine evidence. His advocacy of the Religion of Humanity, together with his view that 'a religion may exist without God', and that 'a religion without a God may be, even to Christians, an instructive and profitable object of contemplation',[4] entailed the repudiation of the very supernaturalism which the traditional theistic arguments presupposed. Among his many references to theism is the following which, as comprehensively as any other, expresses his most consistently held opinion on the subject:

> I do not think it can ever be best for mankind to *believe* what there is not evidence of, but I think that, as mankind improve they will much more recognise two independent mental provinces, the province of belief & the province of imaginative conjecture, that they will become capable of keeping them distinct,

& while they limit their belief to the evidence, will think it allowable to let their imaginative anticipations go forth, not carrying belief in their train, in the direction which experience & the study of human nature shews to be the most improving to the character & the most exalting or consoling to the individual feelings.[5]

It is, however, in his *Three Essays on Religion* that he majors on the subject and from these we shall set out.

These essays, edited by Mill's stepdaughter, Helen Taylor, were published posthumously in 1874. Their appearance prompted a wide variety of responses and caused much ink to flow, as we shall see.[6] What we first need to do is to note carefully their respective dates of composition. The essays on 'Nature' and 'Utility of Religion' were written between 1850 and 1858, at a time when Mill was working on *On Liberty* and on the essays which eventually appeared as *Utilitarianism*. His editor suggests that these essays were not published in the 1850s owing to Mill's reticence in making his religious opinions public, and his reluctance to promulgate half-formed opinions.[7] Whatever the reasons for Mill's silence, the fact of it caused some to challenge him, unaware that he had already dealt with the issues raised. Thus, for example, in his 1866 review of Mill's *Hamilton*, George Grote observed that the author had failed to show how the goodness of God might be reconciled with 'the extent of evil and suffering actually prevailing throughout the earth'.[8] Mill had already tackled this problem in 'Nature' prior to 1858, but the essay was not published until eight years after Grote's criticism. However, in a letter of 21 August 1866 in reply to Robert Pharazyn, Mill said that it had not been to his purpose to address the issue in his study of Hamilton, and then proceeded to present a summary of his position as adumbrated in 'Nature', though without reference to that essay.[9]

The third essay, 'Theism', was drafted at least a decade later, between 1868 and 1870. According to Helen Taylor, while it reveals 'the carefully balanced result of the deliberations of a lifetime',[10] it is, of all Mill's writings, the least polished, for he did not have time to revise it before he died.[11] Although the essays were not intended by Mill to be published together, Miss Taylor, more easily than some of Mill's critics, finds them 'fundamentally consistent'.[12]

The least polished it may have been, but it is in 'Theism' that Mill proceeds through the traditional theistic arguments in the most orderly manner. He discusses in sequence the cosmological, universal consent, ontological and teleological arguments. It might therefore seem appropriate to follow this pattern in our own account. But since Mill's overriding objection to theism (which he often calls deism or natural theology) is moral, and concerns that constellation of issues which gather under the rubric of 'the problem of evil', we shall set out from the indignant onslaught he launches upon God in the first essay, 'Nature'. In this way we shall the more easily be able to detect any changes, even softenings, of view to which Mill became susceptible as the years passed.

I

Mill opens his essay on 'Nature' with an analysis of that ambiguous term. In one sense 'the nature of any given thing is the aggregate of its powers and properties'. It follows that 'Nature in the abstract means the sum of all phenomena, together with the causes which produce them; including not only all that happens, but all that is capable of happening.' Upon examination it is found that phenomena occur with regularity, and by observation and reasoning the conditions which cause the occurrence of many phenomena can be discovered. These, collectively, are denominated the laws of nature. It thus transpires that 'Nature ... in this its simplest acceptation, is a collective name for all facts, actual and possible: or (to speak more accurately) a name for the mode, partly known to us and partly unknown, in which all things take place.'[13] Along this line, human beings are part of nature and all our actions are to that extent natural, and we *could not* fly in the face of nature's laws.

This, however, is not the only sense in which 'nature' is used. In common speech 'Nature is opposed to Art, and natural to artificial.'[14] In art, use is made of natural properties found to hand, and 'the volition which designs, the intelligence which contrives, and the muscular force which executes, are themselves powers of Nature'.[15] In this sense, then, 'Nature' means 'not everything which happens, but only what takes place without the agency, or without the voluntary and intentional agency, of man'.[16]

Mill grants that there are other ambiguities in the term 'nature', but those he has specified are, he believes, its most important denotations. He proceeds to delve briefly into classical antiquity with a view to showing that, historically, nature was widely understood as the foundation of morality. However, 'The Christian theology during the period of its greatest ascendency, opposed some, though not a complete, hindrance to the modes of thought which erected Nature into the criterion of morals, inasmuch as, according to the creed of most denominations of Christians (though assuredly not of Christ) man is by nature wicked.' This doctrine, in turn, provoked the deistic reaction, which is 'almost unanimous in proclaiming the divinity of Nature, and setting up its fancied dictates as an authoritative rule of action'.[17] Mill grants that few could nowadays be found who would develop a system of ethics on the foundation of the so-called 'Law of Nature', but nevertheless the idea that it is good to think, feel and act 'in accordance with nature' is widely prevalent. He raises the possibility of a further sense of 'nature', namely, that which ought to be, only to reject it on the ground that those who appeal to the law of nature do not mean simply to assert that we ought to do what we ought to do; they intend to appeal to an external criterion of right action.

The preliminaries over, Mill announces his major objective in this essay: 'It is proposed to inquire into the truth of the doctrines which make Nature a test of right and wrong, good and evil, or which in any mode or degree attach merit or approval to following, imitating, or obeying Nature.'[18] He has already implied that such doctrines are false, and this is what he sets out to demonstrate.

But first he notes a further ambiguity, namely, that attaching to the term 'law' as in 'law of nature'. This term is used in connection with scientific laws, criminal and civil laws, and the laws of honour, veracity and justice. Scientific laws 'are neither more nor less than the observed uniformities in the occurrence of phenomena'.[19] They are not on all fours with the other usages noted,[20] for we cannot say that the laws of science are obligatory in the way that the others are: we have no option but to live in accordance with the scientific laws of nature. In the first sense of the term, 'There is no mode of acting which is not conformable to Nature' in the sense of acting according to 'the powers and properties of things'.[21]

Is it, then, the case that right action relates to the second sense of 'nature', according to which 'nature' concerns that which, unlike 'art', takes place without any human intervention? No, 'For while human action cannot help conforming to Nature in the open meaning of the term, the very aim and object of action is to alter and improve Nature in the other meaning.'[22] But to amend the created order is to imply its imperfection, and the idea that the created order requires amendment by limited human beings casts doubt upon the idea that nature was instituted by a just, benevolent and omnipotent God.

With this Mill comes to his sustained harangue against the God of the cruelties of nature: 'In sober truth, nearly all the things which men are hanged or imprisoned for doing to one another, are nature's every day performances. Killing, the most criminal act recognized by human laws, Nature does once to every being that lives; and in a large proportion of cases, after protracted tortures.'[23] Nature is clumsy, random, wanton, as hurricanes, floods and the like amply demonstrate. Even if nature's horrors were 'for wise and good ends', this still would not make it right for us to follow nature in ethics: 'Either it is right that we should kill because nature kills; torture because nature tortures; ruin and devastate because nature does the like; or we ought not to consider at all what nature does, but what it is good to do.'[24]

Furthermore, if everything were in the hands of providence, attempts to modify the course of events – by draining a pestilential swamp, curing toothache or putting up an umbrella in the rain – would be impious acts. It is not necessary to deny that good may come from evil ('It is undoubtedly a very common fact' that it does so[25]) but normally good yields good, evil, evil. In any case, natural theologians have been slow to acknowledge that 'if the maker of the world *can* all that he will, he wills misery, and there is no escape from the conclusion'.[26] Again, 'If the Creator of mankind willed that they should all be virtuous, his designs are as completely baffled as if he had willed that they should all be happy.'[27] Utterly appalled by the fact that 'every kind of moral depravity is entailed upon multitudes by the fatality of their birth; through the fault of their parents, of society, or of uncontrollable circumstances, certainly through no fault of their own,' he concludes, 'Not even on the most distorted and contracted theory of good which was ever framed by religious or philosophical fanaticism, can the government of nature be made to resemble the work of a being at once good and omnipotent.'[28] Thus nature, far from being imitated by human beings, is to be amended by them.[29] There is, after all, a 'radical absurdity' in 'attempts to discover, in detail, what are the designs of Providence, in order when they are discovered to help providence in bringing them about.'[30]

In working towards his conclusion, Mill reiterates his view that 'Conformity to nature, has no connection whatever with right and wrong. The idea can never be fitly introduced into ethical discussions at all, except, occasionally and partially, into the question of degrees of culpability.'[31] Thus the suggestion that we 'ought to make the spontaneous course of things' the model of our voluntary actions is 'Irrational, because all human action whatever, consists in altering, and all useful action in improving, the spontaneous course of nature'; and 'Immoral, because the course of natural phenomena being replete with everything which when committed by human beings is most worthy of abhorrence, any one who endeavoured in his actions to imitate the natural course of things would be universally seen and acknowledged to be the wickedest of men.'[32] The upshot is that:

Whatsoever, in nature, gives indication of beneficent design, proves this beneficence to be armed only with limited power; and the duty of man is to co-operate with the beneficent powers, not by imitating but by perpetually striving to amend the course of nature – and bringing that part of it over which we can exercise control, more nearly into conformity with a high standard of justice and goodness.[33]

Mill's devastating critique of Nature convinced a writer in *The Daily Telegraph* that Christians will henceforth rank Mill with Voltaire – indeed, Mill's 'denials go much deeper than those of the doubting Frenchman', for 'He sadly shows that there is a bigotry of science as well as of theology, and that the arrogance of scepticism may be quite as towering as the arrogance of dogma.'[34]

II

A number of specific matters arise from Mill's swingeing critique of nature *qua* moral guide, and we need to proceed carefully, point by point. First, regarding his definitions of 'nature', a number of Mill's critics, with some justification, accused him of special pleading. He grants that the distinction he draws between nature as a thing's 'entire capacity of exhibiting phenomena', and nature as opposed to art 'is far from exhausting the ambiguities of the word'. It is, however, 'the key to most of those on which important consequences depend'.[35] But this latter assertion has been challenged by many writers.[36] It is quite arbitrary, and the suspicion that Mill has simply reached into the bran tub of definitions of 'nature' and drawn out those which most suit his case is difficult to resist. The feeling is accentuated by the fact that he offers no grounds for his selection: we have simply to take his word that he has made the best one. What we have, in fact, is an example of the empiricist–secularist's ploy of ruling out from the beginning, in *a priori* fashion, considerations which are inconvenient – not least, perhaps, to Mill's underlying inductive method, which requires a nature of the most orderly sort.[37] Small wonder that Charles Barnes Upton, the Unitarian philosopher, expostulated,

> As we read Mr. Mill's highly wrought description of Nature's criminalities, the question constantly arises, What right has Mr. Mill, on the principles of his own philosophy, thus to set man's moral judgments and sympathies over against Nature, that he may contrast the two, and show how reckless, cruel and immoral, is the one; and how judicious, benevolent and just, the other? An Intuitional philosopher and a believer in Free-will may possibly contrast his ideal of beauty and goodness with the moral character which he conceives to be displayed in Nature, and may pass a judgment to the disparagement of the latter; but that an Experientialist and Determinist (the writer of the chapter on 'Liberty and necessity'), who must needs regard himself and all his moral ideals and activities, as items in the phenomena which this same Nature has, on the principle of uniformity of sequence, steadily evolved, should thus turn round and revile the system of things which produced him, and of which he is the necessary consequent, seems grotesquely inconsistent and absurd … It is not fair thus to play fast and loose with Intuitive Truth and Moral Freedom; first, to use the doctrine to obtain that severance from the stream of Nature's phenomena, and that independent standard of beauty and righteousness, which enables you to criticise and condemn her for seeming blemishes, and then reject these self-same intuitions when they are brought forward by their advocates as furnishing some solution of the appearances of Evil in creation.[38]

What, then, if human beings are not adequately accounted for when construed as purely natural phenomena? At this point Mill allows an *entrée* to American transcendentalists and philosophical idealists, and to such theologians as Noah Porter of Yale:

> We do not dispute the correctness of Mr. Mill's statement that the word nature signifies *what* is, in the general sense of the properties and capacities of any one, or of the aggregate of the various beings and agents that exist. It is equally obvious that when nature is opposed to art, the means and instruments of art on the one hand, and the operations of art on the other, are limited to the capacities

furnished by nature. We submit, however, that what are called the capacities and constitution of a thing, and also the characteristics or contents of its concept, may as properly include what the thing or agent was intended for, as well as its one or many capacities, which are manifested or employed in actual results. In other words, what a thing *is*, or the nature of a thing, includes what it was made or exists *for*, as well as what it achieves in fact … The frequent and familiar use of the term in this sense, could not possibly be overlooked by a careful reader of the most popular and well-known treatises on morals.[39]

C.B. Upton, expressed the more general point thus:

Over and above that acquaintance with the laws of phenomena which properly constitutes science, there almost inevitably arises in minds that are engrossed with outward observation, and do not frequently or habitually direct their attention to the spiritual side of our being, certain *assumptions*, which, although they cannot be verified and are apparently at variance with the clear deliverance of consciousness, yet by the force of intellectual habit take a powerful hold upon the judgment, and seek to usurp the authority of axiomatic truths. Among these articles of faith, which those of our savants who study only phenomena dogmatically lay down and call upon us to accept on pain of having our views regarded as hopelessly 'unscientific', the principal are, that man must regard himself as a mere series of ideas, feelings and volitions, and not as a substantive *ego*, which thinks, feels and wills, and that he must further believe that this succession of states of consciousness which collectively form himself, is evolved on that principle of uniform sequence which excludes the possibility of true personal causality, or that power of preferential choice between springs of action which we term man's moral freedom.[40]

In partial explanation, though not justification, of Mill's stance we should note a further aspect of his morality-inspired position as confided to his diary on 22 February 1854:

Carlyle is abundantly contemptuous of all who make their intellects bow to their moral timidity by endeavouring to believe Christianity. But his own creed – that everything is right and good which accords with the laws of the universe – is either the same or a worse perversion. If it is not a resignation of intellect into the hands of fear, it is the subornation of it by a bribe – the bribe of being on the side of Power – irresistible and eternal Power.[41]

Others were swift to observe that Mill was guilty of begging the question:

To assert that Nature means the sum of all phenomena, *together with the causes which produce them*, is to assume the main point in dispute, and amounts in fact to saying that Nature includes the causes of Nature. A law of Nature is not the efficient cause – the *vera causa* – of any event. It is only the rule according to which the efficient cause acts.[42]

Leaving on one side for the time being the question how far Mill's view changed in the course of time, it seems undeniable that when he wrote 'Nature' he was, as John Skorupski has declared, committed to the view that human beings are 'entirely part of the natural causal order studied by science'.[43] As he elsewhere explains, 'Mill is a naturalist in the sense that he thinks (i) that beliefs, purposes, sentiments are genuine properties of the human being seen as a natural entity and (ii) that the normative can be grounded in them – nothing *beyond* them is required.'[44] But here a further problem presents itself: how far is it legitimate for Mill, on his own premises, to say that the course of nature is subject to amendment by us? Such language, thought Leslie Stephen, 'would be more consistent in a thorough-going advocate of Freewill, but ... in [Mill's] mouth [it] must be taken as a metaphorical or provisional mode of speech'.[45] Undeterred, we know from others of his writings that Mill's objective was amendment in a utilitarian direction. He even declares that 'No reason can be given why the general happiness is desirable, except that each person, so far as he believes it to be attainable, desires his own happiness'[46] – which, as James Orr saw, 'is surely but another way of saying that he adopts this end, because it is the end that Nature dictates'[47] – notwithstanding his declaration in 'Nature' that nature affords no moral guidance.

Be all that as it may, Mill is persuaded that nature rules herself (to be 'Victorian', for a reason to become clear shortly) out as a moral guide or prompter because of the devastating things she does. In particular, he cannot square any of nature's malign activities with the idea of a good and omnipotent God. This was something which had deeply troubled Mill before he wrote 'Nature'. At some time after George Holyoake's 1847 appeal for subscriptions to his secularist magazine, the *Reasoner and Herald of Progress*, Mill wrote a letter to the editor which remained unpublished. In it he said,

> Anyone who considers the course of nature, without the usual predetermination to find all excellent, must see that it has been made, if made at all, by an extremely imperfect being; that it can be accounted for on no theory of a just ruler, unless that ruler is of extremely limited power, and hemmed in by obstacles which he is unable to overcome.[48]

Whereas a comparable conclusion led Hume to at least theoretical scepticism, and Mansel to reliance upon faith, Mill, at first glance surprisingly, adopts a third position, namely, that the 'principle of Good *cannot* at once and altogether subdue the powers of evil, either physical or moral'.[49] This translates into a limited, non-omnipotent, deity. Even more remarkably, and despite the dire treatment meted out by a Creator upon things inanimate, animal and human alike, Mill continues,

Of all the religious explanations of the order of nature this alone is neither contradictory to itself, nor to the facts for which it attempts to account. According to it, man's duty would consist, not in simply taking care of his own interests by obeying irresistible power, but in standing forward a not ineffectual auxiliary to a Being of perfect beneficence.[50]

What is striking here is that, in apparent contradiction of his general stance, Mill, after all the evils attributed to nature and nature's alleged God, can still posit 'a Being of perfect beneficence'. Indeed, he limits God's power in order to save his benevolence. John Morley was aghast at this tactic: 'Our first objection ... to Mr. Mill's permissive explanation of the facts by a limitation of creative power, is that it springs from a sentiment which is out of place in an enquiry that claims to be scientific.'[51] Morley further notes that 'most of the tremendous indictment against Nature ... must assuredly be considered as cancelled and abandoned'.[52]

We can but surmise that we have here a mixture of Mill's diplomatic reticence regarding the expression of his most deeply held views on religion, and his desire that people shall strive for societal betterment, even if in the name of a dubiously assured deity. But, as so often with Mill, we need to see what he is doing elsewhere. In this case we note that, in the concurrently written essay, 'Utility', as if to invalidate our proffered surmise, he has no qualms at all about lambasting specifically the God of Christianity 'who could make a Hell; and who could create countless generations of human beings with the certain foreknowledge that he was creating them for this fate'.[53] The adjective 'beneficent' is not the first to spring to mind as applicable to such a God. All of which serves to remind us that Mill can be notoriously difficulty to pin down, and suggests that A.M. Fairbairn's verdict would more accurately have been expressed in conjunctive rather than disjunctive terms: 'It was the conflict of nature's way with man's sense of justice that compelled [Mill] to judge her so terribly; it was not its contradiction to a heart of infinite pity in the God who had made man.'[54]

III

Some remarks of Eugene August on 'Nature' will lead us into the next phase of our discussion:

Though the essay's rebelliousness is clear enough, some of its other aspects remain a puzzle. What, for example, brought on this defiant cry of 'No'? Was it written in protest against the consumptive deaths John and Harriet envisaged for themselves in the fifties? And where is that other concept of Nature as the beauty of the world that stirs the soul to ethical grandeur? What of nature lifting the heart to new heights of freedom? What of Nature ministering to a mind diseased? In brief, what of Nature as the Pyrenees and the Lake District? Did Mill, as chapter two of the *Autobiography* suggests, take Nature as a father substitute, transferring to it the ambiguous feelings he felt for James Mill? Certainly 'Nature' is the hardest essay to square with Mill's other works. His love of wilderness, his championing of spontaneity, even his perpetual use of natural organic imagery, belie the hostility towards Nature exhibited here.[55]

August's speculation that Nature may have been to Mill a father substitute should not, perhaps, be pressed too far, though it does engender the thought that the theme of 'substitution' runs rather prominently through Mill's life. We have seen how he wished to substitute the Religion of Humanity for Christianity; and now we must consider the possibility that his deep love for Harriet both fuelled his anger against disease and natural decline, and provided what some commentators have not hesitated to designate a God-substitute – a title from which August stops not far short: 'Given James Mill's fatal harshness, John understandably resisted belief in an omnipotent deity addressed as "Our Father", but he exhibited imaginative skill in worshipping Harriet as Our Lady, a sort of Virgin Mary in the Religion of Humanity.'[56]

There can be no question that in 1854, while Mill was haranguing nature, Harriet was fighting for her life in France. His revision of 'Nature' just completed, Mill, on 14 February, poured out his soul onto the pages of his diary:

> If human life is governed by superior beings, how greatly must the power of evil intelligences surpass that of the good, when a soul and an intellect like hers … *must* perish like all the rest of us in a few years, and *may* in a few months from a mere alteration in the structure of a few fibres or membranes, the exact parallels of which are found in every quadruped.[57]

It is as if, for Mill, Harriet's weakness threw into relief both the cruelty of Nature and her quasi-divine elevation above all things mundane. Certainly it did nothing to lessen Mill's inclination to heap paeans of praise upon his wife, to the mutual puzzlement of his intellectual friends and foes. In his *Autobiography*, for example, he tells us that shortly after meeting Mrs. Taylor he felt her 'to be the most admirable person I had ever known'; she was completely free 'from every kind of superstition', she had a passion for justice, and 'the most genuine modesty combined with the loftiest pride'. In terms of both the ultimate aims of human life and its practical possibilities, 'I have acquired more from her teaching, than from all other sources taken together.'[58] The passage in its entirety resembles nothing so much as the personal testimony of a convert to religious faith. While recognizing all the pitfalls which confront those who would psychologize concerning the long since deceased, it is hard to resist the conclusion that Mill, emotionally cramped by the cerebral power of his father, and allegedly 'misunderstood' by his mother (who, we recall, is entirely absent from his *Autobiography*) when he struck up a friendship with a married woman, was 'converted' by human love.[59] A modern writer has concluded that Harriet 'became for Mill the supreme being in something like a personal religion of humanity'.[60] The same writer quotes Avrom Fleishman's judgment that 'Mill really *believed* in Harriet Taylor, and when we put the case so, we raise the question, what sort of belief is that?'[61]

Replies, not all of them complimentary, came to that question from many quarters. The Lutheran theologian Charles Augustus Stork wrote, 'Many wise and strong men have loved, but it would be hard to find in literature any such expression of affection bordering on idolatry, of homage approaching to intellectual subjection, of reverence showing all the fervour and depth of a religious faith, as Mr. Mill has revealed [in his *Autobiography*].'[62] Pulling no punches, Stork continues, Mill's

> universe was without an Author or Governor; his life was without a Father. What could such a man do? What all men do, when the religious nature is not utterly starved out; he made a God and a religion for himself ... Mr. Mill disdained to be a Christian or even a Theist; it looks very much as if instead of going higher, he had only taken a step lower and become an idolater.[63]

In the opinion of Stork's contemporary, the Baptist C.B. Crane, Mill 'dethroned Jehovah, but he enthroned in his place a woman'.[64] Indignant though these and many other theologians were, they were not without excuse, for Mill, now a widower, had written of Harriet, 'Her memory is to me a religion, and her approbation the standard by which ... I endeavour to regulate my life.'[65] A.M. Fairbairn, however, was a theologian who took a kindlier view: 'has not this tale a moral as true as it is pathetic?' he asked: 'If the logic of incapacity had never a more illustrious victim than John Stuart Mill, man's need for God has never a more veracious witness than the tragic sequel to his disappointed love.'[66]

As for Mill's secular friends, 'perplexed' and 'disappointed' – even 'cheated' – are the words which come to mind to encapsulate their feelings on learning of what to them was an unjustifiable, even an 'addle-brained', attitude on Mill's part. Mill's friend, Alexander Bain spoke for many when he declared that Mill 'outraged all reasonable credibility in describing [Harriet's] matchless genius, without being able to supply any corroborating testimony'.[67] The secularist tractarian, G.W. Foote, invoked W.E. Gladstone to account for the puzzling situation: 'Mr. Gladstone explains Mill's "ludicrous estimate of his wife's powers", by saying that she was a quick receptive woman, who gave him back the echo of his own thoughts, which he took for the independent oracles of truth.'[68]

The extreme Romantic sentimentality which banishes Mill's otherwise eighteenth-century prose style whenever he writes of Harriet returns us to the question of the significance, if any, of Mill's personification of nature. Mid-Victorian writers were fond of personification (and capital letters): ships are 'she', for example, and Mill succumbs to the habit. Not, indeed, that he was unaware of the perils of personification. As early as 1823 Mill had repudiated the use of 'the term *Nature* as denoting some positive, active, if not intelligent being', observing that, 'From the poets, this fictitious personage speedily penetrated into the closets of the philosophers';[69] and in 1825 he thundered, 'Religion, morality, &c. are not persons, either dead or alive, but abstract terms.'[70] This view is reiterated throughout his life, but in 'Nature' it is as if, overcome by intense emotion engendered by Harriet's weakened condition, he sets it on one side, and raves against a personified Nature who at best provides occasions for the development of Victorian 'character' through strife, and at worst is the implacable foe of all that is moral and good.[71] Moreover, all of this stands over against Mill's habitual naturalism: 'Instead of showing that nature is impersonal, which would have been in the interest of naturalism, Mill set out to prove, in effect, that she is a most wicked female, and *therefore* a bad model for human action.'[72]

But have we more than literary convention at work here? Is Mill, in personifying nature, loading the dice in his own favour? A number of his critics declared that he was. Supremely in his invective, Nature is an agent – indeed, a malign one. But, as Mill's contemporary Eustace R. Conder pointed out, there is special pleading here:

> [T]o speak of Nature in the aggregate, or of any physical law or cause, as ruthless, remorseless, merciless, and the like, is absurd. For 'pitiless' implies capacity for pity; 'merciless', power and duty to exercise mercy; and these attributes can exist only in a Personal Being, while their exercise implies the exact opposite of physical law, – the dealing with each case individually on moral considerations.[73]

At this point we may recall August's observation that the Nature of Wordsworth is absent from Mill's essay. Certainly nature as beautiful is absent. W.L. Courtney was not alone in noting 'the absence of all feeling of *the beauty* of the Natural World', something he attributed to Mill's failure, like that of other psychologists with the exception of Bain, to treat systematically of the emotions.[74] But Wordsworth, too, knew of another side to Nature: its ruggedness, its harshness, even its cruelty. However, the point of greatest significance for us is that with the passage of time Mill's view of Nature softened, as we shall see. In the essay on 'Theism' he seems to turn his back on his earlier personification of Nature and reaches a view more consistent with his earliest declarations on the matter: 'There is no ground in Natural Theology for attributing intelligence or personality to the obstacles which partially thwart what seem the purposes of the Creator.'[75] And yet (and how often there is an 'and yet' with Mill) in *On Liberty*, written in the same period as 'Nature', Mill does adopt a more warmly Romantic attitude towards nature, not least human nature: 'Human nature,' he writes, 'is not a machine to be built after a model, and set to do exactly the work prescribed for it, but a tree, which requires to grow and develop itself on all sides, according to the tendency of the inward forces which make it a living thing.'[76]

But, to repeat, this note is not sounded in 'Nature', upon which work Noah Porter returned the following severe verdict:

> We cannot be mistaken when we pronounce it one of the feeblest of Mr. Mill's productions, for the ambitiousness of its pretensions, the narrowness of its definitions, the defectiveness of its logic, and the repulsiveness of its conclusions. Though written in the maturity of the powers of the author, after he had felt and acknowledged the liberalizing and elevating influences of both poetry and love, and had learned to be catholic in judging, and kindly in appreciating, the opinions and feelings of men from whom he differed very widely, this essay seems to reflect the narrowest and most acrid spirit of his unripe youth, as well as the bitterest prejudices against all who believe in God's goodness, which characterized his early manhood. It would seem that his temper must have been for the most part greatly disturbed, while he thought and wrote out this essay.[77]

Porter's last sentence here may contain part of the explanation of the tone of 'Nature', but it raises the further question, why did Mill not further revise 'Nature' in such a way as to make it accord more nearly with his long-entertained views concerning personification, and his appreciation of the examples nature afforded for the discussion of human moral development? However fanciful it may appear to be, my suggestion is that, for all his cerebralism, and notwithstanding the way his emotions were stunted or constrained by his upbringing, Mill was a person of deep feelings, in accordance with which he sometimes allowed himself to act with a degree of conviction and an integrity analogous to Bunyan's when he declared, 'I preached what I felt, what I smartingly did feel.'[78] Mill, not uninfluenced by Harriet's condition, genuinely felt what he wrote in his devastating critique of nature; on another occasion he equally genuinely felt it appropriate to find in the argument from design the most probable support for a benevolent God, and in the deceased Harriet a moral ideal arising in the very midst of nature; and the fact that he left it all standing says much for his personal integrity even as it questions his intellectual consistency. Leaving that possible interpretation on one side, we must now turn to the limitation which Mill places on God's power in 'Nature'.

IV

The *Edinburgh* reviewer correctly observed that the idea of a limited deity was not original to Mill: on the contrary, it had been posited by Soame Jenyns in his *Free Enquiry into the Nature and Origin of Evil* (1757).[79] To the reviewer in *The British and Foreign Evangelical Review*, Mill's 'Nature' 'is the best statement in modern times of Manichaeanism, untinged with Christianity'.[80] In our own time A.G.N. Flew has found Mill to be 'the most considerable thinker to explore this notion [i.e. Manichaeanism] in modern times'.[81] In 1860 Mill summarized his views on the matter in a letter to Florence Nightingale:

> I confess that no religious theory seems to me consistent with the facts of the universe, except (in some form or other) the old one of the two principles. There are many signs, in the structure of the universe, of an intelligent Power wishing well to man and other sentient creatures. I could however shew, not so many perhaps, but quite as decided indications of an intelligent Power or powers with the contrary propensity. But (not to insist on this) the will of the benevolent Power must find, either in its own incompleteness or in some external circumstances, very serious obstacles to the entire fulfilment of the benevolent purpose. It may be, that the world is a battlefield between a good and a bad power or powers, and that mankind may be capable by sufficiently strenuous cooperation with the good power, of deciding, or at least accelerating, its final victory.[82]

However, as Karl Britton pointed out, the 'final result' of this doctrine

> is to divide God from nature and to divide God from man. God and man share many faculties and they share moral aims, but Mill writes of man's actions and efforts as if they were entirely distinct from God's. God is an object in the world; he has great but limited power over other objects.[83]

While this is the ontological situation, in 'Nature' Mill, as we have seen, is more concerned with the moral issue. He summed up his thought on the matter in a late letter of 1871:

> Now the cultivation of the idea of a perfectly good & wise being & of the desire to help the purposes of such a being is morally beneficial in the highest degree though the belief that this being is omnipotent & therefore the creator of physical and moral evil is as demoralizing a belief as can be entertained.[84]

Mill's inclination towards Manichaeism is a further legacy from his father, of whom Mill wrote:

> The Sabaean or Manichaean theory of a Good and an Evil Principle, struggling against each other for the government of the universe he would not equally [with the Christian view] have condemned; and I have heard him express surprise, that no one revived it in our time. He would have regarded it as a mere hypothesis; but he would have ascribed to it no depraving influence.[85]

Needless to say, not all of Mill's readers were content with Mill's attempt to save God's benevolence at the expense of his power. Mill finds that Manichaeism allows it to be believed that all the mass of evil which exists was undesigned by, and exists not by the appointment of, but in spite of the being whom we are called upon to worship. A virtuous human being assumes in this theory the exalted character of a fellow-labourer with the Highest … contributing … towards that progressive ascendency, and ultimately complete triumph of good over evil, which history points to, and which this doctrine teaches us to regard as planned by the Being to whom we owe all the benevolent contrivance we behold in Nature. Against the moral tendency of this creed no possible objection can lie.[86]

But against Mill's logic Leslie Stephen did most certainly object: 'Manichaeism is a clear confession of philosophical bankruptcy. The whole aim of reasoning is to reduce the universe to unity, and this is to admit that there is an ultimate and insoluble dualism.'[87] He later compares Mill and Mansel on the point:

Mill supposes that God must be good, but reconciles this to facts by assuming that God is not all-powerful. Mansel will not give up the power, and to preserve the goodness has to assume a radical incapacity in the intellect – a necessity of believing where there is an impotence of conceiving. Mill, that is, is content with the empirical deity, who is necessarily limited; and Mansel keeps the deity of ontology but admits that he cannot be known.[88]

But long before Stephen wrote, Mill had queried Manichaeism. In 'Theism' he sets out from a strong statement to the effect that monotheism, which he understands as an advance upon polytheism, alone accords with the order in things to which the sciences direct their attention:

The special mode in which scientific study operates to instil Monotheism in place of the more natural Polytheism, is in no way mysterious. The specific effect of science is to show by accumulating evidence, that every event in nature is connected by laws with some fact or facts which preceded it … Now, when once the double conviction has found entry into the mind – that every event depends on antecedents; and at the same time that to bring it about many antecedents must concur … the conviction follows that no one event, certainly no one kind of events, can be absolutely preordained or governed by any Being but one who holds in his hand the reins of all Nature and not of some department only. At least if a plurality be supposed, it is necessary to assume so complete a concert of action and unity of will among them that the difference is for most purposes immaterial between such a theory and that of the absolute unity of the Godhead.[89]

Again, when considering agencies which variously preserve or destroy life, Mill declares that it cannot be supposed 'that the preserving agencies are wielded by one Being, the destroying agencies by another … [T]here is no ground in Natural Theology for attributing intelligence or personality to the obstacles which partially thwart what seem the purposes of the Creator'.[90] After so strong a statement, it is odd to find that almost at the end of

'Theism', when extolling the virtues of the Religion of Humanity, Mill refers once again to the 'battle' which 'is constantly going on' between 'the powers of good and those of evil'.[91] This is a reversion to the position adopted towards the end of 'Utility of Religion',[92] and it provides a further weapon for all who think that Mill is inconsistent – even slippery.

But for all his inclinations towards monotheism, Mill at no time departed from his view that God, if God there be, is limited, less than omnipotent:

> Grant that creative power was limited by conditions the nature and extent of which are wholly unknown to us, and the goodness and justice of the Creator may be all that the most pious believe; and all in the work that conflicts with those moral attributes may be the fault of the conditions which left to the Creator only a choice of evils.[93]

Leaving on one side the puzzle concerning a Creator competent to create the universe but unable to control prevailing conditions within it, it is at this point, albeit Mill displays a more tranquil mood than that evinced in 'Nature', that many critics have protested that Mill's suggestion of a non-omnipotent God misses the Christian target. For, such atypical examples as E.S. Brightman's limited God apart, standard Christian monotheism denies the limitation upon God which Mill introduces to save the deity's benevolence. His friend Alexander Bain, who had no Christian axe to grind, saw the point clearly. Commenting on Mill's idea, 'so repugnant to the religious worshipper, of putting a logical limitation and restriction on the great object of worship', he declares, 'A Being that would not interfere to do us either harm or good can scarcely excite in us any strong regards; at least until we have undergone a new education. The supposed limitations of his power, besides being strangely at variance with the undeniable vastness and complex adjustment of the world, would seem fatal to his ascendency in our minds.'[94] In our own time A.G.N. Flew was even blunter: 'Directly to say that God must be limited by contingently intractable material is to abolish the problem by abandoning an essential doctrine of Christian monotheism.'[95] The Christian philosopher, John Hick, concurs in thinking that Mill's dualism 'is unacceptable for the simple but sufficient reason that it contradicts the Christian conception of God. Mill's type of dualism does not face, and therefore does not solve, the problem of evil as it arises for a religion that understands and worships God as that than which nothing more perfect can be conceived'.[96]

Let it fully be granted that some of the Christian responses to Mill on the problem of evil are unsatisfactory. A.B. Bruce, for example, suggests that 'It might help to cure the dualistic mood if those who suffer from it would make a study of the good that is in evil.'[97] But Mill is not unaware that good may arise from evil. However, he rightly understands that this does not excuse the presence of evil in the first place:

It would be a great moral improvement to most persons, be they Christians, Deists, or Atheists, if they firmly believed the world to be under the government of a Being who, willing only good, leaves evil in the world solely to stimulate the human faculties by an unremitting struggle against every form of it ... If the Divine intention in making man was Effort towards Perfection, the divine purpose is as much frustrated as if its sole aim were human happiness. There is a little of both, but the absence of both is the marked characteristic.[98]

But when, in 'Theism', Mill declares that the evidences of design to be found in nature point towards 'the preservation of the creatures in whose structure the indications are found',[99] he reneges upon the Mill of 'Nature'; and when he admits that good may flow from evil, he aligns himself with Bruce and other Christians when they are in somewhat sentimental mood.

If, as many have suggested, Mill's strictures against a less-than-omnipotent God bypass the Christian God, still less does Mill consider the Christian 'answer' to the problem of evil. To put the point very briefly, this 'answer' does not solve the theoretical problems concerning the suffering of the righteous, and random and apparently quite unmerited natural disasters in relation to a God deemed to be both loving and omnipotent. Rather, it is a practical answer which takes its bearings from the Cross–Resurrection event and turns upon Paul's conviction that because (not 'if') Christ was raised we shall be raised.[100] As C.B. Crane averred, 'Given the facts of man's moral being and man's sin, together with a redemption unmistakably accomplishing, the problem of evil seems always possible of a solution which will not involve a denial of the wisdom and goodness of God.'[101] For his part, T.V. Tymms confessed that 'without appealing to the whole scheme of moral culture and redemption which is inseparably identified with the revelation of God in Christ, I can find no weapon with which to repel Mill's attack'.[102] The answer need not further be elaborated here. Suffice it to say that nothing that Mill says refutes it, for he pays no attention to it at all.

V

We turn now to Mill's discussion of some traditional theistic arguments, a number of which he romps through in 'Theism'. We shall proceed through this essay in order, referring both to Mill's other writings, as appropriate, and to his respondents.

Mill begins by welcoming what he perceives as a 'marked alteration' in present attitudes, as compared with those of the eighteenth and early nineteenth century, towards the dispute over theism. He feels that 'the more softened temper in which the debate is conducted on the part of unbelievers' is generally acknowledged, and 'The reactionary violence, provoked by the intolerance of the other side, has in great measure exhausted itself.' In his next sentence he might almost have been thinking of his earlier self (in some of his moods): 'Experience has abated the ardent hopes once entertained of the regeneration of the human race by merely negative doctrine – by the destruction of superstition.'[103] In particular, 'the more instructed of those who reject the supernatural' now perceive that Christian and theistic views 'can now be done without' : they were not 'things misleading and noxious *ab initio*'.[104]

Whereas the 'war' against religious beliefs turned, in the eighteenth century, upon questions of common sense or logic, it is now scientific advance which has conclusively revealed facts which cannot be reconciled with religious claims. Those who reject religions nowadays discuss them not so much in terms of their truth or falsity, but as phenomena which arise and, when they have had their day, decay. All of this Mill broadly welcomes, but he does not wish to bracket the question of truth altogether. On the contrary, his aim is to bring dogmatic claims to the bar of scientific method:

> It is indispensable that the subject of religion should from time to time be reviewed as a strictly scientific question, and that its evidences should be tested by the same scientific methods, and on the same principles as those of any of the speculative conclusions drawn by physical science. It being granted then that the legitimate conclusions of science are entitled to prevail over all opinions, however widely held, which conflict with them, and that the canons of scientific evidence which the successes and failures of two thousand years have established, are applicable to all subjects on which knowledge is attainable, let us proceed to consider what place there is for religious beliefs on the platform of science.[105]

Manifestly, this is a manifesto! It is the articulation of the basis upon which *believers* in scient*ism*, then as now, go about their business. The position begs the huge question that the methods of science, construed as Mill construes it – that is, naturalistically and empirically – are competent to weigh religious claims. Nowhere does Mill defend his stance; he simply announces it and expects his readers to take it on trust. Furthermore, argument is needed before it be 'granted' that 'the legitimate conclusions of science [construed in Mill's way] are entitled to prevail over all opinions', especially when one considers that many such prominent 'legitimate conclusions' have, with the passage of time, been shown to be ill-advised by developments in science itself. The flat earth comes to mind. Not a few of Mill's critics took exception to the way in which, for all his subsequent argumentation, he had ruled out their position from the start. Of these W.L. Courtney is typical:

> It would be difficult, indeed, for Sensationalism, with its two dogmas of the supremacy of the Individual, and the supremacy of Sensation, to arrive at any such conceptions of the Absolute, and the Infinite, and the Super-sensual, as are implied in the philosophical (and popular) belief in the great First Cause.[106]

But two caveats must be entered at this point. First, in 'Utility of Religion', Mill had listed a considerable number of things which we do not know about the world, and of such presently unavailable knowledge he rhetorically asks, 'Who would not desire this more ardently than any other conceivable knowledge, so long as there appeared the slightest hope of attaining it?'[107] Secondly, as we shall see, Mill's 'Theism' includes the hope that there may be an immortal life which cannot be encapsulated by his science. Thus, declared C.B. Upton, 'the thin end of the wedge was already inserted which must in time have completely rent asunder Necessarian and Experiential dogmas, and given free rein to Intuitional ideas'.[108] These considerations at least hint that Mill was less finally fixed in his opinions than his bold scientistic[109] policy statement might imply. But let us proceed through his account of the theistic arguments.

VI

Following the expression of his preference for monotheism over polytheism, which we have already considered, Mill argues that one version of theism is consistent with the truths made known through science, namely, that God governs the world by invariable laws. But the theistic view which supposes that God governs the world 'by acts of variable will' is inconsistent with science.[110] However, science does not require us to dissent from the view 'that every event which takes place results from a specific volition of the presiding Power, provided that this Power adheres in its particular volitions to the general laws laid down by itself'.[111] Mill grants that there is nothing which can 'disprove the creation and government of Nature by a sovereign will; but is there anything to prove it? Of what nature are the evidences; and, weighed in the scientific balance, what is their value?'[112]

While declaring his intention to investigate impartially both *a priori* and *a posteriori* methods of argument, Mill confesses his 'strong conviction' that, while the latter is scientific in nature, the former is 'not only unscientific but condemned by science'.[113] He cannot endorse the method of those who infer 'external objective facts from ideas or convictions of our minds'.[114] To argue that a benignant God would not have planted in our minds a groundless idea of himself is, by *petitio principii*, to have assumed our desired conclusion in advance. Mill does concede, however, that arguments may be stated in such a way as to combine *a priori* and *a posteriori* elements, as when, in stating the cosmological argument, our experience of the relation of cause and effect in nature is interwoven with an idea of causation as an intuitively apprehended truth of reason.

Turning to the First Cause argument, Mill first points out that while in common parlance we say of both events and objects that they are caused, in fact our experience is only of one event as being caused by another. We have no experience of the coming into existence of the inherent properties of objects. Hence 'Experience ... affords no evidences, not even analogies, to justify our extending to the apparently immutable, a generalization grounded only on our observation of the changeable.'[115] As to the changes we do experience, both the causes and effects are within time, and thus our experience of causation is at first sight repugnant to the idea of a First Cause. But suppose that within all temporal, experienced, causes there is a permanent element which had no beginning, what then? 'Surely this is not very lucid!' expostulated the Baptist apologist, T.V. Tymms: 'In one paragraph we are told that "changes are always the effects of previous changes", and then directly afterwards all these changes are traced up to an unchanging "permanent element"! What would Mill have said about a village preacher who ventured to talk like that?'[116] Undeterred, Mill appeals to 'the last great generalization of science, the Conservation of Force', according to which 'the variety in the effects depends partly upon the *amount* of the force, and partly upon the diversity of the collocations'.[117] This Force is a fixed quantity, which never increases or diminishes, and to it we may 'assign the character of a First Cause'. For 'all effects may be traced up to it, while it cannot be traced up, by our experience, to anything beyond'.[118] It thus transpires that, 'in the only sense in which experience supports in any shape the doctrine of a First Cause, viz., as the primaeval and universal element in all causes, the First Cause can be no other than Force'.[119]

We are not yet out of the wood, however, for it is held by many that Mind alone causes Force; that is, that change results from voluntary action on the part either of humanity or of a more powerful Being. Mill traces this venerable argument to Plato's *Laws*, but it is highly problematic, he thinks: 'Volition either ... does not answer to the idea of a First Cause; since Force must in every instance be assumed prior to it either ... As far as anything can be concluded from human experience Force has all the attributes of a thing eternal and uncreated.'[120] The situation would be otherwise if we could show that while Will does not originate Force, it is co-eternal with it. The problem here is that many other factors, chemical and mechanical, can engender change, and hence 'Volition ... regarded as an agent in the material universe, has no exclusive privilege of origination.'[121] If it be asserted that volition is uncaused, the retort is that so are all the other properties of matter. Accordingly, theism, 'in so far as it rests on the necessity of a First Cause, has no support from experience'.[122]

As for those who propose to base the assertion of a First Cause on intuition, and in particular upon the claim that mind alone can produce mind, they merely invite us to embark upon an infinite regression. Moreover, 'we have no direct knowledge (at least apart from Revelation) of a Mind which is even apparently eternal, as Force and Matter are'.[123] Again, while it is tautologous to say that nothing but mind can consciously produce mind, we cannot assume *ab initio* the impossibility of the unconscious production of mind, for that is what must be proved. Mill thus concludes that on neither *a posteriori* nor *a priori* grounds can the First Cause argument for theism be sustained.

Few Christians pursued Mill as relentlessly, and with such humour, on the First Cause argument as the Presbyterian scholar Daniel Seelye Gregory.[124] His adverse criticism of Mill's cosmological argumentation illustrates his general judgment of the *Three Essays*, namely, that they are dangerous because of the way in which Mill mixes candour and fairness with sophistry and confusion.

Gregory first considers Mill's view that the unchangeable element in nature needs no First Cause. He recasts Mill's argument in syllogistic form thus:

Every thing that has had a beginning requires a cause.
Matter, or the permanent element in nature, has not had a beginning within the range of human experience.
Therefore matter does not require a cause.[125]

Gregory has no difficulty in pointing out that different middle terms – 'had a beginning' and 'had a beginning within the range of human experience' – are used. He dismisses Mill with a homely illustration:

It would be just as logical and conclusive for an ignorant Philadelphian, if there be such a one, who has never been beyond the city limits, standing in the Depot of the Pennsylvania Railway, to reason thus: Whatever has no end is infinite; this railway has *no end within the range of experience*; therefore it is infinite.[126]

What particularly concerns Gregory is that it is by this logical sleight of hand that Mill leaps from narrow human experience to the eternity of matter.

Next, Gregory considers Mill's claim that the changeable element in nature needs no First Cause, and finds that, far from confirming it, our experience seriously questions it. But what disturbs him most of all is Mill's exclusion of efficiency, the power to produce change, from his definition of cause, and his exclusive reference to physical causes: 'he will have nothing to say of *cause* in the sense in which both the common people and the philosophers have always understood the word. It is to be the play of Hamlet with the Prince of Denmark left out'.[127] This is clearly an allusion to Mill's statement, 'To my apprehension, a volition is not an efficient, but simply a physical cause. Our will causes our bodily actions in the same sense, and in no other, in which cold causes ice.'[128]

At this point Gregory has recourse to the definition of 'cause' in Mill's *Logic*:

The Law of Causation, the recognition of which is the main pillar of inductive science, is but the familiar truth, that invariability of succession is found by observation to obtain between every fact in nature and some other fact which has preceded it; independently of all considerations respecting the ultimate mode of production of phenomena, and of every other question regarding the nature of 'Things in themselves'.[129]

But, says Gregory, this admits Reid's objection that night must cause day and vice versa, because these phenomena always invariably succeed one another. In other words, something other than mere succession must be built into the definition, and this Mill proceeds to do. He therefore declares that there must be no 'negative conditions', by which, as he further explains, he means that there must be 'the absence of preventing or counteracting causes'. This leads him to his refined definition: 'We may define, therefore, the cause of a phenomenon to be the antecedent, or the concurrence of antecedents, on which it is invariably and *unconditionally* consequent, and subject only to the absence of preventing or counteracting causes.'[130] On this Gregory pounces with some glee:

> We have at length reached the triumph of logic, in a conditional unconditionality, and a variable invariability, and have found that the last and perhaps most emphatic word in the definition of a *cause* is the word *causes!* If we can understand *that*, the definition is all plain.
>
> This is certainly one of the curiosities of literature, surpassing Hume's celebrated chapter on the same subject. Besides defining *cause* by *causes*, and treating of *causation* without *efficiency*, the author perpetually contradicts himself in his logical jargon, eats up his own first principles and definitions, and in his straits makes constant appeals to *necessity*, or, as one has phrased it, to 'the grand old tortoise, whose mustbeity and perseity are at the bottom of the understanding of all sham science' …
>
> [Mill] is constantly performing the feat of the man trying to ride two horses in precisely opposite directions at the same time, and striving to conceal the fact from himself and others. After devoting half his Logic to proving that there is no causal force, no active power in matter, he turns squarely about, and, in his treatment of *Fallacies*, insists that matter can not only act, but that it can act through absolutely void space, and without any media whatever, and thinks Newton and his scientific adherents a pack of fools for denying it! This is but a single instance of what is to be found everywhere in his writings. in which consistency is certainly a very rare jewel.[131]

The supreme difficulty in Mill's position at this point, Gregory affirms, is that with causal power excluded from his definition, 'no link has any support from its immediate antecedent event, the only connection being that of sequence in time. There are in fact no *links*. The position, therefore, is utterly absurd'.[132]

So Gregory proceeds to Mill's claim that if any First Cause is required for the material universe, Force will suffice. He finds, yet again, that Mill's language changes subtly and significantly as he develops his argument. He moves from saying that a First Cause is 'not sufficient of itself to cause anything', to the claim that it 'may be' the first cause; this 'may be' then becomes a 'must be', and we are finally told, 'after another shake of the juggler's hat', that 'the First Cause can be no other than Force'.[133] Quite apart from the linguistic shifts to which he takes exception, Gregory is perplexed by the confidence with which Mill posits the eternity of matter and of Force. He has no scientific warrant for either claim, and if either or both were true, on the basis of his sensationalist epistemology he could not know that this were so.

Gregory next turns his attention to Mill's argument that so-called 'spiritual phenomena' need no cause other than Force. In particular, Mill wishes to deny that Force is ever originated by Will, and to defend the view that Mind requires only Force as it originating principle. Gregory pursues him relentlessly, concluding that 'The simple and sole scientific fact on which this imposing structure of automatism is reared is, that chemical action in the brain *may accompany* action of will. This *concomitance* is at once confounded by loose thinkers with *equivalence* and *identity*.'[134] He proceeds to deny Mill's claim that other forces may be responsible for what will is frequently thought to do, and repudiates Mill's associated claim that mind is the product of material agencies alone.

Gregory gathers steam and approaches his conclusion with elegant huffs and puffs:

No one can lay down the argument of the great destroyer of theism, after a careful study of it, without mingled feelings of humiliation and indignation – humiliation, that so many of the so-called thinking and educated men of the age should be so incapable of clear thought as to be imposed upon and moulded by such so-called thought; indignation, that men in high places, who ought to know better, are constantly assuming substantially the same views and urging them upon mankind as an addition to, or substitute for, Christian theism.[135]

Nor are theologians innocent in all of this. They have, since Kant's onslaught upon the theistic proofs, too often acquiesced in the belief that the proofs have had their day, 'forgetting that the *proofs* of the divine existence are identical with the *reasons* for the *belief* in God, and that belief without reasons is essentially irrational and absurd'.[136] Accordingly, Gregory concludes that 'One requirement for the return to the old faith in theism is the strong and clear presentation of the proofs that there is a God, together with a merciless exposure of the intricate sophistries of atheism and anti-theism.'[137]

I have thought it well to present Gregory's response to Mill's critique of the cosmological argument in some detail because, of all the many responses, it is among the more logically competent. There can be no doubt that Gregory scores some palpable hits and exposes genuine inadequacies in Mill's presentation of his case. But apart from logical details, it does seem that Mill invites us to take a good deal on trust. In positing the eternity of Matter and of Force he can supply no tenable grounds on the basis of his own epistemology or his naturalism.[138] As James Orr puts it,

We find [Mill] setting up Matter and Force outside of the Deity, though, on his own principles, Matter has no existence apart from the minds apprehending it, and Force has no real existence of any kind, causation being resolved by him into simple antecedence and consequence, and the existence of any causal nexus being denied. The idea of some more intimate connection, of some particular tie, or mysterious constraint exercised by the antecedent over the consequent is, he tells us in the *Logic*, a delusion which the reason repudiates. There is no such compulsion exercised; causes do not draw their effects after them by a mystical tie. Yet here, in the essay on 'Theism,' we find, as we have seen, Force reappearing – nay, hypostasized, and exhibited as a separate existence, co-eternal with God.[139]

On the other hand, Gregory does not offer any defence of the cosmological argument against the legitimate points made against it by Mill – that concerning the regress of causes, for example. Gregory does not consider the possibility that there may be reasons for belief other than those supplied by the traditional proofs. And neither of them considers the possibility that, since the theistic proofs at best yield a First Cause, a prime Mover, a Designer, an undifferentiated Being, they are not concerned with the God worshipped and loved by Christians.[140] In a word, Mill and Gregory between them raise the question of appropriate starting-points in Christian apologetics, but do not answer it.[141] This general judgment applies to Mill's 'Theism' in its entirety.

VII

Before discussing what he regards as the most hopeful theistic argument, namely, the argument from design, Mill disposes of two others. The first of these he labels the 'Argument from the general consent of mankind'. Mill does not deny that on difficult questions people in general may properly be guided by what is generally believed, 'But to a thinker the argument from other people's opinions has little weight.'[142] Many are inclined to infer from the widespread belief in a deity that the belief must be true, for the human mind was made by a God who would not deceive his creatures. Though sanctioned by intuitionist philosophy, this is a precarious, question-begging, conclusion. Moreover, if there exists evidence of other kinds there is no need for this intuitive argument. As for the appeal to the animistic religion of 'savages', this has rightly been superseded, with the result that theists justify their belief either by rational argument or on the basis of evidences drawn from nature. Mill therefore concludes that 'The general consent of mankind does not … afford ground for admitting, even as an hypothesis, the origin in an inherent law of the human mind, of a fact otherwise so more than sufficiently, so amply, accounted for.'[143]

It would seem that very few of Mill's critics, some of them otherwise so vociferously opposed to him, felt inclined to spring to the defence of the argument from universal consent, though W.J. Irons did accuse Mill of failing to deal with the ineradicability of the *fact* of such widespread consent. Irons recognizes that 'It is not an historical or a theoretical difficulty that he has, but to some extent a psychological difficulty. Remove it if you will from the domain of logic, still the fact remains; and science, theological or physical, builds on facts.'[144]

The second argument which Mill considers briefly only to dispense with it is the *a priori* argument from consciousness, otherwise known as the ontological argument. Mill traces it back to Descartes's intuitionism. He summarizes it thus: 'the idea of God implying the union of all perfections, and existence being a perfection, the idea of God proves his existence';[145] and he dismisses it equally curtly: 'This very simple argument, which denies to man one of his most familiar and most precious attributes – of constructing from the materials of experience a conception more perfect than experience itself affords - is not likely to satisfy anyone in the present day.'[146] He elsewhere observes that the Cartesian argument 'would equally prove the real existence of ghosts and of witches'.[147] Noting that there have been later versions of the argument, Mill nevertheless considers that 'they labour under the common infirmity, that one man cannot by proclaiming with ever so much confidence that *he* perceives an object, convince other people that they see it too'.[148]

Mill applauds Kant for seeing the weakness of this argument, and for consistently keeping 'the two questions, the origin and composition of our ideas, and the reality of the corresponding objects, perfectly distinct'.[149] He goes on to explain that to Kant God is 'neither an object of direct consciousness nor a conclusion of reasoning, but a Necessary Assumption; necessary, not by a logical, but a practical necessity, imposed by the reality of the Moral Law'.[150] However, while we are no doubt conscious of the sense of moral obligation, it is not necessary to posit God as its source. On the contrary, duty can be fully acknowledged by many who have no positive belief in God. If it be suggested that our moral feelings make the existence of a god desirable, Mill can agree, but only in a qualified way, for 'surely it is not legitimate to assume that in the order of the Universe, whatever is desirable is true'.[151] Among Mill's critics, M'Cosh was not at all surprised by Mill's rejection of the (so-called) moral argument. For that argument 'derived from the moral faculty in man, so much insisted on by Kant and Chalmers, is no longer available when it is allowed that the moral law has no place in our constitution, and that our moral sentiments are generated by inferior feelings and associated circumstances'.[152]

VIII

At first sight the argument from design in nature commends itself to Mill and, like Kant before him, he speaks of it with respect as being the best and most persuasive of all the theistic arguments.[153] Its character is scientific; it is open to judgment by standard canons of induction; it is entirely rooted in our actual experience of of artefacts made by intelligent persons for a purpose. Its central claim is that the natural order, or considerable parts of it, exhibits qualities which entitle us to assume that it, too, has been fashioned by a power greater than ourselves. Promising though the argument initially appears to be, Mill thinks it is grossly overrated. Paley, for example, puts the case too strongly. Mill says that if he found a watch on a desert island he would infer that it had been left there by a human being, not because the watch reveals evidence of having been designed, but because he knows from direct experience that watches are made by people. Therefore, as far as likenesses between design in nature and design by human beings are concerned, 'All that can be said with certainty is that these likenesses make creation by intelligence considerably more probable than if the likenesses had been less, or than if there had been no likenesses at all.'[154]

But, claims Mill, the argument can be stated more strongly than this. It is not merely an analogy, it is an inductive argument.[155] It turns not upon random circumstances but upon specific instances. Accordingly, Mill considers the claim that the structure of the eye proves a designing mind. It is clear that all the parts of the eye together yield the possibility of sight. 'We are therefore warranted by the canons of induction in concluding that what brought these elements together was some cause common to them all; and inasmuch as the elements agree in the single circumstance of conspiring to produce sight, there must be some connection by way of causation between the cause which brought those elements together, and the fact of sight.'[156]

This is as far as induction can take us. But, Mill continues, since sight is the final result of the design and not its efficient cause, it is an antecedent idea of sight which is the efficient cause; and this leads us to posit an intelligent will behind the process. But this last supposition is not the only candidate; for, as we have learned from the principle of the survival of the fittest, there can be adaptations in nature occurring over time which can yield the phenomena of the world as we know them. Mill grants that the theory of evolution is not an account of creation, and that it is not inconsistent with the idea of creation, but he is not very impressed by it. Even so, 'it is not so absurd as it looks',[157] and if admitted the theory 'would greatly attenuate the evidence for' creation.[158] Mill concludes that 'in the present state of our knowledge, the adaptations in Nature afford a large balance of probability in favour of creation by intelligence. It is equally certain that this is no more than a probability; and that the various other arguments of Natural Theology … add nothing to its force'.[159]

Before passing to the estimates which have been offered of Mill's teleological argument, it is worth noting the absence of that outraged hostility to nature, occasioned by its cruelties and disorderlinesses, which was so apparent in his essay, 'Nature'. This is the more surprising when we recall that it was precisely in connection with the argument from design that

Hume had earlier introduced such considerations, coupling them with the inference that they showed the Designer to be either an infant deity who had not yet fully learned his trade, or a dependent and inferior deity, or a senile god whose competence was much reduced.[160] Mill's omission may, perhaps, be taken as evidence that in this late essay on 'Theism' he is mellower than before, and more intent than he sometimes was on giving religion the most favourable treatment his epistemological principles will allow. This impression is reinforced when he declares, 'it does appear that granting the existence of design, there is a preponderance of evidence that the Creator desired the pleasure of his creatures'.[161] He can even say that 'there is a certain amount of justification for inferring, on grounds of natural Theology alone, that benevolence is one of the attributes of the Creator'.[162] But he immediately proceeds to qualify this by saying that the adverse evidence in nature indicates that, if the happiness of his creatures were his sole motive, he has failed ignominiously.

Before Mill's Christian readers are unduly consoled by what might be termed Mill's passing concessions to theism, let them remember that neither in the case of the First Cause nor of the Designer is there any retreat from Mill's naturalistic anti-supernaturalism, or from the idea of a less-than-omnipotent God. Indeed,

> It is not too much to say that every indication of Design in the Kosmos is so much evidence against the Omnipotence of the Designer. For what is meant by Design? Contrivance: the adaptation of means to an end. But the necessity for contrivance – the need of employing means – is a consequence of the limitation of power. Who would have recourse to means if to attain his end his mere word was sufficient?[163]

Throughout, 'Mill's God is an object in the world, discrete and separable from other objects and other minds'[164] – the very point on which his idealist and theological critics challenged him most urgently. Listen, for example to John Tulloch:

> [I]f mind be a mere quality or outcome of matter, we may certainly ask, with Hume, why should it be made the 'model of the universe'? What right have we to transfer it to natural phenomena? Design is only intelligible as the purposeful operation of an intelligent will ... operating behind the changes of experience; while a philosophy like Mr. Mill's, which *ab initio* denies that there is anything at all behind experience, and makes the will itself merely a phenomenon, really leaves no room for Will in Nature at all. No analogy of mere experience can enable us to find in Nature what we do not recognise in ourselves. The whole fabric of Mr. Mill's Theism therefore tumbles to the ground ... Blot out the Divine in Man, and no Divine can be found in Nature. Soul and God are essentially co-relative, and if soul is denied, God, or a Creative Mind, can nowhere be found.[165]

From his very different point of view, Alexander Bain judged that Mill's treatment of the argument from design was unsatisfactory. He was not persuaded by Mill's attempt to show that the argument is inductive, not merely analogical, and Mill ought to have disposed of the the objections lodged against the argument by Hume and Kant. For his part, John Morley thought that 'it can never be sufficiently deplored that the author did not find time to give us the result of his meditations as to the effect upon his own long-settled line of thought of the theory of Evolution and its moral and sociological applications'.[166] As Morley elsewhere averred, 'In face of the Darwinian hypothesis, with the immense mass of evidence already accumulated in its favour, the inference from contrivance exists, to say the best of it, in a state of suspended animation.'[167] More particularly, Morley observes that 'The scientific principles which lead to the doctrine of Evolution, are not logically consistent with Theism', and that Mill's account of the argument from design has not answered the objection that the argument 'implies a transfer to regions beyond experience, of an idea which springs from experience and is limited by it'.[168] It remained for the freethinker, B.V., both to denounce Mill's inadequate treatment of the argument from design and to chide any Christians who might draw comfort from it:

> Such is the Deity offered to Theists famishing for logical sustenance. A vague Mind, a mere probability, not creative but simply adaptive; certainly limited in power, perhaps limited in skill and will; whose benevolence is by no means his strongest motive of action; who has no other moral attribute. As to whether this Intelligence is embodied or not; how, if embodied, its body is not worn out by its life; how, if not embodied, it works on Matter and Force … not a word, not a single compassionate conjecture. Verily, some Christians are grateful for very minute mercies; the smallest contributions are by them thankfully received.[169]

IX

In 'Theism' Mill devotes an entire chapter to 'Immortality'. He explains that some understandings of immortality 'are independent of any theory respecting the Creator and his intentions', while others 'depend upon an antecedent belief on that subject'.[170] Regarding the former, such intimations are long-standing, and it is impossible to adduce conclusive evidence for or against them; for 'Experience furnishes us with no example of any series of states of consciousness, without … contingent sensations attached to it.'[171] Again the fact that many through the human ages have desired immortality affords no rational grounds for believing in it.

As to views of immortality which suppose a God, Mill recalls his view that the existence of a Creator is no more than a probability; that the overall benevolence of such a Being is open to question; and that the pleasure of his creatures, for which there is some evidence, is not God's sole objective. The evidence does suggest, however, that he is a limited Being. What, then, of the claim that such a Being would not wish to annihilate his greatest work, human beings, or doom their desires for immortality to disappointment? Mill replies, 'These might be arguments in a world the constitution of which made it possible without contradiction to hold it for the work of a Being at once omnipotent and benevolent. But they are not arguments in a world like that in which we live.'[172] Nevertheless (and at this point Mill's intellectual friends and foes alike detected a *volte face*),

> Appearances point to the existence of a Being who has great power over us …
> and of whose goodness we have evidence though not of its being his predominant
> attribute: and as we do not know the limits either of his power or of his goodness,
> *there is room to hope that both the one and the other may extend to granting us*
> *this gift* [immortality] *provided that it would be really beneficial to us*.[173]

Any such future life, he affirms, will have nothing to do with the apportioning of rewards and punishments, but it will preserve 'the best feature of our present life, improvability by our own efforts'.[174] As for the notion that at death, by a miracle, we shall be made perfect: while a duly authenticated revelation might justify such an aspiration, it 'is utterly opposed to every presumption that can be deduced from the light of Nature'.[175]

It is hardly surprising that Mill's contemporary critics were puzzled to the point of dumbfounded by Mill's gentle advocacy of the hope of immortality. It is, in a way, even more surprising to us, for we know that in 1854 Mill had written the following in his *Diary*:

> A person longing to be convinced of a future state, if at all particular about
> evidence, would turn with bitter disappointment from all the so-called proof of it.
> On such evidence no one would believe the most commonplace matters of fact.
> The pretended philosophical proofs all rest on the assumption that the facts of the
> universe bear some necessary relation to the fancies of our own minds.[176]

At the very least he accorded more space to the fancies some 14 years later, and this despite his assertion at the end of 'Utility of Religion' to the effect that, when the Religion of Humanity is established, 'not annihilation, but immortality, will be the burdensome idea'.[177] He now even thinks that these 'supernatural hopes, in the degree and kind in which what I have called rational scepticism does not refuse to sanction them, may still contribute not a little to this religion [of Humanity] its due ascendency over the human mind'.[178] It is important for us to note that in speaking of 'hope' Mill is employing the term to distinguish hope from belief. To him, 'The whole domain of the supernatural is … removed from the region of Belief into that of simple Hope.'[179] This is consistent with his view that 'To my mind the only permanent value of religion is in lightening the feeling of total separation which is so dreadful in a real grief.'[180] C.B. Upton pounced on Mill's hope as being 'the thin end of the wedge ... which must in time have completely rent asunder Necessarian and Experiential dogmas, and given free access to Intuitional ideas.'[181]

Did Mill himself espouse the hope of immortality, or did he continue to think that we are somehow fulfilled in the continuing life of the human race?[182] I suspect that his longing for renewed fellowship with Harriet, together with his feeling that apart from this hope there was no relief from 'the disastrous feeling of "not worth while"',[183] may have tilted him, against all his philosophical presuppositions, in the direction of hope.[184] But, as Alan Millar has rightly pointed out, 'It is one thing to be hopeful about what for all we know might be the case when we think there is at least some chance that it may be so. It is another to indulge hope where we have no reason to think there is such a chance.'[185] Mill's philosophical presuppositions gave him no such reasons, the fact that he thought the hope 'philosophically defensible'[186] notwithstanding.

Small wonder that freethinking B.V. could scarcely believe what he was reading: 'Not a few will rub their eyes in wonder at beholding how he, whom they have regarded as the champion of Empiricism and Positivism, carries on this contest from the high vantage-ground of Idealism and Transcendentalism, with potent and finely-tempered weapons from the armouries of Berkeley and Fichte.' His own view is that 'The whole scientific view of cosmic life and development is not merely antagonistic, but scornfully antagonistic, to this thought born of petty fear and desire, that a man having lived shall live again. And the whole moral view of humanity rejects it with certainly not less disdain.' He concludes that Mill's 'amiable' recommendation of hope and imagination 'has nothing to do with the dialectic on Theism'.[187]

Alexander Bain was quite dismissive of his former master: 'Mill hardly does justice to the natural difficulties of reproducing human existence, after death, for an eternal duration; and yet casts doubt on the omnipotence of the Power that is to perform the miracle.'[188] John Morley felt affronted – even betrayed – by Mill, and argued that 'Theism' contained views utterly inconsistent with those Mill had expressed in his earlier essays, a view not shared by Helen Taylor, as we have seen. While ruefully admitting that 'we cannot *disprove* the possibility of the immortality of the soul', Morley added, 'But then no more can we disprove any other propositions whatever, that anybody may choose to make as to regions outside of our own experience.'[189]

Confronted by Mill's apparent softening on the matter, the theologian James Orr resorts to understatement, thus:

It is an interesting circumstance that Mr. J.S. Mill, who, in his treatment of [immortality], took evident delight in reducing the logical evidence to a minimum, yet practically brings all those arguments which he had thrust out of the door of the head back by the door of the heart, and uses them to found the duty of cherishing this hope of a future life.[190]

Orr's reference to 'the door of the heart' calls to mind Upton's pertinent observation:

> There is a curious parallelism between [Mill's] case and that of many orthodox Christians. They likewise find themselves in the meshes of a logical network from which they can see no escape; yet, if they are pure-minded, loving natures, they are constantly devising kindly sophistries which may appear to harmonize the sentiments of their hearts and the requirements of their creed.[191]

But, for Mill, any quasi-supernatural hope was literally groundless. Hence, to Henry Reeve the chapter on immortality was 'not the least singular and painful portion of this volume,' and it drew from him the driest critical remark I have found: 'A writer who would speak of the immortality of the soul labours under some difficulty when he entertains doubts of the existence of any spiritual faculties and nature in man.'[192] Reeve ends his review in sepulchral tones, crafting Victorian cadences which, for all their flavour of yesteryear, nevertheless make the crucial epistemological point:

> The primary condition of religious belief is the Truth of the objects to which it is directed … To substitute a dream of imagination, or a thrill of emotion, for that which is, if it exist at all, the foundation of all Being and all Knowledge, appears to us to be but a feeble attempt to dispel the gloom of this philosophy of despair. When the light that should lighten the world is darkened, how great is that darkness![193]

As Mill said in his most concise, if most puzzling, statement on the matter, 'I think [Theism] a legitimate subject of imagination, & hope, & even belief (not amounting to faith) but not of knowledge.'[194] What is puzzling here is the confusion caused by Mill's failure to analyse 'faith'. He clearly does not have in mind *fiducia*, trust; but if he intends *assensus*, the difference between faith in this sense and belief is not clear. What is clear is that by construing the mind as a 'series of feelings',[195] Mill's 'official' pan-phenomenalism militates against what, in Christian terms, might be called the assurance of faith in God conceived as real, revealed and personal.

X

Mill turns next to 'Revelation', a subject concerning which he seems particularly anxious to deal fairly with those who take the opposing view to his own. He first explains the restricted nature of his interest here. He is not concerned with the positive evidences of any particular religion, but confines his attention to matters pertinent to revelation in general. He further points out that, since there are independent grounds for supposing that a divine being probably exists, subscribers to a revelation do not have to prove that such a being exists before making their claims.

The common distinction, Mill continues, is between external and internal revelation: 'External evidences are the testimony of the senses or of witnesses. By the internal evidences are meant the indications which the Revelation itself is thought to furnish of its divine origin.'[196] While internal evidences are important, and while they may afford conclusive grounds for rejecting a revelation – for example, if their allegedly revealed doctrines are morally perverting – they cannot warrant the acceptance of a revelation as divine. The only acceptable evidence is external evidence, comprising the exhibition of supernatural facts. The question therefore is, are there any such facts, and what evidence would prove them?

Mill argues that while the possibility of proving a supernatural fact by our senses cannot be ruled out, the evidence of miracles, as understood in Protestant circles, 'is not the evidence of our senses, but of witnesses, and even this not at first hand, but resting on the attestation of books and traditions.'[197] He recounts Hume's objection that the testimony of witnesses is frequently, intentionally or unintentionally, false, and notes Hume's advice that 'When ... the fact to which testimony is produced is one the happening of which would be more at variance with experience than the falsehood of testimony, we ought not to believe it.'[198] This is to behave prudently, not with credulity. Further, since miracles, according to the argument which Hume attacks, are contrary to experience, entailing as they do a breach in the natural law, we should disbelieve them.

At this point Mill appears as balanced adjudicator. In the first place he notes that the appeal here is to negative experience, which is more inconclusive than positive evidence. Furthermore, 'facts of which there had been no previous experience are often discovered, and proved by positive experience to be true'.[199] Again, the testimony of past experience is not entirely negative, and the evidence for it ought to be fairly examined. Indeed, 'The question can only be stated fairly as depending on a balance of evidence: a certain amount of positive evidence in favour of miracles, and a negative presumption from the general course of human experience against them.'[200] The fact remains, however, that owing to the progress of science we understand that all phenomena are amenable to law. To this defenders of miracles reply that miracles may not entail violations of known law, but may occur in accordance with laws unknown to us. This, says Mill, cannot be disproved, but it runs counter to our normal understanding of both law and miracle. He thus comes to his test:

> The test of a miracle is: Were there present in the case such external conditions, such second causes as we may call them, that whenever these conditions or causes reappear the event will be reproduced? If there were, it is not a miracle; if

there were not, it is a miracle, but it is not according to law; it is an event produced, without, or in spite of law.[201]

The objection that we ourselves, and God, alter the cause of events by the exercise of volition does not stand, he continues, for in neither case is it necessary to suppose that the laws of nature are violated. We could prove that God interferes with nature if we had evidence identical to that which we have in the case of human interferences; but all we have in the case of God are more or less speculative inferences. The upshot is that 'There is ... nothing to exclude the supposition that every alleged miracle was due to natural causes.'[202]

Mill admits that this is a limited conclusion. It demonstrates that 'The existence of God cannot possibly be proved by miracles, for unless a God is already recognized, the apparent miracle can always be accounted for on a more probable hypothesis than that of the interference of a Being of whose existence it is supposed to be the sole evidence.'[203] To this point Hume's position is unassailable. But if, on independent evidence, it can be shown that there is probably a God, then the possibility of his miraculous intervention is no longer an arbitrary hypothesis but a serious possibility.[204] But supernatural explanations remain matters of inference and speculation, and mysteries are susceptible to non-supernatural explanations. Supernatural explanations would appear more probable than not if they accorded with what we know of, or may surmise concerning, the methods of the supernatural agent. But in fact, all that we know, from the evidence of nature, concerning his ways, is in harmony with the natural theory and repugnant to the supernatural:[205] 'There is, therefore, a vast preponderance of probability against a miracle'.[206] When to this consideration we add the ambiguities in the world and the perilous nature of the testimony of eye witnesses, many of them unknown to us and none of them competent to analyse what they had seen, the only tenable conclusion can be that 'miracles have no claim whatever to the character of historical facts and are wholly invalid as evidences of any revelation'.[207] Such evidences as there are that a benevolent, though non-omnipotent, divine being exists, when coupled with the fact of the gift of Christ to the world, entitle us to say 'that there is nothing so inherently impossible or absolutely incredible in this supposition [in favour of miracles] as to preclude anyone from hoping that it may perhaps be true'. But Mill immediately adds, 'I say from hoping; I go no further; for I cannot attach any evidentiary value to the testimony even of Christ on such a subject, since he is never said to declare any evidence of his mission (unless his own interpretations of the prophecies be so considered) except internal conviction.'[208] In writing thus Mill demonstrates intellectual consistency over a number of years. For example, as early as 1849 he had written to W.G. Ward, protesting his innocence of any inclination to speak irreverently of Jesus:

He is one of the very few historical characters for whom I have a real & high respect. But there is not, to me, the smallest proof of his ever having said that he worked miracles – nor if he did, should I feel obliged either to believe the fact or to disbelieve his veracity.[209]

Fourteen years later we find him saying to Henry Chenevix,

Unless I could pretend to know either that there is no supernatural power or that such Power never works but in one way, I cannot presume to say that Christ may not have worked miracles: & I confess if I could be convinced that he ever *said* he had done so, it would weigh a great deal with me in favour of the belief. But in my opinion there is not a single miracle in either the Old or New Testament the particular evidence of which is worth a farthing. Those of Christ seem to me exactly on a level with the wonderful stories current about every remarkable man, & repeated in good faith in times when the scientific spirit scarcely existed.[210]

H.J. McCloskey was not out of order in declaring that 'Mill was committed by his arguments to the strangely paradoxical conclusion that there may well be miraculous events, and that we shall never have adequate grounds for accepting them as such.'[211] The earlier critic, W.L. Courtney, was to the point in observing, 'It is this playing with probabilities, this deliberate attempt to live in a twilight land of semi-faith, which caused so much consternation among those of Mill's disciples who had fed themselves on his earlier work.'[212]

As we might expect, criticisms of Mill's position have taken various forms. For example, the medical man, John T. Seccombe, pointed out that

We have the same evidence for miracles as we have for the life and teaching of Christ, and these are admitted [by Mill] to be unique. The miraculous element is so closely interwoven with the gospel narrative that no criticism can separate them on any other principle than that of taking it for granted beforehand that miracles are impossible or what cannot be proved, and this assumption is shown in the Essays to be groundless.[213]

James Orr concurs, and uses Mill's own words against his claim that the witnesses to Christ were incompetent. Mill writes,

It is of no use to say that Christ as exhibited in the Gospels is not historical and that we know not how much of what is admirable has been superadded by the tradition of his followers … [W]ho among his disciples or among his proselytes was capable of inventing the sayings ascribed to Jesus or of imagining the life and character revealed in the Gospels? Certainly not the fishermen of Galilee.[214]

On which Orr quite properly remarks,

It is useless to ascribe the sayings to Christ while attempting to explain the miracles as assertions of a 'later tradition' … If the sayings could not be invented by the fishermen of Galilee, as little certainly could the miracles, which, for the most part, bear precisely the same impress of simplicity, originality, dignity, and superiority to anything which credulous minds were likely to invent, as do the other acts and words of Christ.[215]

In any case, as Eustace Conder argued, to assert that because some alleged miracles have been impostures, all are, is to prove too much: 'The first question for a jury should be, not whether the witnesses are competent and honest, but whether what they state is probable, according to whatever standard of probability each particular set of jurymen is pleased to set up.'[216]

But the underlying problem concerns Mill's recourse to natural law. He claims that the phenomena of the universe are governed by laws, that God governs the world through such laws, and that miracles are violations of such laws. But, to quote McCloskey, 'This is what is in dispute between Mill and the theist; hence Mill's argument ... is a simple *petitio principii*.'[217] Much ink has been spilled over the questions, what is a natural law, what counts as a violation of natural law and how can we determine when such a violation has occurred? There is no need to pursue these questions here. Rather, an exercise in lateral thinking is more theologically appropriate. We need to start somewhere else: in fact with the notion of a miracle not as a violation of natural law, not as evidence apt to convince a sceptic, but as a 'sign' (to use the Johannine term) to those who believe on other grounds. It is unfortunate that in working towards this point a distinguished biblical scholar perpetrates a question-begging non sequitur, thus: 'It is inappropriate to describe miracle as a violation of natural law, since most societies, including those represented in the Bible, believed in the direct action of God (or gods) in history.'[218] The question is what miracles are, not what people have believed them to be. The conclusion, however, is more satisfactory: 'Throughout the Bible ... miracles are presented as means by which God discloses and fulfils his purpose in the world.'[219] If this is the case, then many of the arguments lodged against miracles – not least those of Hume and Mill – bypass their target and leave it unscathed. Of course, antagonists cannot be blamed for attacking claims regarding the miraculous which were held by many Christians of their day, and which continue to be articulated in some quarters in ours.

XI

Before leaving Mill's 'Theism', it is appropriate to dwell a little longer on his complimentary remarks concerning Jesus Christ. We have already noted one or two of them, but there are others elsewhere in his writings. As early as 1834 we find him informing Carlyle that he has been reading the New Testament. He continues,

I have for years had the very same idea of Christ, & the same unbounded
reverence for him as now; it was because of this reverence that I sought a more
perfect acquaintance with the records of his life, that indeed gave new life to the
reverence, which in any case was becoming or was closely allied with all that was
becoming a living principle in my character.[220]

In *On Liberty* he refers to the impression of 'moral grandeur' which Christ
left upon his followers;[221] and in 'Utility of Religion' he declares that 'some
of the precepts of Christ as exhibited in the Gospels ... carry some kinds of
moral goodness to a greater height than had ever been attained before'.[222] In
the latter essay Mill further speaks of 'the noble and beautiful beneficence
towards our fellow-creatures which [the Christ of the Gospels] so
impressively inculcates', though he feels bound to regret that 'even' Christ
'holds out the direct promise of reward from heaven as a primary
inducement' to such beneficence.[223] Indeed, in this regret there resides one
of Mill's primary charges against Christianity: as compared with the
Religion of Humanity, it is selfish.[224]

For all that, when he comes to 'Theism', his final word on the subject, it
is not surprising to find that Mill finds in Christ 'a standard of excellence and
a model for imitation, [which] is available even to the absolute unbeliever
and can never more be lost to humanity'.[225] None of which is to imply that
if Christianity were to fail morality would fall with it; in fact, Christian
morality falls short of the morality of Christ: it is negative and passive.[226]
As we have seen, throughout his life Mill consistently contended that 'a
large portion of the noblest and most valuable moral teaching has been the
work, not only of men who did not know, but of men who knew and rejected,
the Christian faith'.[227] Nevertheless, the 'Prophet of Nazareth' is found 'in
the very first rank of men of sublime genius of whom our species can
boast'.[228] Mill, going even further, famously declares,

When this pre-eminent genius is combined with the qualities of probably the
greatest moral reformer, and martyr to that mission, who ever existed upon earth,
religion cannot be said to have made a bad choice in pitching on this man as the
ideal representative and guide of humanity; nor, even now, would it be easy, even
for an unbeliever, to find a better translation of the rule of virtue from the abstract
into the concrete, than to endeavour so to live that Christ would approve our
life.[229]

As if to prevent his Christian readers from being lulled into thinking that
Mill has become their ally, he goes on to say that the impressions received
from Christ 'seem to me excellently fitted to aid and fortify that real, though
purely human religion, which sometimes calls itself the Religion of
Humanity and sometimes that of Duty'.[230] Supernatural hopes, he
concludes, may well function in a similar manner.

The secularist G.W. Foote zealously reminded his readers of Mill's
retractions in a tract partly designed to pour cold water on Christians who

felt that Mill was 'coming over': 'Here is Mill's testimony to Christ,' they cry, 'and we fling it like a bombshell into the Freethought camp.' We propose to pick up this bombshell, to dissect and analyse it, and to show that it is perfectly harmless.[231] Foote attributed any appearance of softening on Mill's part to Harriet, who 'disturbed his judgment in life and perverted it after death'.[232]

Other critics were more restrained. Bain accused Mill of purveying a reduced Christology:

> It seems, at first glance, a bold proceeding to take to pieces the Christ of Christianity, and to appropriate just so much of him as suits a 'rational criticism' … We are, of course, at liberty to dissent from the prevailing view, which makes Christ a divine person. But to reduce a Deity to the human level, to rank him simply as a great man, and to hold intercourse with him in that capacity, is, to say the least of it, an incongruity.[233]

To Morley, Mill's low Christology was still too high: it was, in fact 'one of the puzzles and perplexities' of 'Theism'.[234] He took particular exception to Mill's openness to the possibility that, while Christ was not God, he was 'a man charged with a special, express and unique commission from God to lead mankind to truth and virtue'.[235] '[N]o theist,' thundered Morley, 'can believe in the possibility of a science of social development, or in there being scientific laws of ethological growth, if he believes also that a most critical and important step in that development was due to special, express, and unique intervention on the part of the Supreme Being.'[236] All of this, thinks Morley, flies in the face of the sixth book of Mill's *Logic*.[237] Moreover, in selecting Christ as his moral exemplar, Mill behaves in a quite arbitrary way, for there have been many other morally exemplary people.

James Orr was concerned that Mill had abstracted from Christ all that was most religiously important:

> Christ did not come into the world merely to be a teacher and guide to virtue, as Mr. Mill in his rationalizing way supposes, but to be a Redeemer from sin; and it is through his weak hold on the idea of sin that Mr. Mill misses the clue to all the higher aspects of the Saviour's character and work. With all his mental and moral progress, this defect of his early training remained with him. We cannot wonder at it. The truer marvel is that he advanced so far.[238]

Others were intrigued by what they regarded as Mill's undermining of his own customary position. Of these C.B. Upton is typical. Mill, he says, asserts that there is nothing in the idea of duty or in religious experience

> which may not be explained by subjective and emotional processes. Yet, strange to say, after he has laid down this general principle, he suddenly startles us by an insinuation utterly subversive of his own philosophy. Speaking of the advent of Christianity, and of the comforting and ennobling views which it professed to

bring to mankind, he declares that there are some features in the character and teachings of Christ which do not appear to have arisen in the natural course of social evolution, and which therefore demand some other explanation.[239]

In justification of his opinion Upton quotes Mill's own words:

> when we consider further that a gift, extremely precious, came to us which though facilitated was not apparently necessitated by what had gone before, but was due, as far as appearances go, to the peculiar mental and moral endowments of one man, and that man openly proclaimed that it did not come from himself but from God through him, then we are entitled to say that there is nothing so inherently impossible or absolutely incredible in this supposition as to preclude any one from hoping that it may perhaps be true.[240]

Upton continues:

> Mr. Mill's words clearly involve the virtual surrender of the one great assumption which supports and animates all the researches of Positivists into the origin and development of mankind, and shew that their deceased chieftain had conceived and cherished a fatal doubt whether, after all, there are not elements in human nature which must ever prove inaccessible to so-called 'scientific' investigation.[241]

For his part, Morley was aghast at the suggestion which, he was convinced, entailed a *volte face* from Mill's earlier stated view that Christianity 'appeared at the appointed time by natural development'.[242] Like Upton, Morley detects encroaching idealism here, but unlike Upton, he strongly disapproves of it. Mill, he says, makes an 'appeal to a mystic sentiment which in other parts of the book he had shown such good reason for counting superfluous'.[243]

It would seem, however, that both Upton and Morley, in ignoring Mill's qualifying terms, 'not apparently necessitated' and 'as far as appearances go', were jumping too quickly to their conclusions. Consistently with his necessarianism, Mill could hold that certain things come to pass in what seems to us to be an undetermined way, though in fact they are predetermined to occur when they do. On the other hand, when Mill, thinking of the fishermen of Galilee and Paul, denies that these were 'capable of inventing the sayings ascribed to Jesus or of imagining the life and character revealed in the Gospels',[244] the *Edinburgh* reviewer understandably asks, 'If all the phenomena of life succeed each other with undeviating regularity, whence came this astounding apparition?'[245] There is sufficient ambivalence in Mill's writings to account for alternative interpretations of his meaning. The following are among such interpretations:

Just as the Experientialism and Utilitarianism of Hartley and Priestley ... underwent of necessity a gradual transformation into the religious philosophy of Channing and Martineau, so we believe that Mr. Mill's admission of a possible communion between Christ and God would probably in the course of time have expanded into a like admission in the case of every man, and that in this way his soul would have finally disengaged itself from the trammels of Sensationalism, and become prepared to study and appreciate those internal evidences of the truths of Religion, in the light and warmth of which his faint probabilities would have ripened into satisfying faith.[246]

By contrast, the *Westminster* reviewer was more realistic:

The concessions which Mr. Mill offers will, in all probability, be turned to account by the despairing champions of Orthodoxy; but Truth is patient, and can smile composedly at temporary delays to her progress, or ineffectual efforts to arrest her triumph. And what, after all, do these concessions amount to? A Probable Deity: a hope of Immortality which cannot be disproved, but for which there is no warrant; a possible revelation, from which miracle is discarded, and which is discredited by flagrant moral difficulties and perversions; a revelation mutilated by the removal of atonement, redemption, original sin, and vicarious punishment. Are these concessions calculated to nerve the failing arm or revive the drooping energies of the Theological Giant Despair?[247]

Leaving on one side the tendentious term 'vicarious punishment' and the question-begging term 'original sin', this statement does seem to encapsulate Mill's position accurately, and points, somewhat inaccurately and certainly incompletely, to factors in Christian faith to which Mill pays no attention whatsoever. We need not doubt that Mill's reverence for Jesus Christ was sincere. What is remarkable, however, in persons of his persuasion, then as now, is that they appear to see no inherent incongruity in a person whose ethical teaching is 'on the ball' to the point of sublimity, whilst his convictions as to his own person and mission are 'up the pole' to the point of insanity.[248] However that may be, it cannot be denied either that Mill's habitual method is to annexe Christ to his Religion of Humanity whenever it suits him, or that the Christ he reveres is a pared-down Christ, adapted to the confines of that Religion of wishful thinking. In the end, Mill's Christ is one who has relatively little to do with Christian faith or life. Basil Willey was not, therefore, without justification in declaring that Mill's statement about Christ, 'in its guarded hesitancy contrasts almost ludicrously with the Christian creed, and yet ... coming from Mill, represents an astonishing concession'.[249] It would seem that, if Mill had been able to do more than *hope* that in Christ God had acted uniquely, his entire philosophical edifice would have collapsed:

[I]f there was one thing more than any other which the sixth book of Mill's *Logic* was intended to teach, it was the notion of a science of social development, in which there could be no breaks, no want of continuity in the natural order. A science of historical sociology could not admit that, at a given period in the world's development, a character arose which had no relation to the past, and no roots in the existing social conditions.[250]

It would in fact only be necessary to admit that Jesus was not fully explained by the past or by existing social conditions, and this would guard against Docetism. But the main thrust of Courtney's overstated remark is to the point.

If many of those we have considered concluded that Mill had little to offer the theologians, a writer in the *Pall Mall Gazette* declared that 'the final judgment on these Essays must be deeply unfavourable to Mr. Mill as a philosopher'. Mill, he is persuaded, has failed in that capacity by allowing his feelings to get the better of him. Many of those who have mistaken feeling for thought 'know well enough that it is a mere anodyne and not a cure, and they will question the philosophy of a teacher who tells them otherwise as they would question the science of the physician who prescribed a diet of anaesthetics'.[251] In similar vein a writer in *The Daily Telegraph* suspected that 'the Pharisees of the inductive philosophy will be scandalised at the courtesies which their chief exchanges with the camp of the orthodox'.[252]

XII

On the posthumous publication of Mill's *Three Essays*, numerous and varied responses appeared from intellectual friends and foes alike.[253] As C.B. Upton accurately put it,

> From neither the friends nor the foes of the Experiential Philosophy has it received a warm and unequivocal welcome. It does not make that clean sweep of theological sentiments and beliefs which thorough-going Positivists desiderate; nor, on the other hand, do its faint probabilities seem of any worth to those who believe that only in the immediate apprehension of a righteous and sympathizing God is to be found the basis of that Theistic faith which is worthy to overthrow and replace the decaying orthodoxy of our time.[254]

From the other side, Morley expresses his 'rather keen surprise' at the spirit of Mill's theistic conclusions, and affirms that Mill's 'reconstruction ... results in a very modest and unsubstantial fabric'.[255] A contributor to *The Pall Mall Gazette* wrote of the 'mingled feelings of surprise, disappointment, and of something closely bordering on irritation' with which Mill's acolytes greeted the publication of the *Three Essays*.[256] Leslie Stephen, it is said, angrily paced up and down his study, while his wife, not very helpfully, remarked, 'I always told you John Mill was orthodox.'[257] Most dismissive of all is the remark in *The Dublin Review*:

[W]e are bound to admit that it is by far the weakest thing he has ever published. His philosophical principles lead to antitheism by legitimate consequence; and his passionate attempts to construct some kind of religious edifice do more credit … to his heart than to his head. Such attempts, we think, are due to that passionate emotionalism, which was so very prominent and so very singular a part of his character.[258]

The classification of the responses is extraordinarily difficult not only because of the variety of challenges posed, but also because they cannot be grouped neatly under such headings as 'Christian' and 'Agnostic'. Within either camp some disagreed with others, while between the camps there was agreement on some points. Consider the charge of doctrinal reductionism, for example. This was levelled in different ways by the agnostic, Leslie Stephen, and the Unitarian philosopher, C.B. Upton. Stephen argues that

A theory must have some definite support in facts. It must at lowest be not only consistent with the known facts, but inconsistent with some otherwise imaginable facts. If it fits every conceivable state of things, it can throw light on none. But this is obviously the case with Mill's theory. He makes way for a good being by an arbitrary division of nature into two sets of forces. He saves the benevolence by limiting the power of the deity; but then the limits are, by his own admission, unknowable … In fact, on Mill's showing, a power omnipotent but not benevolent, or an indefinite multitude of powers of varying attributes, or a good and a bad power eternally struggling, or, in short, any religious doctrine that has ever been held among men, would suits the facts.[259]

Upton's point is that the essay, 'Utility of Religion'

is utterly vitiated by the fact, that in his estimate of Christianity [Mill] never leaves the obsolete standpoint of Deism, whereas his own conception of religion, so far indeed as he can be said to have one, is an incipient and imperfect Theism, in which Hopes take the place of Beliefs, and the ideal imaginations of spiritual realities.[260]

Upton further finds Mill psychologically or spiritually incompetent to speak of Christianity in any other than a reductionist way:

His view is not even a caricature of Christian Theism, for it involves no reference to true spiritual experience, to the consciousness of personal obligation, and to that immediate insight of the affections, apart from which the reality of that which he attempts to criticise is wholly absent.[261]

Another Unitarian writer, Frances Power Cobbe, concurred. Of Mill she lamented, 'great philosopher as he was, when he comes to deal with a subject on which the rude tinker of Bedford has instructed the world, [he] writes like a blind man discoursing of colours, or a deaf man criticising the contortions of a violinist wasted on the delusion of music'.[262]

Not, indeed, that all of Mill's religious critics were Unitarians. The
Scottish divine, John Tulloch, also complained of the doctrinal reductionism
of Mill's 'pallid Theism', whereby Mill 'recognised a Creator, but denied to
Him either full benevolence, or the power to carry his benevolent purposes
into effect. A God thus limited – whose hand is shortened that it can not save,
is no God at all, and no religion worth speaking of could rest on such a
basis'.[263] But Tulloch thought that Mill had performed a useful service, too.
He had made clearer than before the competing postulates, 'Man is either
divine from the first – a free spiritual being standing apart from all nature, –
or he is essentially material. On the latter basis, no religion in the old sense
can be based.'[264] None travelled further along this line than a writer in the
popular magazine, *The Leisure Hour*:

> To the Christian [*Three Essays*] is a confirmation of the truth of God's word that
> man is made for God and eternity, and that no less good than the highest will
> really satisfy him long. If there are any timid Christians who think that the
> tendency of such a book as this of Mr. Mill's is to promote scepticism we can
> only say that our impression is the very reverse. It is, in fact, a testimony to the
> truth of Revelation, and though Mr. Mill does not break off with the same
> conclusion as Augustine in his 'Confessions', every line in it leads that way.
> *Fecisti nos ad te et inquietum est cor nostrum donec requiescat in te.*'[265]

Two prominent views emerge in explanation of the weaknesses in Mill's
theistic case. First, some attribute this to his personal characteristics, and to
his great desire to be fair to religion. Thus, a reviewer of the *Three Essays*
testifies in general that 'we are conscious of increased admiration for the fine
intellectual faculty, the beautiful moral nature, the docility, the patience, the
moderation, and the aesthetic or romantic enthusiasm of their lamented
author.' He goes on to speak of the 'wonderful caution in investigation' and
the 'prodigious boldness of thought' which are here united. But he feels
forced to temper his verdict where the third essay is concerned:

> Its philosophical infirmities we are disposed to ascribe to the unconscious
> despotism of delicate personal predilections, to the tyranny of transcendental
> sentiment, to the shuddering recoil at the presence of the world's misery, and the
> amiable desire to deal tenderly with the fair humanities of religious faith.[266]

Somewhat more technically, a later writer similarly found that 'in his own
effort to formulate a theology [Mill] did not make use of the "high degree of
probability" allegedly established by his induction. He chose instead the
more compelling, if less rigorous basis of his personal yearning for the fruits
of the spirit'.[267]

J. Baldwin Brown, a prominent Congregational minister, interpreted the
situation thus:

It may sound like a paradox, but I believe that Mr. Mill's many and palpable inconsistencies as a philosopher are the true key to the influence which he exerted on the world outside his school. Had he been merely the cold, bright, logical machine which his father did his very best to make him, the interest of the world at large in his life and labours would have been but limited … What Necessarian ever before pleaded so passionately for liberty and for the free play of individuality, and all that can develop individuality in the ordering of the great world's affairs? … It is not too much to say that Mr. Mill did as much to break down the narrow bounds of his philosophy with the one hand as he did to establish them with the other … Mr. Mill has rendered an essential service to religion: he has demonstrated and brought home to the hearts of his readers the poverty, the worthlessness of life without it.[268]

More recently, Karl Britton was similarly persuaded of the importance for his religious thought of the affective strand in Mill's character:

Mill's attitude towards religion involves, in the last analysis, not belief but the 'cultivation of feelings. Wordsworth – the poet of *The Prelude*, not the poet of the *Ecclesiastical Sonnets* – remains a powerful influence … [However] Wordsworth had Faith and Mill had not. And Mill always assumed that Faith must rest on *an inference* – upon an inference from experience to the existence of a remote and separate being. He was unable to see any logical justification for such an inference. But does Faith always rest upon an inference, logical or illogical? Was it essential to Wordsworth's religion to believe something *about* his experiences? It would surely be more accurate to say simply that he *believed in* them.[269]

No doubt; but with the proviso that unless belief be irrational, the connection in principle between 'belief in' and 'belief that' must ever be maintained.[270]

Secondly, others were much more inclined to emphasize the adverse effects of the contraints which Mill's philosophical presuppositions placed upon him. These, they allege with some justification, made it difficult if not impossible for him adequately to treat religion, and led him into inconsistencies, a number of which we have already noticed. Few produced as long a list of Mill's alleged inconsistencies as the *Spectator* writer, to whom Mill was

an empiricist who attached more importance to the secondary than to the primary forms of satisfaction; a Utilitarian who was more of a believer in the sacredness of disinterested emotion than the transcendentalists themselves … a necessarian who was the most passionate advocate of liberty … a sceptic who held the character of Christ all but divine … [The way he eulogizes the emotions is] more like the enthusiasm of fever than the enthusiasm of health.[271]

Such complaints emerge from disparate sources. John Cabot, for example detected in Mill's later writings glimpses of a far different end for human life than happiness: namely, the purpose to bring human beings themselves nearer to 'the ideal conception embodied in them'. Such a thought ... seems fitted to take away the sense of hostility in the forces that govern our lives, and so to dispose of the indictment which Mr. Mill brings against Providence. Such ideas, however, are excluded by the postulates of Mr. Mill's philosophy, and remain only as hopes, aspirations to be indulged in the region of the imagination; or as probabilities, not in the sense of facts imperfectly proved, but in the sense of haunting conjectures which reason can neither sanction nor shake off.[272]

Again, in the opinion of Henry Shaen Solly, the Unitarian, Mill 'would have risen superior alike to the stifling influences of education and the repellant force of perverted theology, and have ultimately grasped the pure creed of a reasonable faith, had he not been fatally encompassed and blinded by his Necessarian, Emperistic, and Eudaimonistic tenets'.[273] From a more conservative theological position came Noah Porter's stinging verdict:

To us it is no matter of wonder that a system made up of associational psychology, empirical metaphysics, prudential ethics, and necessitarian fatalism should be incompetent to lay the foundations or rear the superstructure of a religious theory of the universe ... A telescope which stands upon an unstable pedestal, and is furnished with imperfect lenses, and moved by imperfect machinery, must of necessity give images of vague outlines and blurred surfaces. Mr. Mill's philosophy appears to a bad advantage when it is applied in the service of a science of nature considered as the aggregate of finite, physical, and spiritual existence. It is not surprising that it should fail altogether to justify the belief in a self-existent Originator and Moral Ruler of this finite universe, who is unlimited in power and perfect in goodness.[274]

Lest the impression be given that theologians alone expressed such concerns, let us heed the logician, W. Stanley Jevons:

I will no longer consent to live silently under the incubus of bad logic and bad philosophy which Mill's Works have laid upon us. On almost every subject of social importance – religion, morals, political philosophy, political economy, metaphysics, logic – he has expressed unhesitating opinions, and his sayings are quoted by his admirers as if they were the oracles of a perfectly wise and logical mind ... But in one way or another Mill's intellect was wrecked. The cause of injury may have been the ruthless training which his father imposed upon him in tender years; it may have been Mill's own life-long attempt to reconcile a false empirical philosophy with conflicting truth. But, however it arose, Mill's mind was essentially illogical.[275]

Brand Blanshard later took exception to Jevons's charge of illogicality, at the same time, somewhat oddly, granting Mill's self-contradictoriness: 'Beneath the logic-chopping, and even when he contradicts himself, one feels the pulse of an honest and able mind toward a more rational theory.'[276]

A final complication concerns the question of the degree to which Mill's views on, and attitudes towards, religion may have changed over time. We have already detected a softening of his attitude towards religion in his later writings, and I have suggested that this may not be unconnected with his sense of loss following Harriet's death, something which quickened his *hope* that religious claims concerning God and immortality might be well founded.[277] Whatever the reason, Mill's friend, Alexander Bain, spoke for many when he wrote of 'Theism':

> It was a more extraordinary revelation of departure from opinions that he had been known to maintain, than had been his Bentham and Coleridge articles; and, while it might be grateful to some of his friends and the opposite to others, it was certainly hard to reconcile with his former self.[278]

But however it may have been with his attitudes, where his views were concerned Mill remained in thrall to his philosophical presuppositions. Basil Willey's elegant words both capture something of Mill's situation and require serious qualification:

> All through his life, like some ungifted Moses, he had tried to strike water out of dry rocks – altruism out of self-love, liberty out of bondage – and now here, in culminating frustration, he tries to draw faith out of reason. The rod taps and taps; the rock yields no drop; while – hidden from his shortsighted eyes – the spring bubbles up close at his back. If any proof were needed of St. Paul's proposition that by wisdom (reasoning) no man finds God, here is an admirable one. Yet Mill's strength was perfected in weakness, for, precisely by overworking his intellectual machine, he showed that he was not finally enslaved to it.[279]

But he *was* – intellectually. In 'Theism', his most 'softened' work, he puts his cards on the table in no uncertain manner. He declares that 'the legitimate conclusions of science are entitled to prevail over all opinions, however widely held, which conflict with them', and this governs his method: 'let us proceed to consider what place there is for religious beliefs on the platform of science; what evidences they can appeal to, and what foundation there is for the doctrines of religion, considered as scientific theorems'.[280] The enormity of the question begged in the last phrase there seems to have made no impression upon him at all. The humanist, Dorothea Krook, was, however, alive to it. While believing that Mill's *Three Essays on Religion* showed 'the humanist aspect of his mind and temper' more clearly than any other of his writings, and while deeming the collection 'as carefully considered and scrupulously fair as it is thoroughly argued' (too high praise on each count), she nevertheless concluded that Mill 'remained too much the scientist, too little the humanist (in the common sense of that term) to be quite flexible or quite imaginative enough in the employment of his spiritual resources' – a product of 'a deficiency of what one may call *religious culture*'.[281]

C.B. Upton thought there could be little doubt that 'had it not been for the shackles of early intellectual habit, which fettered his mind', Mill might have become 'a powerful expounder and defender of Christianity as it is set forth in the Sermon on the Mount'.[282] But, as we have just seen, from Mill's own mouth we have the testimony that, however oiled by emotion – even, in later years, by sentimentalism – the shackles remained in place. John Morley hit the mark when speaking of 'Mr. Mill's creed of low probabilities and faintly cheering potentialities.'[283]

Notes

1   So J.S. Mill, *Autobiography*, early draft, CW, I, p.74.
2   Letter of Mill to Carlyle of 12 January 1834, CW, XII, p.206.
3   J.S. Mill, *Autobiography*, CW, I, pp.41, 43.
4   J.S. Mill, *Auguste Comte and Positivism*, CW, X, p.332.
5   Idem, Letter of 21 August 1866 to Robert Pharazyn, CW, XVI, pp.1195–96.
6   For a varied selection of responses, to some of which reference will be made below, see Alan P.F. Sell (ed.), *Mill and Religion. Contemporary Responses to Three Essays on Religion*, Bristol: Thoemmes Press, 1997.
7   H. Taylor, 'Introductory notice' to the *Three Essays*, CW, X, p.372.
8   G. Grote, 'John Stuart Mill on *The Philosophy of Sir William Hamilton*', *Westminster Review*, N.S. XXIX, January 1866, 18.
9   See CW, XVI, 1195.
10 Ibid.
11 This authorial chronology amply justifies Karl Britton in taking Bertrand Russell to task. In a paper published in the *Proceedings of the British Academy* in 1955 (p.46), reprinted in J.B. Schneewind (ed.), *Mill. A Collection of Critical Essays*, London: Macmillan, 1968, pp.1–21, Russell had expressed surprise that 'in his three *Essays on Religion* written very late in his life' Mill had made no reference to Darwin's evolutionary hypothesis. But only the third essay was published late in Mill's life, and in it he did refer to the principle of the survival of the fittest (CW, X, p.449). See K. Britton, 'Perpetuating a mistake about Mill's *Three Essays on Religion*', *The Mill News Letter*, V, no. 2, Spring 1970, 6–7.
12 CW, X, p.371.
13 J.S. Mill, 'Nature', CW, X, p.374.
14 Ibid., 375.
15 Ibid.
16 Ibid.
17 Ibid., 376.
18 Ibid., 377–8.
19 Ibid., 378.
20 Mill accuses Montesquieu and George Combe of overlooking this fact and confusing the senses.
21 J.S. Mill, 'Nature', CW, X, p.379.
22 Ibid., 380.
23 Ibid., 385.
24 Ibid., 386.
25 Ibid., 387.
26 Ibid., 388.
27 Ibid., 389.

28   Ibid.
29   Ibid., 391, 397.
30   Ibid., 397.
31   Ibid., 400.
32   Ibid., 402.
33   Ibid.
34   Anon, *The Daily Telegraph*, 20 October 1874, p.4.
35   J.S. Mill, 'Nature,' CW, X, p.375.
36   Among them, Robert T. Harris, '*Nature*: Emerson and Mill', *The Western Humanities Review*, VI, 1952, 3.
37   Cf. Thomas Woods, *Poetry and Philosophy. A Study in the Thought of John Stuart Mill*, London: Hutchinson, 1961, p.184.
38   C.B. Upton, 'Mr. Mill's Essays on Religion – I', *The Theological Review*, XII, 1875, 132, 133.
39   N. Porter, 'John Stuart Mill as a religious philosopher', *Dickinson's Theological Quarterly*, 1875, 494, 495.
40   C.B. Upton, 'Mill's Essays on Religion – II. Theism: *The Theological Review*, XII, 1875', 259. Cf. Charles Douglas, John Stuart Mill. *A Study of his Philosophy*, (1895), reprinted with an Introduction by Andrew Pyle, Bristol: Thoemmes Press, 1994, 273: 'the inclusion of man in nature is fatal to that perverse cleavage of reality which makes the world independent of God'.
41   J.S. Mill, *Diary*, CW, XXVII, p.656.
42   [Henry Reeve] in *The Edinburgh Review*, no. CCLXXXVII, January 1875, 10.
43   J. Skorupski, *John Stuart Mill*, London: Routledge, 1989, p.5.
44   Idem, Introduction to his edited volume *The Cambridge Companion to Mill*, Cambridge: CUP, 1998, p.6. Cf. Philip Kitcher, 'Mill, mathematics and the naturalist tradition', : 'Mill is not only one of the most important naturalists in the history of philosophy, but also, perhaps, the most thoroughly consistent' (ibid., 58).
45   L. Stephen, *The English Utilitarians*, London: Duckworth, 1900, III, p.437.
46   J.S. Mill, *Utilitarianism*, CW, X, p.234.
47   J. Orr, 'John Stuart Mill and Christianity – II', *Theological Monthly*, VI, 1891, 111. Cf. R.T. Harris, '*Nature*: Emerson and Mill', 12–13.
48   CW, XXIV, p.1083.
49   CW, X, p.389.
50   Ibid.
51   J. Morley, 'Mr. Mill on religion', *Critical Miscellanies. Second Series*, London: Chapman and Hall, 1877, p.318.
52   Ibid., 322.
53   J.S. Mill, 'Utility', CW, X, p.424.
54   A.M. Fairbairn, *The Philosophy of the Christian Religion*, 5th edn, London: Hodder and Stoughton, (1902), 1907, p.96.
55   E. August, *John Stuart Mill. A Mind at Large*, London: Vision, 1976, pp.250–51.
56   Ibid., 245.
57   CW, XXVII, p.654.
58   J.S. Mill, *Autobiography*, CW, I, pp.193, 195, 197.
59   In other words, just as psychologists have frequently noted the way in which those hostile to a religion may, if converted to it, become the most ardent, even fanatical, adherents (Saul of Tarsus/Paul the apostle being a classic case), so something analogous may explain Mill's attitude towards, and his 'over the top' writing about, Harriet.
60   James Eli Adams, 'Philosophical forgetfulness: John Stuart Mill's *Nature*', *Journal of the History of Ideas*, LIII no. 3, July–September 1992, 453.
61   Ibid., 450 n., quoting A. Fleishman, *Figures of Autobiography: the Language of Self-Writing in Victorian and Modern Britain*, Berkeley: University of California Press, 1983, p.151.

62 C.A. Stork, 'Mr. Mill's Autobiography as a contribution to Christian evidences', *Quarterly Review of the Evangelical Lutheran Church*, IV, 1874, 274.
63 Ibid., 276, 277.
64 C.B. Crane, 'John Stuart Mill and Christianity', *The Baptist Quarterly* (Philadelphia), VIII, 1874, 351, 361.
65 J.S. Mill, *Autobiography*, CW, I, p.251.
66 A.M. Fairbairn, *Studies in Religion and Theology. The Church: In Idea and in History*, New York: Macmillan, 1910, 613.
67 A. Bain, *John Stuart Mill. A Criticism with Personal Recollections*, London: Longmans, 1882; reprinted Bristol: Thoemmes Press, 1993, 171.
68 G.W. Foote, *What was Christ? A Reply to John Stuart Mill*, London: Progressive Publishing Company, 1887, p.5. For Foote see MR; J. M. Wheeler, *A Biographical Dictionary of Freethinkers of all Ages and Nations*, London: Progressive Publishing Co., 1889; Jim Herrick, *Vision and Realism: A Hundred Years of The Freethinker*, London: G.W. Foote, 1982.
69 J.S. Mill, letter to *The Republican* of 3 January 1823, in CW, XXII, pp.8, 9.
70 Idem., 'Law of libel and liberty of the press', CW, XXI, p.21.
71 The point is developed by J.E. Adams, 'Philosophical forgetfulness', 440–41.
72 R.T. Harris, '*Nature*: Emerson and Mill', 9.
73 E.R. Conder, *The Basis of Faith. A Critical Survey of the Grounds of Christian Theism*, London: Hodder and Stoughton, 1877, p.282. Cf. Linda C. Raeder, *John Stuart Mill and the Religon of Humanity*, Columbia, MO: University of Missouri Press, 2002, p.99: 'It does not seem to have occurred to Mill that the forces of nature, unlike human beings, are not conscious beings, endowed with minds and will.' She observes that 15 years later Mill spoke more tentatively on the matter.
74 W.L. Courtney, *The Metaphysics of John Stuart Mill*, London: C. Kegan Paul, 1879; reprinted Bristol: Thoemmes Press, 1990, p.149.
75 J.S. Mill, 'Theism' CW, X, p.455.
76 Idem, *On Liberty*, CW, XVIII, p.263.
77 N. Porter, 'John Stuart Mill as a religious philosopher', 493.
78 John Bunyan, *Grace Abounding to the Chief of Sinners*, London: SCM Press, 1955, p.124.
79 [Henry Reeve], *The Edinburgh Review*, January 1875, 19n. For Reeve (1813–95) see MR.
80 *The British and Foreign Evangelical Review*, XXIV, 1875, 172.
81 A.G.N. Flew, *God and Philosophy*, London: Hutchinson, 1966, p.51.
82 J.S. Mill, Letter of 23 September 1860 to Florence Nightingale, CW, XV, p.709.
83 K. Britton, 'John Stuart Mill on Christianity', in John M. Robson and Michael Laine (eds), *James and John Stuart Mill. Papers of the Centenary Conference*, Toronto: University of Toronto Press, 1976, p.29.
84 Letter of 24 August 1871: Mill to Joseph Giles, CW, XVII, p.1829.
85 J.S. Mill, *Autobiography*, CW, I, p.43.
86 Idem, 'Utility of Religion', CW, X, p.425.
87 L. Stephen, *The English Utilitarians*, III, 438.
88 Ibid., 450.
89 J.S. Mill, 'Theism', CW, X, p.432.
90 Ibid., 455.
91 Ibid., 488.
92 Ibid., 425–6.
93 Ibid., 456.
94 A. Bain, *John Stuart Mill. A Criticism*, 135
95 A.G.N. Flew, *God and Philosophy*, 51.
96 J.H. Hick, *Evil and the God of Love* (1966), London: Collins Fontana, reprinted 1968, p.35; cf. 171.

97   A.B. Bruce, *The Moral Order of the World in Ancient and Modern Thought*, London: Hodder and Stoughton, 1899, p.337. For Bruce (1831–99) see DHT, DSCHT, ODNB; W.M. MacGregor, *Persons and Ideals*, Edinburgh: T. & T. Clark, 1939, ch. 1; Alan P.F. Sell, *Defending and Declaring the Faith. Some Scottish Examples 1860–1920*, Exeter: Paternoster Press and Colorado Springs: Helmers & Howard, 1987, ch. 5.
98   J. S. Mill, Letter to Florence Nightingale, CW, XV, p.709. Cf. 'Theism', CW, X, 458–9.
99   Idem, 'Theism', CW, X, p.455.
100 Cf. C.A. Stork, 'Mill's *Autobiography*', 274. P.T. Forsyth's *The Justification of God*, (1917), London: Independent Press, 1957, is a classic statement along this line. A number of Mill's critics accused him of not taking due account of the devastating consequences of human sin – the cause of so much misery in the world. No doubt it is; but apparently random and inequitably distributed disasters would still remain to be accounted for. The humanist, Dorothea Krook, charged that Mill failed to take account of 'the Christian answer to the problem [of evil] supplied by the Fall and the doctrine of Original Sin'. See her *Three Traditions of Moral Thought*, Cambridge: CUP, 1959, p.198. But even if the *explanation* were to be sought where she suggests, Christians look to the Cross for the (practical) *answer*.
101 C.B. Crane, 'John Stuart Mill and Christianity', 358.
102 T.V. Tymms, *The Mystery of God*, London: Elliot Stock, 1890, p.105. For Tymms (1842–1921) see *The Baptist Handbook*, 1922, 274; DNCBP; J.O. Barrett, *Rawdon College (Northern Baptist Education Society) 1804–1954. A Short History*, London: Carey Kingsgate, 1954; Alan P.F. Sell, *Philosophy, Dissent and Nonconformity 1689–1920*, Cambridge: James Clarke, 2004.
103 J.S. Mill, 'Theism', CW, X, p.429.
104 Ibid.
105 Ibid., 430–31.
106 W.L. Courtney, *The Metaphysics of John Stuart Mill*, 148–9.
107 J.S. Mill, 'Utility of Religion', CW, X, p.419.
108 C.B. Upton, 'Mill's *Essays on Religion* – II. Theism', *The Theological Review*, XII, 1875, 266.
109 This ugly word distinguishes the scientist as such from those scientists who subscribe to scientism, an inherently reductionist position, in the sense just described.
110 J.S. Mill, 'Theism', CW, X, p.433.
111 Ibid., 434.
112 Ibid.
113 Ibid.
114 Ibid., 435.
115 Ibid., 436.
116 T.V. Tymms, *The Mystery of God*, 79.
117 J.S. Mill, 'Theism', CW, X, p.437.
118 Ibid.
119 Ibid.
120 Ibid., 438.
121 Ibid.
122 Ibid., 439.
123 Ibid.
124 For Gregory (1832–1915) see DAB, MR.
125 D.S. Gregory, 'John Stuart Mill and the destruction of theism', *The Princeton Review*, N.S. 1878, 419.
126 Ibid.
127 Ibid., 425.
128 J.S. Mill, *A System of Logic*, CW, VII, p.355.
129 Ibid., 326–7.
130 Ibid., 340.

131   D.S. Gregory, 'John Stuart Mill and the destruction of theism', 426–7.

132   Ibid., 427–8.

133   Ibid., 429. The linguistic shifts to which Gregory refers are found in one paragraph in 'Theism', CW, X, p.437.

134   Ibid., 442.

135   Ibid., 447–8.

136   Ibid., 448.

137   Ibid.

138   Cf. James Orr, 'John Stuart Mill and Christianity', 115.

139   Ibid., 110. Cf. T.V. Tymms, *The Mystery of God*, 80–81.

140   In connection with the argument from universal consent, Mill thunders, 'The religious belief of savages is not belief in the God of Natural Theology.' See 'Theism', CW, X, p.442. We may with equal confidence retort, 'The God of Natural Theology is not the God of Christians.'

141   I have attempted a trilogy in which this question is addressed. See Alan P.F. Sell, *Philosophical Idealism and Christian Belief*, Cardiff: University of Wales Press and New York: St. Martin's Press, 1995; *John Locke and the Eighteenth-Century Divines*, Cardiff: University of Wales Press, 1997; *Confessing and Commending the Faith. Historic Witness and Apologetic Method*, Cardiff: University of Wales Press, 2002.

142   J.S. Mill, 'Theism', CW, X, p.441.

143   Ibid., 443.

144   W.J. Irons, *An Examination of Mr. Mill's Three Essays on Religion*, London: Robert Hardwicke, 1875, p.36.

145   J.S. Mill, 'Theism', CW, X, p.444.

146   Ibid.

147   Idem, *A System of Logic*, CW, VIII, p.813.

148   Idem, 'Theism', CW, X, p.444.

149   Ibid., 445.

150   Ibid.

151   Ibid., 446.

152   J. M'Cosh, *An Examination of Mr. J. S. Mill's Philosophy*, London: Macmillan, 1866, p.396. Cf., for example, Mill's *Utilitarianism*, CW, X, pp.229–33.

153   J.S. Mill, *An Examination of Sir William Hamilton's Philosophy*, CW, IX, p.439.

154   Idem, 'Theism', CW, X, p.447.

155   In his *An Examination of Sir William Hamilton's Philosophy*, Mill refers to the design argument only as an analogy. He agrees with Hamilton that 'the Divine Intelligence is but an assumption, to account for the phaenomena of the universe; and that we can only be warranted in referring the origin of those phaenomena to an intelligence, by analogy to the effects of human intellect' (CW, IX, pp.440–41; cf. 192, 438–9). But he does not agree with Hamilton that the analogy can suggest complete identity in conditions and modes of action as between God and ourselves; and he does not see how Hamilton's inference is consistent with Hamilton's customary view that God is absolute, unrestricted by conditions, and unknowable and inconceiveable by us.

156   Ibid., 448.

157   Ibid., 449.

158   Ibid., 450.

159   Ibid.

160   D. Hume, *Dialogues Concerning Natural Religion*, Indianapolis: Hackett, 1986, pp.37–8.

161   J.S. Mill, 'Theism', CW, X, pp.457–8.

162   Ibid., 458.

163   Ibid., 451. We may note the *a priori* cast of this argument.

164   Karl Britton, 'John Stuart Mill on Christianity', p.26.

165 J. Tulloch, *Movements of Religious Thought in Britain During the Nineteenth Century* (1885), reprinted Leicester: Leicester University Press, 1971, 241–2.

166 J. Morley, 'Mr. Mill's Three Essays on Religion – Pt. I', *The Fortnightly Review*, XVI, November 1874, 649.

167 Idem, 'Mr. Mill on religion', 324.

168 Ibid., 326.

169 B.V., 'Mill on Religion', *The National Reformer*, N.S. XXIV, 1874, 391.

170 J.S. Mill, 'Theism', CW, X, p.460.

171 Ibid., 462.

172 Ibid., 466.

173 Ibid., my italics.

174 Ibid.

175 Ibid., 467.

176 Idem, *Diary*, 1854, CW, XXVII, p.663.

177 Idem, 'Utility of Religion', CW, X, p.428.

178 Idem, 'Theism', CW, X, p.489.

179 Ibid., 483.

180 Quoted by A. Bain, *John Stuart Mill. A Criticism*, 140.

181 C.B. Upton, 'Mill's Essays on Religion – II', 266.

182 See, for example, 'Utility of Religion', CW, X, p.420.

183 J.S. Mill, 'Theism', CW, X, p.485. I am not alone in suspecting this. See, for example, *The Daily Telegraph*, 22 October 1874, p.5.

184 Cf. Robert Carr, 'The religious thought of John Stuart Mill: a study in reluctant scepticism', *Journal of the History of Ideas*, XXIII, 1962, 490–91. For the alternative view see Alan Ryan, *J.S. Mill*, London: Routledge, 1974, p.247. Linda C. Raeder thinks that the 'softened' character of 'Theism' is explained by the fact that, as a widower, Mill was no longer under the influence of the 'aggressively antireligious' Harriet. See her *John Stuart Mill and the Religion of Humanity*, 364. I am more inclined to think that Mill was devastated by the loss of Harriet, and cast around for whatever straws of consolation he could find.

185 A. Millar, 'Religion', in J. Skorupski (ed.), *The Cambridge Companion to Mill*, p.198.

186 J.S. Mill, 'Theism', CW, X, p.485.

187 B.V., 'Mill on Religion', 404.

188 A. Bain, John Stuart Mill. A Criticism, 134.

189 J. Morley, 'Mr. Mill on religion', 331.

190 J. Orr, *The Christian View of God and the World*, Edinburgh: Elliot, 1897, p.156.

191 C.B. Upton, 'Mill's Essays on Religion – II', 264.

192 [Henry Reeve], *The Edinburgh Review*, January 1875, 26.

193 Ibid., 30, 31.

194 Letter of Mill to Arthur W. Greene of 16 December 1861, CW, XV, 755. On the previous page we read: 'neither in the Logic nor in any other of my publications had I any purpose of undermining Theism; nor, I believe, have most readers of the Logic perceived any such tendency in it … [Nor] would I willingly weaken in any person the reverence for Christ, in which I myself very strongly participate.' Even Mill's slender hope places him at a remove from his father. C.B. Upton described James Mill's scientific prejudices as 'mental disabilities' which, in his case, impaired religious insight to the point of 'congenital spiritual blindness. Such natures, accordingly, hardly feel the want of the truths they fail to see, and he would probably have viewed with pity, if not with disdain, his son's anxiety to retain by the faint tenure of hope doctrines of which his philosophy allowed him no right of possession'. See 'Mill's Essays on Religion – II', 261.

195 See J.S. Mill, *An Examination of Sir William Hamilton's Philosophy*, CW, IX, p.190.

196 Idem, 'Theism', CW, X, pp.469–70.

197 Ibid., 471.

198   Ibid.
199   Ibid., 472.
200   Ibid.
201   Ibid., 474.
202   Ibid., 477.
203   Ibid.
204   Cf. Mill's Letter to Joseph Napier of 24 December 1862, CW, XV, p.814.
205   Cf. Mill's Letter to Standish O'Grady of 16 January 1869, CW, XVII, pp.1545–6.
206   Idem, 'Theism', CW, X, p.478.
207   Ibid., 481.
208   Ibid.
209   Letter of Mill to Ward of [Spring, 1849], W.G. Ward, CW, XIV, p.27.
210   Letter of 4 November 1863 to Henry Chenevix, CW, XV, p.895.
211   H.J. McCloskey, *John Stuart Mill: A Critical Study*, London: Macmillan, 1971, p.166.
212   W.L. Courtney, *Life of John Stuart Mill*, London: Walter Scott, 1889, 169–70.
213   J.T. Seccombe, *Science, Theism, and Revelation, considered in relation to Mr. Mill's Three Essays on Nature, Religion, & Theism*, London: Simpkin, Marshall, 1875, p.76. For Seccombe (b. 1834) see MR.
214   J.S. Mill, 'Theism', CW, X, p.487.
215   J. Orr, 'John Stuart Mill and Christianity', 120.
216   E.R. Conder, *The Basis of Faith*, 451.
217   H.J. McCloskey, *John Stuart Mill: A Critical Study*, 167. For a discussion of the subject in which reference is made to more recent writers, see P.J. McGrath, 'John Stuart Mill and the concept of a miracle', *The Irish Theological Quarterly*, LIX, no. 3, 1993, 211–17.
218   Howard Clark Kee, 'Miracle', in *The Oxford Companion to the Bible*, ed. Bruce M. Metzger and Michael D. Coogan, Oxford: OUP, 1993, p.519.
219   Ibid., 520.
220   Letter of Mill to Carlyle of 12 January 1834, CW, XII, pp.208–09; cf. ibid., 182.
221   J.S. Mill, *On Liberty*, CW, XVIII, p.235.
222   'Utility of Religion', CW, X, p.416.
223   Ibid., 423. It is more accurate to regard the reward as the consequence of beneficent acts performed for their own sake.
224   See, for example, 'Utility of Religion', CW, X, p.423.
225   Idem, 'Theism', CW, X, p.487.
226   Idem, *On Liberty*, CW, XVIII, p.255.
227   Ibid., 257.
228   Idem, 'Theism', CW, X, pp.487–8.
229   Ibid., 488.
230   Ibid.
231   G.W. Foote, *What Was Christ? A Reply to John Stuart Mill*, 3.
232   Ibid., 4.
233   A. Bain, *John Stuart Mill: A Criticism*, 138.
234   J. Morley, 'Mr. Mill on religion', 315.
235   J.S. Mill, 'Theism', CW, X, p.488.
236   J. Morley, 'Mr. Mill on religion', 307.
237   Ibid., 308.
238   J. Orr, 'John Stuart Mill and Christianity', 121. In his essay of 1833 on 'Blakey's history of moral science', Mill writes of the people of Christ's day, 'It was out of the hardness of their hearts that they needed signs [Mark 3: 5]. Had all been right within, the precepts themselves would have sufficed to prove their origin.' See CW, X, p.29. Mill makes scant use of the idea of the noetic effects of sin elsewhere in his writings.
239   C.B. Upton, 'Mill's Essays on Religion – II', 269.
240   J.S. Mill, 'Theism', CW, X, 481; quoted by Upton, art.cit., 270.

241   C.B. Upton, art.cit., 270.
242   J. Morley, 'Mr. Mill on religion', 307–8.
243   Idem, 'Mill's Three Essays', 637.
244   J.S. Mill, 'Theism', CW, X, p.487.
245   *The Edinburgh Review*, January 1875, 30.
246   C.B. Upton, 'Mill's Essays on Religion – II', 272.
247   [Wathen Mark Wilks Call], 'John Stuart Mill, Three Essays on Religion', *The Westminster and Foreign Quarterly Review*, 1 January, 1875, 28. For Call (1817–90) see MR.
248   I have recourse, in uncharacteristic fashion, to these cheerful slang expressions by way of indicating that I am more amused than devastated by this circumstance. (But sometimes those who should know better can be tiresome!)
249   B. Willey, *Nineteenth-Century Studies*, London: Chatto & Windus, 1949, p.185.
250   W.L. Courtney, *Life of John Stuart Mill*, 170.
251   Anon., 'Mr. Mill on Religion', *The Pall Mall Gazette*, 23 October 1874, p.10. *The Pall Mall Budget* was a weekly paper comprising articles from the *Gazette*, together with a news summary. The items on Mill are in the issues for Saturday 24 October 1874, 8–9, and Saturday 31 October, 9–10.
252   *The Daily Telegraph*, 20 October 1874, p.5.
253   For a selection of these, see MR.
254   C.B. Upton, 'Mill's Essays on Religion – I', 127.
255   J. Morley, 'Mr. Mill on religion', 287, 304.
256   *The Pall Mall Gazette*, 23 October 1874, p.10.
257   Recounted in S. Parkes Cadman, *Charles Darwin and Other English Thinkers with reference to their Religious and Ethical Value*, London: James Clarke, 1911, p.131. Stephen's brother, James Fitzjames Stephen, was of similar opinion: 'John Mill in his modern or more humane mood – or, rather, I should say, in his sentimental mood ... is a deserter from the proper principles of rigidity and ferocity in which he was brought up.' See a letter quoted in L. Stephen, *The Life of Sir James Fitzjames Stephen*, London: Smith, Elder, 1895, p.308.
258   Anon., review of *Three Essays on Religion*, in *The Dublin Review*, XXIV, January–April 1875, 223.
259   L. Stephen, *The English Utilitarians*, III, 445.
260   C.B. Upton, 'Mill's Essays on Religion – I', 142.
261   Ibid., 141.
262   F.P. Cobbe, *The Hopes of the Human Race, Hereafter and Here: Essays on the Life After Death*, London: Williams and Norgate, 1880, p.38. For F.P. Cobbe (1822–1904) see ODNB, MR. The 'rude tinker of Bedford' is, of course, John Bunyan.
263   J. Tulloch, *Movements of Religious Thought in Britain during the Nineteenth Century*, 243. Cf. Anon., 'Mr. Mill's religious confession', *The Spectator*, 24 October 1874, 1325: 'while he doubted everything from the existence of God and the divine mission of Christ to the immortality of the soul, he distinctly rejected nothing except the divine omnipotence'.
264   Ibid., 244. By 'standing apart' we are presumably meant to understand 'distinct from,' not 'utterly divorced from'. If the latter were the case that would be no basis for a religion either – or even for humanity as we know it.
265   Anon., *The Leisure Hour*, 1875, 119.
266   *The Westminster and Foreign Quarterly Review*, 1 January 1875, 2–3.
267   Robert Carr, 'The religious thought of John Stuart Mill', 493.
268   J.B. Brown, 'Mr. John Stuart Mill's legacies', *The Evangelical Magazine and Missionary Chronicle*, N.S. V, 1874, 716, 717, 718. For Brown (1830–84) see MR, ODNB; *The Congregational Year Book*, 1885, 181–4. Brown was on the liberal wing of Victorian Congregationalism.
269   K. Britton, *John Stuart Mill*, Harmondsworth: Penguin Books, 1953, 216, 218.

270 The allusion here is to often popular, but sometimes more uncritical, theological discussions in which much is made of the undeniable fact that 'Christianity is not merely a matter of intellectual assent to credal assertions; it is belief in, and commitment to, a person.' Quite so; but, for example, were the proposition, 'Jesus never existed' true, continued belief in him would be, to say the least, odd. Cf. Hebrews 11: 6.

271 Anon, 'Mr. Mill's religious confession', 1326. In *The Spectator* of 7 November 1874, 1396–7, William Wordsworth, writing from Rydal Lodge on 1 November 1874, replies to this article, and the editor appends a rejoinder.

272 James E. Cabot, review of *Three Essays on Religion*, in *North American Review*, no. 120, 1875, 468.

273 H.S. Solly, review of *Three Essays on Religion*, in *The Inquirer*, 28 November 1874, p.774. Solly adds, 'The contradiction between an assured religion and such philosophy, was felt in a similar way by the followers of Priestley. There were two positions which could not be held together. They surrendered the one, Mill gave up the other.' For Solly (1848–1925) see MR. Solly's co-religionist, C.B. Upton, concurred. See 'Mr. Mill's Essays on Religion – I', 130.

274 N. Porter, 'John Stuart Mill as a religious philosopher', 499.

275 W. S. Jevons, 'John Stuart Mill's philosophy tested. Portions of an examination of John Stuart Mill's philosophy', in Robert Adamson and Harriet A. Jevons (eds), *Pure Logic and Other Minor Works*, London: Macmillan, 1890, p.201. Jevons is nothing if not direct: 'I do not believe that Mill's immense philosophical influence, founded as it is on confusion of thought, will readily collapse. I fear that it may remain as a permanent obstacle in the way of sound thinking' (ibid., 273). Cf. W.L. Courtney, *The Metaphysics of John Stuart Mill*, 149–50.

276 Brand Blanshard, *Four Reasonable Men*, Middletown, CT: Wesleyan University Press, 1984, p.78.

277 Among many who detected this attitudinal change were C.B. Upton, 'Mr. Mill's Essays on Religion – II', 250; E. August, *John Stuart Mill. A Mind at Large*, 247.

278 A. Bain, *John Stuart Mill: A Criticism*, 158.

279 B. Willey, *Nineteenth-Century Studies*, 177. While in general agreement with Willey, Dorothea Krook, referring to the fact that Enlightenment Christians were happy to regard 'rational explanations' of the faith, offered on the basis of unquestioned assumptions concerning the existence and attributes of God, as confirmatory of faith, regretted that Willey 'nowhere allows that if Mill did have hold of the wrong end of the stick, the same end had been firmly grasped by thoughtful Christians for nearly two hundred years before'. See her *Three Traditions of Moral Thought*, 198.

280 J.S. Mill, 'Theism', CW, X, p.431.

281 D. Krook, *Three Traditions of Moral Thought*, 181, 200, 201.

282 C.B. Upton, 'Mr. Mill's Essays on Religion – II', 267.

283 J. Morley, 'Mr. Mill's Three Essays on Religion – I', *The Fortnightly Review*, 637. Cf. Karl Britton, 'John Stuart Mill on Christianity', 23: '"Religion in the region of mere hope" is John Stuart Mill's contribution to philosophical theology.'

Chapter 5

Conclusion: Pervasiveness and Elusiveness

This investigation of Mill's views on God and religion, and with it an attempt to enter into discussion with his critics, friendly and hostile, contemporary and subsequent, is almost complete. It should by now be clear that the sub-title of this study was not casually chosen. I think it has been amply demonstrated that God and religion were fairly constant preoccupations of Mill's, and that his thoughts on these subjects were by no means confined to his posthumous *Three Essays on Religion*. On the contrary, they permeate his letters and his *Autobiography*; they inform his crusade against intuitionism in his *Examination of Sir William Hamilton's Philosophy* and elsewhere; his *Utilitarianism* comprises the statement of his creed, while his writings on education concern his mission to establish the Religion of Humanity, a cause which is discussed in his essay on Comte and alluded to in other places, notably in the essays on 'Utility of Religion' and 'Theism', and in his letters. Not even the *Logic* is innocent of religious reflection. It may thus reasonably be suggested that those who write studies of Mill which neglect his religious thought while claiming comprehensiveness are in fact overlooking a dimension of his work which was significant, and a motivation both positive (in favour of the Religion of Humanity) and negative (opposed to Christianity) apart from which Mill himself cannot fully be understood. To put it otherwise, for all the abstracting from his pages of arguments concerning utilitarianism, political thought and the like, we have not finished with *Mill* until we have asked, for example, how suitable in theory and in practice is utilitarianism as the creed of a Religion of Humanity? Pervasive though his thoughts on God and religion are, it has not been argued that they are of the first rank in terms of depth and critical acumen. Mill does not have the incisiveness of Hume, and he is more influenced by emotion (in 'Nature', for example) and sentiment (supremely in 'Theism') than other adverse critics of religion have been.

Above all, Mill outstrips many others in the elusiveness of his thought on God and religion. Evidence of this elusiveness has been supplied in some detail in a variety of connections, and there is no need to reproduce it here. The reasons for the elusiveness may, however, briefly be recapitulated. First, as we have seen, Mill, influenced here as elsewhere by his father, was reticent as regards those religious opinions which he was willing publicly to articulate in speech and writing. This accounts for those differences to be found between statements in his publications and in his writings or his *Diary*. Here he looks for the time when Christianity will be entirely banished from the scene, and theologians with it; there, wearing the hat of a practical man of affairs, he understands that as moral cement and as a dissuasive to societal anarchy, religion may have a continuing usefulness for some time, even though its doctrinal claims are false. In his later years, following Harriet's death, Mill's attitude towards religion softens somewhat. Having shown to his own satisfaction that there probably is a limited God, he now, however inconsistently with his philosophical principles, entertains, in an elusive way, the hope of immortality.

Secondly, the elusiveness emerges from his method. As Martineau pointed out, Mill, unlike his father and Bentham, does not set out from utilitarian first principles and adhere to them unflinchingly. His disinclination for metaphysical speculation on the one hand, and on the other his desire to carry as many people as possible with him on socio-political issues, combine to render his thought intriguingly and sometimes elusive. We thus detect a leaven of Romanticism here, a dose of positivism there, a doffing of his hat to Christ at fairly regular intervals: and all of this with a view to bringing together people of differing, even of opposing, views in the cause of social advancement. Hence his oscillations between empiricism and idealism, necessarianism and libertarianism; hence also many of the inconsistencies sprinkled through his writings: they result from his intellectual hospitableness to almost everything except responsible Christian theology.

What of the new religion which Mill advocated? Certainly he does not swallow Comte whole. As a committed associationist, he resents Comte's denigration of psychology; he thinks Comte deficient in failing to allow for proper self love, and for appearing to place the individual at the mercy of society. Above all, however, he cannot stomach Comte's cultus or his exaggerated sense of his own importance. As to his own version of the utilitarian creed: here, once again, he is eclectic if not elusive; for with his view that values may be graded he opens the door to intuitionism, thereby undercutting his general hostility to that philosophy. Of the human beings for whom his new religion is, he frequently takes a dim view, and in aristocratic fashion looks to the 'philosopher kings' – and above all to a particular 'philosopher queen' – to exemplify and encourage the educative mission whose end he cannot see. Sometimes he advocates the inculcation of values, at others he wishes individuals to find their own ways to growth of character, whilst reserving the right to moan about the inadequate choices many of them make. Elsewhere his emphasis is so strongly upon human nature as progressive that his sense of optimism verges upon the unrealistic (he overlooks sin, intoned many theologians).

The question how far Mill was really committed to the inauguration of a new religion has exercised a number of scholars. No doubt he desired such an outcome, but he did not do much to bring it about. We know that he abhorred Comte's cultus, and that he held himself aloof from the English practitioners of the Religion of Humanity. Whereas John Wesley organized his preachers, called conferences, and rode thousands of miles on horseback to proclaim his message; and whereas in Mill's own day William Booth was organizing his Salvation Army, and encouraging his soldiers to play brass instruments and visit public houses for the Gospel's sake, what does Mill propose to do? He thinks he may write a book when the time is ripe. In a letter to Comte of 17 January 1845 we find him optimistic that the time may soon come when past doctrines and with them the supernatural might be jettisoned. 'All we need is a little daring,' he says, 'and I might not be averse to making the attempt myself' – immediately adding, 'But I would do so in a book.'[1] It seems unlikely that Mill envisaged anything more in the foreseeable future than the propagation, largely by writing, of his credal idea, which he had good reason to think would appeal only to a certain 'advanced' section of the community.

All of which seems to suggest a gnostic pipe-dream religion of an armchair kind. The actual conditions of society were not such as to give the Religion of Humanity any more than a toe-hold, and Mill's temperament, as indicated by his reticence, was not that of martyrs, who may draw a following of at least a few for at least a time. His endorsement of Comte's prophecy that 'the moral and intellectual ascendency, once exercised by priests, must in time pass into the hands of philosophers, and will naturally do so when they become sufficiently unanimous, and in other respects worthy to possess it'[2] awaits fulfilment, on both counts. Indeed, Mill's reminder to the editor of *The Morning Chronicle* of 'what every schoolboy knows', namely, 'that the philosophers of a creed are seldom its successful politicians',[3] has a direct application to himself. It appears that for Mill the Religion of Humanity remained more a theory to be propagated than a way (with its organizational implications) to be walked in company with others.

So much for the new religion, but what of the old? We need to think about this under two aspects. First, Mill quite frequently lands telling and deserved blows against reactionary attitudes and hypocritical practices in the institutional Church. He also sees a place for the teaching of religion, provided that it be done with integrity and in a non-proselytizing way. His advocacy of fuller religious liberty is to be applauded. But none of this rises above good, forward-looking journalism, which much of it actually was. Although it is entirely compatible with the main thrust of his utilitarianism (with supplementary resources annexed from elsewhere, notably from Christianity, by way of commending his ideas to the public) it is the work of one who can 'get up a brief' and then move on to other topics.

Secondly, there are his views – many of them strong – on theological and doctrinal matters. Here he is quite out of his depth, and for this he had only himself to blame. However formative Mill's contribution in other fields (the theory of induction, political thought and sociology, for example) on the field with which this book has been concerned he was at best a thoughtful amateur, and at worst a self-blinkered opponent. The fact that Mill, consistently with his philosophical principles, dispenses with the supernatural in his Religion of Humanity, and with an omnipotent God in his discussion of evil and the theistic arguments, and declines to break out of his naturalism when pondering immortality, both makes his eschatological hope intellectually insecure and reveals an undeniable weakness in his strategy. He does not consider Christian (not merely theistic) doctrines in their strongest expression, and this in defiance of his self-serving self-estimate:

> I ... thought myself much superior to most of my contemporaries in willingness and ability to learn from everybody; as I found hardly any one who made such a point of examining what was said in defence of all opinions, however new or however old, in the conviction that even if they were errors there might be a substratum of truth underneath them.[4]

This is the more serious because, as we have seen, Mill wished to eradicate theology (if not immediately Christianity) as soon as possible. The least he might have done, therefore, would have been to examine responsible theological and doctrinal claims with as much care as possible. This he signally failed to do. Time and again he lambasts a bizarre version of Calvinism, yet Calvinism was in his day undergoing significant revision, and by no means all Christian theology was Calvinistic; he scorns Christian ethics for its allegedly 'carrot and stick' and selfish character, and its negativity, while annexing as much of the ethical teaching of Jesus as he can, and introducing not a few prohibitions into his utilitarianism. But his lack of careful attention to Christian claims regarding sin, eternal life and, above all, the person and work of Jesus Christ, renders his anti-Christian strictures tangential to what Christians traditionally have believed. One illustration of this is that the undifferentiated Being of natural theology is not 'the God and Father of our Lord Jesus Christ'.[5] Another is Mill's failure ever to relate the problem of evil to the doctrine of the Cross. As A.M. Fairbairn wrote of Mill, 'As he misconceived the religion, he never judged it impartially, nor could he. He thought he was neutral when he was not; and where he failed to appreciate he was quite unable to criticize.'[6] In fairness to Mill, however, it must be granted that he was not entirely without excuse:

> He might criticize Christianity in a wooden way, but if he had got hold of the wrong end of the stick he was surely holding it by the same end as the [more accurately, 'many'] Victorian Christian apologists. It was they who repeated the two-centuries-old arguments for the existence of God ... It was they who entangled themselves in moral dilemmas by declaring God omnipotent and then maintaining that his mercy must be limited to the Elect.[7]

Nevertheless, the more general verdict which Martineau pronounced against Comte applies to Mill also as far as theology is concerned. Towards this discipline 'he presents only a blind or negative side ... and he is content to do this *dogmatically* ... he presents no front for attack or discussion on this side; for it is impossible to refute mere oracular contempt'.[8] Such an attitude ill becomes a professedly anti-dogma person like Mill, but in philosophy as elsewhere mirror images abound. Certainly I have found little evidence to support Brand Blanshard's claim that Mill 'wanted to know why thoughtful Christians believed as they did, and in this he largely succeeded'.[9]

Even Mill's humanist friend, Alexander Bain, was adversely critical of him in this connection: 'I think … he was too little versed in the writings of Theologians, to attack their doctrines with any effect.' In fact he seldom even states their doctrines accurately. This is not surprising, for as Bain recalls, 'He scarcely ever read a Theological book.'[10] A reviewer vainly wished that the now deceased Mill 'had ever come into real contact with Christian ideas'.[11] It really does seem that we must look to Mill's a-theistic education at the hand of his father for the explanation of this lacuna: hence his impaling on a *tu quoque* by the ebullient C.A. Stork:

> Mr. Mill has written some very eloquent passages on the benumbing and cramping effects of receiving our beliefs on tradition; but the best illustration of what he has so well portrayed, in the abstract, he has himself furnished in the history of the adoption of his own beliefs concerning religion. No man of equal capacity … was to the end of his life more influenced by the lessons imbibed in youth. He was, as far as his religious opinions are concerned, a 'made man'.[12]

Since what Martineau said concerning Mill's anti-Coleridgian reasonings has a wider application, we shall do well to heed his crisp observation: 'The keen aim and the steady hand are of no avail when there is an optical displacement of the thing aimed at.'[13] This brings us to the heart of the matter, and to the chief methodological lesson to be learned from this study. While Mill was culpable, and untrue to his proclaimed even-handedness in argument, in not giving Christian teaching a fair hearing, he was not lazy. Rather, he was habitually and methodologically disinclined to give Christianity its due. This was a function of the scientism with which he was indoctrinated from his earliest years. From his very method he could draw the inference that nothing which Christians might say or write on doctrinal matters could qualify as rational, so why pay them much attention? Let us recall his typical words:

> It is indispensable that the subject of religion should from time to time be reviewed as a strictly scientific question, and that its evidences should be tested by the same scientific methods, and on the same principles as those of any of the speculative conclusions drawn by physical science [for] the legitimate conclusions of science are entitled to prevail over all opinions, however widely held, which conflict with them.[14]

As I said, 'Manifestly this is a manifesto!' It begs the question of science's competence for the task Mill gives it in his understanding of it, and it rules out fundamental Christian claims *ab initio*. Moreover, Mill offers no justification of this elevation of science. The upshot is that, having devised the rules in such a way that Christians cannot play the game, he has no need to concern himself with what their moves, as suggested by their best authors in their actual works, might have been. In this he is not alone. If R.P. Anschutz is correct in saying that Mill 'regards as an empiricist a man who, failing or refusing to recognize any distinction between the scientific and unscientific ways of experience, inevitably treats it in the unscientific way',[15] we may say that Mill does recognize the distinction, and ignores it in the interest of scientific imperialism. What Mill does, dramatically, is to throw into relief the importance for Christian apologetics of the question of starting-points, and for this we may be grateful.[16]

As to the adverse criticisms levelled against Mill's *Three Essays on Religion*, it must be granted that it takes a particular skill to alienate Christians, agnostics and secularists in roughly equal measure, but this is what Mill did. Some of his critics were astonished – even dumbfounded – that he could write as he did, and a number were hard put to judge what his deepest intentions were. All of this is further testimony to his elusiveness. Indeed, it is not too much to say that a large part of the interest of Mill's religious thought lies in the fluttering in very diverse dovecotes which it prompted. The final irony is that the prophet of a Religion of Humanity, which was inherently social, was, as far as religious questions are concerned, left in intellectual isolation at the last.

If one more elusive matter may be tolerated, it is this: was Mill a religious person? He certainly was not a Christian, either in the sense of committed discipleship of Christ in the fellowship of the Church or in the sense of affirming major Christian doctrines. On the other hand, I take his word that, like his father before him, he was not a dogmatic atheist, for they both knew that the non-existence of God cannot be proved. But Mill certainly claimed to have religious feelings,[17] and he had a genuine admiration for Jesus, and a genuine concern for liberty in matters of belief. Some have labelled Mill an out-and-out secularist, and it seems to me that this is to go too far. Perhaps the circle can be squared by saying that Mill's religiosity was secular in character. But that is not, perhaps, all (it seldom is with the elusive Mill). His philosophical principles notwithstanding, Mill was reluctant to exclude God altogether – at least the God of theism – even if the God he retained was one whose existence was probable only, and whose power was limited. Again, despite his customary anti-supernaturalism, at times the eighteenth-century man was almost routed by the Romantic, the hard-headed empiricist by the wistful sentimentalist, who could even hope that there may be immortal life. In view of these occasions it is not altogether fanciful to say that if, as Novalis said, Spinoza was a God-intoxicated man, and if, as Mill said, Comte was a morality-intoxicated man,[18] John Stuart Mill was, at least from time to time, a God-haunted man.

Notes

1   O.A. Haac (ed.), *The Correspondence of John Stuart Mill and Auguste Comte*, New Brunswick: Transaction Publishers, 1995, p.288.
2   J.S. Mill, *Autobiography*, CW, I, p.219.
3   Idem, 'Puseyism – I', CW, XXIV, p.814.
4   Idem, *Autobiography*, CW, I, pp.251, 253.
5   I Peter 1: 3.
6   A.M. Fairbairn, *Studies in Religion and Theology. The Church: In Idea and History*, New York: Macmillan, 1910, p.612.
7   Noel Annan, recounting the position of Dorothea Krook, in J. B. Schneewind (ed.), *Mill*, London: Macmillan, 1968, p.17.
8   James Martineau, *Types of Ethical Theory*, 3rd revised edn, Oxford: Clarendon Press, 1891, I, p.399.
9   B. Blanshard, *Four Reasonable Men*, Middletown, CT: Wesleyan University Press, 1984, p.100.
10 A. Bain, *John Stuart Mill. A Criticism: with Personal Recollections*, London: Longmans, Green, 1882, p.139. Mill does confess to having read Ward's *On Nature and Grace* right through. See his letter to Ward of 18 November 1859, CW, XV, p.647. Noah Porter made a similar point to that of Martineau, but more bluntly. See his 'John Stuart Mill as a religious philosopher', *Dickinson's Theological Quarterly*, 1875, 504. H.L. Mansel applied a similar judgment to Mill's treatment of metaphysics. See his *The Philosophy of the Conditioned*, London: Alexander Strahan, 1866, pp.182–3.
11 *The British Quarterly Review*, LXI, January 1875, 274.
12 C.A. Stork, 'Mr. Mill's *Autobiography*', *Quarterly Review of the Evangelical Lutheran Church*, IV, 1874, 264.
13 J. Martineau, *Essays, Reviews and Addresses*, London: Longmans, 1891, III, p.504.
14 J.S. Mill, 'Theism', CW, X, pp.430–31.
15 R.P. Anschutz, *The Philosophy of J.S. Mill*, London: OUP, 1953, p.76.
16 I described my trilogy on Christian apologetic method as to a considerable extent 'a tale of alternative starting-points'. See above, ch.4 n.141.
17 See for example, *Auguste Comte and Positivism*, CW, X, p.333.
18 Ibid., 336.

References

Adams, James Eli, 'Philosophical forgetfulness: John Stuart Mill's *Nature*', *Journal of the History of Ideas*, LIII, no. 3, July–September 1992, 437–54.

Adamson, William, *The Life of the Rev. Joseph Parker*, Glasgow: Inglis, Ker, 1902.

Alexander, Edward, *John Stuart Mill: Literary Essays*, Indianapolis: Bobbs-Merrill, 1967.

Annan, Noel, 'John Stuart Mill', in H.S. Davies and G. Watson (eds), *The English Mind*, Cambridge: CUP, 1964, reprinted in J.B. Schneewind, *Mill. A Collection of Critical Essays*, 22–45.

Anon., 'Christian ethics and John Stuart Mill', *Dublin University Magazine*, LIV, October 1859, 387–410.

—— 'John Stuart Mill on religion', *Daily Free Press* (Aberdeen), 20 October 1874, 2.

—— 'On Mill's *Three Essays on Religion*', *The Daily Telegraph*, 20 October 1874, 4–5; 22 October 1874, 5.

—— 'Mr. Mill on religion', *The Pall Mall Gazette*, 22 October 1874, 10; 23 October 1874, 9–10; and in the *Pall Mall Budget*, 24 and 31 October 1874, 8–9 and 9–10 respectively.

—— 'Mr. Mill's religious confession', *The Spectator*, 24 October 1874, 1325–7.

—— 'Review of Mill's *Three Essays on Religion*', in *The Dublin Review*, XXIV, January–April 1875, 223.

—— 'Review of Mill's *Three Essays on Religion*', in *The Leisure Hour*, XXIV, 1875, 117–19.

—— 'Review of Mill's *Three Essays on Religion*', in *The British Quarterly Review*, LXI, January 1875, 271–4.

—— 'Review of Mill's *Three Essays on Religion*', in *The British and Foreign Evangelical Review*, XXIV, 1875, 172–6.

—— *Is Theism Immoral? An Examination of Mr. J.S. Mill's Arguments against Mansel's View of Religion*, Swansea: E. E. Rowse, 1877.

Anschutz, R.P. *The Philosophy of J.S. Mill*, London: OUP, 1953.

Atkinson, R.F., 'J.S. Mill's "proof" of the principle of utility', *Philosophy*, XXXII, April 1957, 158–67.

August, Eugene, *John Stuart Mill: A Mind at Large*, London: Vision, 1976.

Bain, Alexander, *James Mill. A Biography*, London: Longmans, 1882.

—— *John Stuart Mill. A Criticism with Personal Recollections* (1882), reprinted Bristol: Thoemmes Press, 1992.

Baptist Handbook, The, London: The Baptist Union of Great Britain and Ireland, 1922, p.274.

Barrett, J.O., *Rawdon College (Northern Baptist Education Society) 1804–1954. A Short History*, London: Carey Kingsgate, 1954.

Barros, Carolyn A., *Autobiography. Narrative of Transformation*, Ann Arbor: University of Michigan Press, 1998.

Blackstone, William, *Commentaries on the Laws of England*, ed. Thomas A. Green, Chicago: University of Chicago Press, 1979.

Blakey, Robert, *An Essay shewing the Intimate Connexion between our Notions of Moral Good and Evil, and our Conception of the Freedom of the Divine and Human Wills*, Edinburgh: Adam Black, 1831.

Blanshard, Brand, *Four Reasonable Men*, Middletown, CT: Wesleyan University Press, 1984.

Bocking, Ronald, 'Sydney Cave (1883–1953), missionary, principal, theologian', *Journal of the United Reformed Church History Society*, VII, no. 1, October 2002, 28–35.

Bradley, F.H., *Ethical Studies* (1876), reprinted London: OUP, 1962.

Bridges, J.H., *The Unity of Comte's Life and Doctrine. A Reply to Strictures on Comte's Later Writings, Addressed to John Stuart Mill*, London: Trübner, 1866.

Brink, David O., 'Mill's deliberative utilitarianism', *Philosophy and Public Affairs*, XXI, 1992, 67–103, reprinted in C.L. Ten (ed.), *Mill's Moral, Political and Legal Philosophy*, 357–93.

Britton, Karl, *John Stuart Mill*, Harmondsworth: Penguin, 1953.

—— 'J.S. Mill: A debating speech on Wordsworth', *Cambridge Review*, LXXIX, March 1958, 418–23.

—— 'Utilitarianism: the appeal to a first principle', *Proceedings of the Aristotelian Society*, N.S. LX, 1959–60, 141–54.

—— *Philosophy and the Meaning of Life*, Cambridge: CUP, 1969.

—— 'Perpetuating a mistake about Mill's *Three Essays on Religion*', *The Mill News Letter*, V, no. 2, Spring 1970, 6–7.

—— 'John Stuart Mill on Christianity', in J.M. Robson and M. Laine (eds), *James and John Stuart Mill. Papers of the Centenary Conference*, Toronto: University of Toronto Press, 1976, 21–34.

Brodie, George, *A History of the British Empire*, Edinburgh: Bell and Bradfute, 1822.

Brown, J. Baldwin, 'Mr. John Stuart Mill's legacies', *The Evangelical Magazine and Missionary Chronicle*, N.S. V, 1874, 715–18.

Bruce, A.B., *The Moral Order of the World in Ancient and Modern Thought*, London: Hodder and Stoughton, 1899.

Bunyan, John, *Grace Abounding to the Chief of Sinners*, London: SCM Press, 1955.

Burston, W.H. (ed.), *James Mill on Education*, Cambridge: CUP, 1969.

Cabot, James E., 'Review of Mill's *Three Essays on Religion*', in *North American Review*, no. 120, 1875, 461–9.

Cadman, S. Parkes, *Charles Darwin and Other English Thinkers with reference to their Religious and Ethical Value*, London: James Clarke, 1911.

Caird, Edward, *The Social Philosophy and Religion of Comte*, Glasgow: Maclehose, 1893.

Calderwood, Henry, *The Philosophy of the Infinite*, Edinburgh: T. Constable, 1854.

Calderwood, W.L. and David Woodside, *The Life of Henry Calderwood, LLD, FRSE*, London: Hodder and Stoughton, 1900.

[Call, Wathen Mark Wilks], 'John Stuart Mill's Three Essays on Religion', *The Westminster and Foreign Quarterly Review*, N.S. XLVII, January 1875, 1–28.

Calvin, John, *Institutes of the Christian Religion*, trans. Ford Lewis Battles, ed. J.T. McNeil, Philadelphia: Westminster Press, 1961.

Cameron, Nigel M. de S. (ed.), *Dictionary of Scottish Church History and Theology*, Edinburgh: T.&T. Clark, 1993.

Carlyle, Thomas, *Sartor Resartus*, London: Chapman and Hall, 1858.

Carr, Robert, 'The religious thought of John Stuart Mill: a study in reluctant scepticism', *Journal of the History of Ideas*, XXIII, 1962, 475–95, reprinted in V. Sánchez-Valencia (ed.), *The General Philosophy of John Stuart Mill*, Aldershot: Ashgate, 2002, p.413–33.

Cashdollar, Charles D., *The Transformation of Theology, 1830–1890. Positivism and Theological Thought in Britain and America*, Princeton: Princeton University Press, 1989.

Cathcart, William, *The Baptist Encyclopaedia*, Philadelphia: Louis H. Everts, 1881.

Cave, Sydney, *The Christian Estimate of Man*, London: Duckworth, 1944.

Chalmers, Thomas, *Considerations on the System of Parochial Schools in Scotland, and on the advantage of Establishing Them*, Glasgow: James Hedderwick, 1819.

Chapman, Edward Mortimer, *English Literature and Religion 1800–1900*, London: Constable, 1910.

Christian Life, The, Appreciation of William MacCall, 1888, 557.

Church, R.W., 'Mill on liberty', *Bentley's Quarterly Review*, II, 1860, reprinted in A. Pyle (ed.), *Liberty. Contemporary Responses to John Stuart Mill*, Bristol: Thoemmes Press, 1994, pp.210–54.

Clarke, M.L., *Paley: Evidences for the Man*, Toronto: University of Toronto Press, 1974.

Cobbe, F.P., *The Hopes of the Human Race, Hereafter and Here: Essays on the Life After Death*, London: Williams and Norgate, 1880.

Coleridge, E.H. (ed.), *Letters of Samuel Taylor Coleridge*, London: Heinemann, 1895.

Coleridge, S.T., *Confessions of an Inquiring Spirit*, London: William Pickering, 1840.

Comte, Auguste, *Cours de Philosophie Positive*, Paris, 1830, etc.

—— *The Positive Philosophy of Auguste Comte*, freely trans. and condensed by Harriet Martineau, London: J. Chapman, 1853.

—— *System of Positive Polity, or, Treatise on Sociology, Instituting the Religion of Humanity*, trans. J.H. Bridges *et al.*, London: Longmans, 1875–7

—— *The Catechism of Positive Religion*, 2nd edn, trans. Richard Congreve, London: Trübner, 1883.

Conder, Eustace R., *The Basis of Faith. A Critical Survey of the Grounds of Theism*, London: Hodder and Stoughton, 1877.

Congregational Year Book, The, London: Congregational Union of England andWales, 1885, 181–4; 1903, 208 (b)–(e); 1954, 506–7.

Courtney, W.L., *The Metaphysics of John Stuart Mill* (1879), reprinted Bristol: Thoemmes Press, 1990.

—— *Life of John Stuart Mill*, London: Walter Scott, 1889.

Cowling, Maurice, *Mill and Liberalism*, Cambridge: CUP, 1963.

Crane, C.B., 'John Stuart Mill and Christianity', *The Baptist Quarterly* (Philadelphia), VIII, 1874, 348–62.

Crimmins, James E., 'Bentham on religion: atheism and the secular society', *Journal of the History of Ideas*, XLVII, January–March 1986, 95–110.

—— *Secular Utilitarianism: Social Science and the Critique of Religion in the Thought of Jeremy Bentham*, Oxford: Clarendon Press, 1990.

—— *Utilitarians and Religion*, Bristol: Thoemmes Press, 1998.

—— (ed.), *Religion, Secularization and Political Thought. Thomas Hobbes to J.S. Mill*, London: Routledge, 1989.

Cumming, R.D., 'Mill's history of his ideas', *Journal of the History of Ideas*, XXV no. 2, April–June, 1964, 235–56.

Cunningham, William, *The Reformers and the Theology of the Reformation* (1862), reprinted London: The Banner of Truth Trust, 1967.

Davidson, W.L., 'Mill, James and John Stuart', *Encyclopaedia of Religion and Ethics*, VII, ed. James Hastings, Edinburgh: T. & T. Clark, 1915.

Davies, H.S. and G. Watson (eds), *The English Mind*, Cambridge: CUP, 1954.

Dawson, Albert, *Joseph Parker. His Life and Ministry*, London: S.W. Partridge, 1901.

De Burgh, W.G., *From Morality to Religion*, London: Macdonald & Evans, 1938.

Douglas, Charles, *John Stuart Mill. A Study of his Philosophy* (1895), reprinted, with an Introduction by Andrew Pyle, Bristol: Thoemmes Press, 1994.

—— *The Ethics of John Stuart Mill*, Edinburgh: Blackwood, 1897.

Drummond, James and C.B. Upton (eds), *The Life and Letters of James Martineau*, London: Nisbet, 1902.

Dumont, P.E.L., *Traités de Législation civile et pénale*, Paris: Bossange, Masson andBesson, 1802.

Elliot, Hugh S.R. (ed.), *The Letters of John Stuart Mill, With a Note on Mill's PrivateLife by Mary Taylor* [Harriet's granddaughter], London: Longmans, 1910.

Evans, George Eyre, *Vestiges of Protestant Dissent*, Liverpool: F. and E. Gibbons, 1897.

Ewing, A.C., *Ethics*, London: English Universities Press, 1953.

Fairbairn, A.M., *The Philosophy of the Christian Religion*, 5th edn, London: Hodder and Stoughton, 1907.

—— *Studies in Religion and Theology. The Church: In Idea and in History*, New York: Macmillan, 1910.

Fleishman, A., *Figures of Autobiography: the Language of Self-Writing in Victorian and Modern Britain*, Berkeley: University of California Press, 1983.

Flew, A.G.N., *God and Philosophy*, London: Hutchinson, 1966.

—— 'Review of J. Skorupski, *John Stuart Mill*', in *The Philosophical Quarterly*, XLI, no. 162, January, 1991, 97–100.

Flint, Robert, *Anti-Theistic Theories*, Edinburgh: Blackwood, 6th edn, 1899.

Foote, G.W., *What was Christ? A Reply to John Stuart Mill*, London: Progressive Publishing Company, 1887.

Forsyth, P.T., *The Justification of God* (1917), reprinted London: Independent Press, 1957.

Gray, John, *Mill on Liberty: A Defence* (1983), reprinted London: Routledge, 1996.

Green, T.H., *Prolegomena to Ethics*, Oxford: Clarendon Press, 4th edn, 1899.

Gregory, Daniel S., 'John Stuart Mill and the destruction of theism', *The Princeton Review*, N.S. II, 1878, 409–48.

Grote, George, 'John Stuart Mill on *The Philosophy of Sir William Hamilton*', *Westminster Review*, N.S. XXIX, January 1866,1–39.

—— [pseud. Philip Beauchamp], *An Analysis of the Influence of Natural Religion on the Temporal Happiness of Mankind*, London: R. Carlile, 1822.

Haac, Oscar A. (ed.), *The Correspondence of John Stuart Mill and Auguste Comte*, New Brunswick: Transaction Publishers, 1995.

Halliday, R.J., *John Stuart Mill*, London: Allen and Unwin, 1976.

Hamburger, Joseph, 'Religion and *On Liberty*', in Michael Laine (ed.), *A Cultivated Mind. Essays on J.S. Mill resented to John M. Robson*, Toronto: University of Toronto Press, 1991, pp.139–81.

—— *John Stuart Mill on Liberty and Control*, Princeton: Princeton University Press, 1999.

Hamilton, Andy, 'Mill, phenomenalism and the self', in J. Skorupski (ed.), *The Cambridge Companion to Mill*, Cambridge: CUP, 1998, pp.138–75.

Hamilton, William, *Discussions on Philosophy and Literature, Education and University Reform*, 2nd enlarged edn, London: Longman, Brown, Green and Longmans, 1853.

—— *Lectures on Metaphysics and Logic*, Boston: Gould and Lincoln, 1860.

Harris, Robert T., '*Nature*: Emerson and Mill', *The Western Humanities Review*, VI, 1952, 1–13.

Harrison, Ross, 'Review of Alan P.F. Sell, *Mill on Religion*', in *The British Journal for the History of Philosophy*, VII, no. 2, June 1999, 386–7.

Hart, Trevor (ed.), *The Dictionary of Historical Theology*, Carlisle: Paternoster, 2000.

Hayek, F. A. (ed.), *J.S. Mill and Harriet Taylor*, London: Routledge, 1951.

Herrick, Jim, *Vision and Realism: A Hundred Years of The Freethinker*, London:G.W. Foote, 1982.

Heyd, Thomas, 'Mill on Comte and psychology', *Journal of the History of the Behavioural Sciences*, XXV, 1989, 125–38, reprinted in V. Sánchez-Valencia (ed.), *The General Philosophy of John Stuart Mill*, Aldershot: Ashgate, 2002, pp.171–84.

Hick, John H., *Evil and the God of Love* (1966), reprinted London: Collins Fontana, 1968.

Hicks, G.D., *The Philosophical Bases of Theism*, London: Allen and Unwin, 1937.

Himmelfarb, Gertrude, *On Liberty and Liberalism: The Case of John Stuart Mill*, San Francisco: ICS Press, 1990.

Hoag, Robert W., 'Mill's conception of happiness as an inclusive end', *Journal of the History of Philosophy*, XXV, 1987, 417–31, reprinted in C.L. Ten (ed.), *Mill's Moral, Political and Legal Philosophy*, Aldershot: Ashgate, 1999, pp.341-55.

Hoeveler, James D., Jr, *James M'Cosh and the Scottish Intellectual Tradition*, Princeton: Princeton University Press, 1981.

Horton, R.F., *An Autobiography*, London: Allen and Unwin, 1917.

Hume, David, *Dialogues Concerning Natural Religion* (1779), reprinted Indianapolis: Hackett, 1986.

Hutton, R.H., 'Mill on liberty', *The National Review*, 1859, reprinted in A. Pyle (ed.), *Liberty. Contemporary Responses to john Stuart Mill*, Bristol: Thoemme Press, 1994, pp.81–117.

—— *Criticisms on Contemporary Thought and Thinkers selected from The Spectator*, London: Macmillan, 1894.

Huxley, T.H., *Lay Sermons, Addresses and Reviews*, London: Macmillan, 1883.

Inquirer, The, 'Appreciation of William MacCall', 1888, 755.

—— 'On Henry Ireson': 3 September 1892, 573–4; 10 September 1892, 591–2; 5 November 1892, 712; 12 November 1892, 729.

Ireson, Henry, 'The religious views of John Stuart Mill', *The Unitarian Review and Religious Magazine*, I, no. 2, April 1874, 101–12.

Irons, W.J., *An Examination of Mr. Mill's Three Essays on Religion*, London: Robert Hardwicke, 1875.

Jevons, W.S., *Pure Logic and Other Minor Works*, ed. Robert Adamson and Harriet Jevons, London: Macmillan, 1890.

Johnson, Allen (ed.), *Dictionary of American Biography*, London: OUP, 1928, etc.

Johnson, Dale A., *The Changing Shape of English Nonconformity, 1825–1925*, New York: OUP, 1999.

Jones, H.S., 'John Stuart Mill as moralist', *Journal of the History of Ideas*, LIII, no. 2, April–June 1992, 287–308.

Kaye, Elaine, *Mansfield College. Its Origin, History and Significance*, Oxford: OUP, 1996.

Kee, Howard Clark, 'Miracle', in *The Oxford Companion to the Bible*, ed. Bruce M. Metzger and Michael D. Coogan, Oxford: OUP, 1993, pp.519–20.

Kitcher, Philip, 'Mill, mathematics and the naturalist tradition', in J. Skorupski (ed.), *The Cambridge Companion to Mill*, Cambridge: CUP, 1998, pp.57–111.

Krook, Dorothea, *Three Traditions of Moral Thought*, Cambridge: CUP, 1959.

Laird, John, *Theism and Cosmology*, London: Allen and Unwin, 1940.

Lenzer, Gertrude, *Auguste Comte and Positivism: The Essential Writings*, New York: Harper, 1975.

Lewes, G.H., *The History of Philosophy from Thales to Comte*, London, 1867.

Lidgett, J. Scott, *The Christian Religion its Meaning and Proof*, London: Robert Culley, [1907].

Lipkes, Jeff, *Politics, Religion and Classical Political Economy in Britain. John Stuart Mill and his Followers*, Basingstoke: Macmillan, 1999.

[Lucas, Edward], 'Review of Mill's *On Liberty*', in *The Dublin Review*, N.S. XIII,1869, reprinted in A. Pyle (ed.), *Liberty. Contemporary responses to John Stuart Mill*, Bristol: Thoemmes Press, 1994, pp.255–70.

MacCall, William, *The Elements of Individualism. A Series of Lectures*, London: John Chapman, 1847.

McCloskey, H.J., *John Stuart Mill: A Critical Study*, London: Macmillan, 1971.

M'Cosh, James, *An Examination of Mr. J.S. Mill's Philosophy. Being a Defence of Fundamental Truth*, London: Macmillan, 1866.

McGrath, P.J., 'John Stuart Mill and the concept of a miracle', *The Irish Theological Quarterly*, LIX, no. 3, 1993, 211–17.

MacGregor, W.M., *Persons and Ideals*, Edinburgh: T. & T. Clark, 1939.

Mackenzie, J.S., *A Manual of Ethics*, 6th edn, London: University Tutorial Press, 1929.

Mackintosh, Robert, *From Comte to Benjamin Kidd. The Appeal to Biology or Evolution for Human Guidance*, London: Macmillan, 1899.

Mallock, W.H., 'Is life worth living?', *The Nineteenth Century*, II, September 1877, 251–73 and III, January 1878, 146–68.

Mander, W.J. and Alan P.F. Sell (eds), *Dictionary of Nineteenth-Century British Philosophers*, Bristol: Thoemmes Press, 2002.

Mansel, H.L., *The Limits of Religious Thought Examined in Eight Lectures* (1858), reprinted 5th edn, London: John Murray, 1870.

—— *The Philosophy of the Conditioned*, London: Alexander Strahan, 1866.

Manson, T.W., *Ethics and the Gospel*, London: SCM Press, 1960.

Marmontel, J-F., *Mémoires d'un Père pour servir à l'instruction de ses enfans*, Paris, 1804.

Martineau, James, *Essays Philosphical and Theological*, New York: Henry Holt, 1879.

—— *Types of Ethical Theory*, (1885), 3rd revised edn, Oxford: Clarendon Press, 1891.

—— *The Seat of Authority in Religion*, London: Longmans, Green, 1890.

—— *Essays, Reviews and Addresses*, London: Longmans, 1891.

Matthews, W.R., *The Religious Philosophy of Dean Mansel* (Friends of Dr. Williams's Library, 10th Lecture, 1956), London: OUP, 1956.

Maurice, F.D., *What is Revelation?*, Cambridge: Macmillan, 1859.

—— *Sequel to the Inquiry, What is Revelation?*, Cambridge: Macmillan, 1860.

Metzger, Bruce M. and Michael D. Coogan (eds), *The Oxford Companion to the Bible*, Oxford: OUP, 1993.

Michelet, Jules, *Histoire de France*, trans. W.K. Kelly, London, 1844–6.

Mill, James, 'Periodical literature: *Edinburgh Review*', *Westminster Review*, I, January 1824, 206–49.

—— *Analysis of the Phenomena of the Human Mind*, London: Longmans,Green and Dyer, 1829.

Mill, John Stuart, The following volumes from the *Collected Works of John Stuart Mill*, Toronto: University of Toronto Press and London: Routledge & Kegan Paul:

I, *Autobiography and Literary Essays*, ed., John M. Robson and Jack Stillinger, 1981.

II, III, *Principles of Political Economy with some Applications to Social Philosophy*, Introduction by V.W. Bladen, textual ed., J.M. Robson, 1965.

VI, *Essays on England, Ireland and the Empire*, ed. J.M. Robson, Introduction by Joseph Hamburger, 1982.

VII, VIII, *A System of Logic Ratiocinative and Inductive*, ed. J.M. Robson, Introduction by R.F. McRae, 1974.

IX, *An Examination of Sir William Hamilton's Philosophy*, ed. J.M. Robson, Introduction by Alan Ryan, 1979.

X, *Essays on Ethics, Religion and Society*, ed. J.M. Robson, Introduction by F.E.L. Priestley, 'Essay on Mill's *Utilitarianism*' by D.P. Dryer, 1969.

XII, XIII, *The Earlier Letters of John Stuart Mill 1812–1848*, ed. Francis E. Mineka, Introduction by F.A. Hayek, 1963.

XIV to XVI, *The Later Letters of John Stuart Mill 1849–1873*, ed. F.E. Mineka and Dwight N. Lindley, 1972.

XVIII, *Essays on Politics and Society*, ed. J.M. Robson, Introduction by Alexander Brady, 1977.

XXI, *Essays on Equality, Law, and Education*, ed. J.M. Robson, Introduction by Stefan Collini, 1984.

XXII, XXIV, XXV, *Newspaper Writings*, ed. Ann P. Robson and J.M. Robson, Introduction by A.P. Robson, Textual Introduction by J.M. Robson, 1986.

XXVI, XXVII, *Journals and Debating Speeches*, ed. J.M. Robson, 1988.

XXVIII, *Public and Parliamentary Speeches, November 1850–November 1868*, eds. J.M. Robson and Bruce L. Kinzer, Introduction by B.L. Kinzer, Textual Introduction by J.M. Robson, 1988.

—— *Utilitarianism, Liberty and Representative Government*, Introduction by A.D. Lindsay, London: Dent, n.d.

—— *The Autobiography of John Stuart Mill*, ed. A.O.J. Cockshut, Krumlin, Halifax: Ryburn Publishing, 1992.

Millar, Alan, 'Mill on religion', in John Skorupski (ed.), *The Cambridge Companion to Mill*, Cambridge: CUP, 1998, pp.176–202.

Miller, D.E., 'Mill, John Stuart', in W.J. Mander and Alan P.F. Sell (eds), *Dictionary of Nineteenth-Century British Philosophers*, Bristol: Thoemmes Press, 2002, pp.792–9.

Morley, John, 'Mr. Mill's Three Essays on Religion', *The Fortnightly Review*, N.S. XVI, November 1874, 634–51 and XVII, January 1875, 103–31.

—— *Critical Miscellanies. Second Series*, London: Chapman and Hall, 1877.

—— *Critical Miscellanies*, London: Macmillan, 1898.

—— *Recollections*, London: Macmillan, 1917.

Mueller, Iris Wessel, *John Stuart Mill and French Thought*, Urbana: University of Illinois Press, 1956.

National Cyclopaedia of American Biography, XVI, New York: James T. White, 1937.

Nicholson, Peter, *The Political Philosophy of the British Idealists: Selected Studies*, Cambridge: CUP, 1990.

—— 'The reception and early reputation of Mill's political thought', in J. Skorupski (ed.), *The Cambridge Companion to Mill*, Cambridge: CUP, 1998, pp.464–96.

Oliphant, Mrs. (Margaret Oliphant Wilson Oliphant), *A Memoir of the Life of John Tulloch, D.D., LL.D*, Edinburgh: Blackwood, 1889.

Orr, James, 'John Stuart Mill and Christianity – II', *Theological Monthly*, VI, 1891, 108–21.

—— *The Christian View of God and the World*, 4th edn, Edinburgh: Andrew Elliot, 1897.

Oxford Dictionary of National Biography, forthcoming 2004.

Packe, M. St.J., *The Life of John Stuart Mill*, London: Secker and Warburg, 1954.

Paley, William, *Principles of Moral and Political Philosophy* (1785), 19th edn, London: J. Faulder *et al.*, 1811.

Pappé, H.O., *John Stuart Mill and the Harriet Taylor Myth*, Parkville: MelbourneUniversity Press, 1960.

Parker, Joseph, *John Stuart Mill on Liberty. A Critique*, London: F. Pitman, 1865.

—— *Job's Comforters. Scientific Sympathy*, London: Hodder and Stoughton, 1874.

—— *A Preacher's Life. An Autobiography and an Album*, London: Hodder and Stoughton, 1899.

Plamenatz, John, *The English Utilitarians* (1949), reprinted Oxford: Blackwell, 1966.

Porter, Noah, 'John Stuart Mill as a religious philosopher', *Dickinson's Theological Quarterly*, 1875, 492–507.

Priestley, Joseph, *The Theological and Miscellaneous Works of Joseph Priestley*, ed. J.T. Rutt (1817–31), reprinted Bristol: Thoemmes Press, 1999.

Pringle-Pattison, A.S., *The Idea of God in the Light of Recent Philosophy*, 2nd revised edn, New York: OUP, 1920.

Pyle, Andrew (ed.), *Liberty. Contemporary Responses to John Stuart Mill*, Bristol: Thoemmes Press, 1994.

Raeder, Linda C., *John Stuart Mill and the Religion of Humanity*, Columbia, MO: University of Missiouri Press, 2002.

Raphael, D.D., 'Fallacies in and about Mill's *Utilitarianism*', *Philosophy*, XXX, October 1955, 344–57.

Reardon, B.M.G., *Religious Thought in the Nineteenth Century*, Cambridge: CUP, 1966.

Rees, J.G., *Mill and his Early Critics*, Leicester: University College Leicester, 1956.

—— 'A phase in the development of Mill's ideas on liberty', *Political Studies*, VI, February 1958, 33–44.

—— 'The reaction to Cowling on Mill', *The Mill News Letter*, I, no. 2, Spring 1966, 2–11.

[Reeve, Henry], 'Review of Mill's *Three Essays on Religion*', in *The Edinburgh Review*, CCLXXXVII, January 1875, 8–31.

Robson, John M. and Michael Laine (eds), *James and John Stuart Mill. Papers of theCentenary Conference*, Toronto: University of Toronto Press, 1976.

Ross, W.D., *Foundations of Ethics*, Oxford: Clarendon Press, 1939.

Russell, Bertrand, 'My mental development', in P.A. Schlipp (ed.), *The Philosophy of Bertrand Russell*, Evanston and Chicago: Northwestern University Press, 1944, p.10.

—— 'John Stuart Mill', *Proceedings of the British Academy*, 1955, reprinted in J.B. Schneewind (ed.), *Mill. A Collection of Critical Essays*, London: Macmillan, 1968, pp.1–21.

Ruston, Alan, *The Inquirer. A History and Other Reflections*, London: Inquirer Publishing Co., 1992.

Ryan, Alan, *J.S. Mill*, London: Routledge, 1974.

Sánchez-Valencia, Víctor (ed.), *The General Philosophy of John Stuart Mill*, Aldershot: Ashgate, 2002.

Scharff, Robert C., 'Mill's misreading of Comte on "interior observation"', *Journal of the History of Philosophy*, XXVII, no. 4, October 1989, 559–72.

—— 'Positivism, philosophy of science and self-understanding in Comte and Mill', *American Philosophical Quarterly*, XXVI, 1989, 235–68, reprinted in V. Sánchez-Valencia (ed.), *The General Philosophy of John Stuart Mill*, Aldershot: Ashgate, 2002, pp.155–70.

Schlipp, P.A. (ed.), *The Philosophy of Bertrand Russell*, Evanston and Chicago: Northwestern University Press, 1944.

Schneewind, J.B., 'Review of J. Skorupski, *John Stuart Mill*', *The Philosophical Review*, CI, no. 4, October 1992, 873–5.

—— (ed.), *Mill. A Collection of Critical Essays*, London: Macmillan, 1968.

Scorgie, Glenn G., *A Call for Continuity: The Theological Contribution of James Orr*, Macon, GA: Mercer University Press, 1988.

Seccombe, J.T., *Science, Theism, and Revelation, considered in relation to Mr. Mill's Three Essays on Nature, Religion, & Theism*, London: Simpkin, Marshall, 1875.

Sedgwick, Adam, *A Discourse on the Studies of the University*, London: Parker, 1834.

Selbie, W.B., *The Life of Andrew Martin Fairbairn*, London: Hodder and Stoughton, 1914.

Sell, Alan P.F., *Robert Mackintosh: Theologian of Integrity*, Berne: Peter Lang, 1977.

—— *The Great Debate: Calvinism, Arminianism and Salvation* (1982), reprinted Eugene, OR: Wipf & Stock, 1998.

—— *Theology in Turmoil. The Roots, Course and Significance of the Conservative-Liberal Debate in Modern Theology* (1986), reprinted Eugene, OR: Wipf & Stock, 1998.

—— *Defending and Declaring the Faith. Some Scottish Examples 1860–1920*, Exeter: Paternoster and Colorado Springs: Helmers & Howard, 1987.

—— *Dissenting Thought and the Life of the Churches. Studies in an English Tradition*, Lewiston, NY: Edwin Mellen, 1990.

—— *Commemorations: Studies in Christian Thought and History*, Calgary: University of Calgary Press and Cardiff: University of Wales Press, 1993; reprinted Eugene, OR: Wipf & Stock, 1998.

—— *Philosophical Idealism and Christian Belief*, Cardiff: University of Wales Press, 1995.

—— *John Locke and the Eighteenth-Century Divines*, Cardiff: University of Wales Press, 1997.

—— *Christ Our Saviour*, Shippensburg, PA: Ragged Edge Press, 2000.

—— *Confessing and Commending the Faith: Historic Witness and Apologetic Method*, Cardiff: University of Wales Press, 2002.

—— *Philosophy, Dissent and Nonconformity 1689–1920*, Cambridge: James Clarke, 2004.

—— (ed.), *Mill and Religion. Contemporary Responses to Three Essays on Religion*, Bristol: Thoemmes Press, 1997.

Semmel, Bernard, *John Stuart Mill and the Pursuit of Virtue*, New Haven: Yale University Press, 1984.

Seth, James, *A Study of Ethical Principles*, 5th edn, Edinburgh: Blackwood, 1899.

Short, H.L., 'Presbyterians under a new name', in C. Gordon Bolam, Jeremy Goring, H.L. Short and Roger Thomas, *The English Presbyterians. From Elizabethan Puritanism to Modern Unitarianism*, London: Allen and Unwin, 1968, pp.219–286.

Sidgwick, Arthur and Eleanor Mildred Sidgwick, *Henry Sidgwick: A Memoir*, London: Macmillan, 1906.

Sidgwick, Henry, *The Methods of Ethics*, London: Macmillan, 1930.

Skorupski, John, *John Stuart Mill*, London: Routledge, 1989.

—— (ed.), *John Stuart Mill*, London: Routledge, 1989, p.5.

Solly, Henry Shaen, 'Review of Mill's *Three Essays on Religion*', in *The Inquirer*, 18 November, 1874, 774–75.

Stephen, James Fitzjames, *A History of the Criminal Law of England*, London: Macmillan, 1883.

—— 'Mr. Mill on political liberty', *The Saturday Review*, 19 February 1859, reprinted in A. Pyle (ed.), *Liberty*, *Contemporary Responses to John Stuart Mill*, Bristol: Thoemmes Press, 1994, pp.15–24.

Stephen, Leslie, *The Life of Sir James Fitzjames Stephen*, London: Smith, Elder, 1895.

—— *The English Utilitarians*, London: Duckworth, 1900.

Stork, C.A., 'Mr. Mill's *Autobiography* as a contribution to Christian evidences', *Quarterly Review of the Evangelical Lutheran Church*, IV, 1874, 258–77.

Ten, C.L., 'Mill and liberty', *Journal of the History of Ideas*, XXX, 1969, 47-68, reprinted in C.L. Ten (ed.), *Mill's Moral, Political and Legal Philosophy*, Aldershot: Ashgate, 1999, pp.293–314.

Thomas, William, 'John Stuart Mill and the uses of autobiography', *History*, LVI, no. 188, October 1971, 341–59.

Thomson, J. Radford, *Utilitarianism: An Illogical and Irreligious Theory of Morals*, London: The Religious Tract Society (bound in *Present Day Tracts*, VII, no. 40, 1886).

—— *A Dictionary of Philosophy in the Words of the Philosophers*, London: R.D. Dickinson, 1887.

—— *Auguste Comte and 'The Religion of Humanity'*, London: The Religious Tract Society (bound in *Present Day Tracts*, VIII, no. 47, 1887).

Tinkles, John F., 'J.S. Mill as a nineteenth-century humanist', *Rhetorica*, X, no.2, Spring 1992, 165–91.

Tulloch, John, *Modern Theories in Philosophy and Religion*, Edinburgh: Blackwood, 1884.

—— *Movements of Religious Thought during the Nineteenth Century*, (1885), reprinted Leicester: Leicester University Press, 1971.

Tymms, T. Vincent, *The Mystery of God*, London: Eliot Stock, 1890.

Upton, Charles Barnes, 'Mr. Mill's Essays on Religion', *The Theological Review*, XII, 1875, 127–145, 249–272.

—— *Dr. Martineau's Philosophy: A Survey*, London: Nisbet, 1905.

Urmson, J.O., 'The interpretation of the philosophy of J.S. Mill', *The Philosophical Quarterly*, III, 1953, reprinted in J.B. Schnewind (ed.), *Mill. A Collection of Critical Essays*, London: Macmillan, 1968, 190–98.

V., B, [i.e. James Thomson], 'Mill on religion', *The National Reformer. Secular Advocate and Freethought Journal*, 1874, 290–92, 309–10, 329–30, 345–47, 362–68, 377–79, 390–91, 403–04.

Veitch, John, *Hamilton*, Edinburgh: Blackwood, 1882.

Vernon, R., 'J.S. Mill, and the Religion of Humanity', in J. E. Crimmins (ed.), *Religion, Secularization and Political Thought. Thomas Hobbs to J.S. Mill*, London: Routledge, 1989, pp.167–82.

Vickers, John A., *A Dictionary of Methodism in Britain and Ireland*, Peterborough: Epworth, 2000.

Wainwright, Valerie, 'Discovering autonomy and authenticity in *North and South*: Elizabeth Gaskell, John Stuart Mill and the liberal ethic', CLIO, XXIII, no. 2, Winter 1994, 149–65.

Ward, W.G., *On Nature and Grace. A Theological Treatise. Book I. Philosophical Introduction*, London: Burns and Lambert, 1860.

Wentz, Abdel Ross, *Gettysburg Evangelical Lutheran Seminary, I. The History 1826–1965*, Harrisburg, PA: The Evangelical Press 1826–1926 [1927].

Westminster Shorter Catechism, 1647, many editions.

Wheeler, J.M., *A Biographical Dictionary of Freethinkers of all Ages and Nations*, London: Progressive Publishing Co., 1889.

Whewell, William, *The Elements of Morality including Polity*, London: John Parker, 1845.

Whittaker, Thomas, Comte and Mill, (1908), reprinted Bristol: Thoemmes Press, 1993.

Who Was Who in America, New Providence, NJ: Marquis.

Willey, Basil, *Nineteenth-Century Studies*, Lodnon: Chatto & Windus, 1949.

Wilson, Fred, 'Mill and Comte on the method of introspection', *Journal of the History of the Behavioural Sciences*, XXVII, 1991, 107–29, reprinted in V. Sánchez-Valencia (ed.), *The General Philosophy of John Stuart Mill*, Aldershot: Ashgate, 2002, pp.185–207.

Woods, Thomas, *Poetry and Philosophy. A Study in the Thought of John Stuart Mill*, London: Hutchinson, 1961.

Wright, T.R., *The Religion of Humanity. The Impact of Comtian Positivism on Victorian Britain*, Cambridge: CUP, 1986.

Index of Persons

Acland, T.D. 61–3.
Adams, J.E. 165–6
Adamson, Robert 64, 172
Adamson, William 21
Alcibiades 99
Alexander, Edward 24
Allen, John 34, 62
Annan, Noel 50, 66, 179
Anschutz, R.P. 24, 178–9
Aristotle 4, 14, 55, 71
Atkinson, R.F. 112
August, Eugene 21, 60, 127–8, 130, 165, 172
Augustine of Hippo 160
Austin, John

Bain, Alexander 4, 9, 17, 20, 22, 25, 39, 46, 52–3, 61, 63, 67, 77, 92, 109, 113, 129–30, 134, 146, 148, 155, 163, 166, 169–70, 172, 177, 179
Barros, Carolyn A. 21
Bates, Frederick 29, 61
Battles, Ford Lewis 64
Beattie, James 11
Beauchamp, Philip (pseud.)
    See Grote, G.
Beesly, E.S. 105
Belsham, Thomas 17
Bentham, Jeremy 7–8, 11, 20–1, 23–4, 49, 56, 87, 89–90, 92–3, 97, 100, 106, 112–13, 163, 174
Berkeley, George 8, 79, 148
Blackstone, William 60
Blakey, Robert 31
Blanshard, Brand 162, 172, 177, 179
Bocking, Ronald A.H. 117
Boethius 99
Bolam, C.G. 25
Booth, William 175

Bradlaugh, Charles 29, 46, 61
Bradley, F.H. 91–2, 113–14
Bridges, J.H. 108
Brightman, E.S. 134
Brink, David O. 113
Britton, Karl 24–5, 42, 64, 86, 89–91, 111–13, 132, 161, 164, 166, 168, 171–2
Brodie, George 68
Brown, J. Baldwin 160, 171
Brown, Thomas 8, 89
Bruce, A.B. 134–5, 167
Bulwer, E.L. 14, 24, 113
Bunyan, John 166, 171
Burns, Robert 11
Burston, W.H. 22
Byron, George G. 13

Cabot, John 161, 172
Cadman, S. Parkes 171
Caird, Edward 75, 84, 86, 108, 111
Calderwood, Henry 67–8
Calderwood, W. L. 67
Call, W.M.W. 171
Calvin, John 37, 42, 64, 99
Campbell, John McLeod 38
Carlyle, Thomas 17, 21, 24, 40, 63, 68, 90, 113–14, 119, 125, 153, 164, 170
Carr, Robert 110, 169, 171
Cashdollar, Charles D. 107, 110
Cave, Sydney 106, 117
Chalmers, Thomas 61, 115
Channing, William Ellery 17, 45, 157
Chapman, E.M. 3, 14, 21, 23–4
Chenevix, Henry 152, 170
Church, R.W. 49, 65–6
Clarke, M.L. 112
Cobbe, Frances Power 159, 171
Cockshut, A.O.J. 11, 16, 23–5

Coleridge, E.H. 24
Coleridge, S.T. 13–17, 24, 32, 38, 49,
    58–9, 68, 80–1, 98, 113, 163
Combe, George 164
Comte, Auguste 10, 18, 28, 35, 52, 56,
    58, 60–3, 67–86, 93, 95, 97,
    103–4, 107–11, 174–6
Conder, Eustace R. 130, 153, 166, 170
Condorcet, Marquis de 71, 98
Congreve, Richard 84, 105, 111
Connell, Mr. 46
Coogan, Michael D. 170
Cooper, Anthony Ashley 89
Coulson, Walter 62
Courtney, W.L. 48, 66, 79, 89, 92, 109,
    112–13, 130, 136, 152, 166–7,
    171–2
Cowling, Maurice 47, 66
Cowper, William 11
Crane, C.B. 17, 23, 25, 37, 63, 96,
    98–9, 114–15, 129, 135, 166–7
Cranfield, Graham 61
Crimmins, James E. 22–3, 66, 111–12
Cumming, R.D. 21
Cunningham, William 42–3, 64

Dale, R.W. 38
Dante Alighieri 16
Darwin, Charles 69, 164
Davidson, William L. 88, 112
Davies, H.S. 66
Dawkins, Richard 22
Dawson, Albert 21
De Burgh, W.G. 5, 22, 84, 105, 111,
    116
D'Eichthal, G. 38, 57, 63, 68–9, 109
Demosthenes 4
Descartes, René 143
Diderot, Denis 41
Donner, Wendy 113
Douglas, Charles 41, 62, 64, 79, 91,
    109, 112–14, 165
Drummond, James, 25, 41, 64
Dryer, D.P. 87, 112
Dumont, P.E.L. 7

Elliott, Hugh S. R. 25
Evans, G.E. 64
Ewing, A.C. 92, 113

Fairbairn, A.M. 22, 127, 129, 165–6,
    176, 179
Fichte, J.G. 40, 52, 148
Fleishman, Avrom 129, 165
Flew, A.G.N. 20, 22, 131, 134, 166
Flint, Robert 69–71, 73–4, 79, 84–5,
    107–9, 111
Foote, G.W. 129, 154–5, 166, 170
Forsyth, P.T. 167
Fox, R.B. 61
Fox, W.J. 16, 36
Frederic of Prussia 3
Fuller, Andrew 37

Gibbon, Edward 3
Gladstone, W.E. 129
Goethe, J.W. von 40
Goldsmith, Oliver 11
Gomperz, T. 52, 67
Gray, John 66
Gray, Thomas 11, 16
Green, T.A. 60
Green, T.H. 89, 91, 113
Greene, Arthur W. 33, 62, 169
Gregory, D.S. 139–42, 167–8
Grote, George 4, 8, 31, 46, 70, 120,
    164
Grote, Harriet 14

Haac Oscar, 60, 108, 179
Halliday, R.J. 90,113
Hamburger, Joseph 25, 47–8, 60, 65–6,
    102, 115–16
Hamilton, Andy, 67
Hamilton, William, 35, 52–4, 64, 67–8,
    79, 88, 110, 119, 168
Harris, Robert T. 165–6
Harrison, Frederic 105
Harrison, Ross 20
Hartley, David 8, 13, 17, 78, 157
Hayek, F.A. 25
Hegel, G.W. F. 52, 73, 81
Helvetius, C.A. 89
Herford, Edward 115
Herrick, Jim 166
Heyd, Thomas 109
Hick, John H. 134, 166
Hicks, G.D. 85, 111
Himmelfarb, Gertrude 63

Hoag, Robert W. 113
Hobbes, Thomas 4
Hoeveler, James D., Jr. 108–9
Holyoake, George J. 62, 126
Hooke, Nathaniel 3
Horace (Horatius Flaccus, Q.) 99, 115
Horton, R.F. 116
Humboldt, Wilhelm von 40 43
Hume, David 3, 8, 20, 69, 71, 79, 89.
    126, 140, 145–6, 150–1, 153, 168,
    173
Hume, Joseph 7
Hutton, R.H. 2, 15, 20–1, 24, 26, 48–9,
    65–6, 94, 98, 114
Huxley, T.H. 82, 110

Ignatius Loyola 80
Ireson, Henry 111
Irons, Joseph 23
Irons, W.J. 10, 23, 143, 168

Jenyns, Soame 131
Jevons, Harriet A. 64, 172
Jevons, W. Stanley 40, 64, 162, 172
Johnson, Dale A. 62
Jones, H.S. 49, 66, 111
Jones, Henry 93, 96, 113–14

Kant, Immanuel 14, 52, 73, 141, 143,
    146
Kaye, Elaine 22
Kee, H.C. 170
Kitcher, Philip 165
Krook, Dorothea 163, 167, 172, 179

Laine, Michael 24, 116, 166
Laird, John 85 111
Lambert, Elizabeth 61
Lenzer, Gertrude 107
Lewes, G.H. 62, 72, 108
Lidgett, John Scott 96, 114
Lindsay, A.D. 20, 26, 48, 66, 89, 113
Lipkes, Jeff 35, 65
Locke, John 14, 46, 73, 78, 89, 112
Lucas, Edward 46, 65
Lucretius Carus, T. 16
Lyttelton, W.H. 67

Mabbott, J.D. 112

Macaulay, T.B. 21
MacCall, William, 64
McGrath, P.J. 170
MacGregor, W.M. 167
Mackenzie, J.S. 93, 114
Mackintosh, Robert 74–6, 108
McCloskey, H.J. 152–3, 170
Mcneil, J.T. 64
M'Cosh, James 73, 98, 108–9., 115,
    143, 168
M'Crie, Thomas 3
Mallock, W.H. 90, 113
Mander, W.J. 112
Mansell, H.L. 35, 52, 54–5, 61, 67–8,
    88, 126, 133, 179
Manson, T.W. 112
Marmontel, J.–F. 10
Marshall, Richard 61, 116
Martineau, Harriet 108
Martineau, James 17, 19, 25–6, 41, 55,
    60, 63–4, 67, 74, 88, 94, 108, 114,
    157, 174,
176–7, 179
Matthews, W.R. 67
Maurice, F.D. 16, 55, 67
Metzger, Bruce M. 170
Michelet, Jules 58
Mill, Harriet (*see* Taylor, Harriet)
Mill, James 1–9, 16, 19–22, 28, 56–7,
    68, 90, 93, 104, 113, 115, 119,
    128, 162, 169, 177–8
Mill, John Stuart
    his elusiveness, 28–30, 60, 88, 127,
        173–4, 178
    his intellectual opinions, see Select
        Index of Subjects
    his life, ch. 1
    his optimism, 98–9. 148. 163, 169,
        172, 176
    on Harriet Taylor, 17–18, 128–9
    on his father, 16
    Works (abbreviated titles):
        Autobiography 1, 3, 21, 99, 128,
            173
        Hamilton 29, 78, 120, 168, 173
        Liberty 13, 18, 40, 43–50, 100,
            120, 130, 154
        Logic 41–2, 46, 76–7, 109–10,
            119, 139, 142, 155

'Nature' 120–3, 126, 130–2, 134–5, 144, 173
Political Economy 18, 110
Review of Blakey's *Essays* 31
'Theism' 84, 120, 130, 133–5, 137, 146, 148, 153–4, 163, 169, 173
Three Essays 1, 12, 20–1, 120, 139, 158, 160, 163, 173, 178
Utilitarianism 1, 13, 87, 91, 100, 110, 120, 173
'Utility' 8, 44, 47, 63, 81, 112, 120, 127, 134, 137, 147, 154, 159, 173
Mill, Wilhelmina 3
Millar, Alan 21, 110, 148, 169
Miller, Dale 88, 112
Montesquieu, C.L. deS. de 164
Morley, John 8, 15, 19, 23–5, 33, 40, 62–3, 110, 127, 146, 148, 155–6, 158, 164–5, 169–72
Mozley, J.R. 60
Mueller, Iris Wessel 108

Napier, Joseph 170
Newman, J.H. 21
Newton, Isaac 140
Nichol, J.P. 24, 62
Nicholson, Peter 47, 65
Nightingale, Florence 132, 166–7
Novalis (Hardenberg, F.L. von) 61, 178

O'Grady, Standish 170
Oliphant, M.O.W. 24
Orr, James 47, 66, 84, 111, 126, 141, 148–9, 152, 155, 165, 168–70
Owen, Robert 45

Packe, M.St. J. 6, 20–2, 25
Paley, William, 87, 111–12, 119, 144
Pappé, H.O. 25
Parker, Joseph 2, 21, 37, 46–7, 63, 65–6, 101, 115
Pharazyn, Robert 120, 164
Plamenatz, John 48, 66, 91, 93, 113–14
Plato 4, 138
Poole, Thomas 13, 24
Porter, Noah 83, 110, 124, 131, 162, 165–6, 172, 179

Priestley, Joseph 17, 46, 65, 89, 157, 172
Pringle-Pattison, A. S. 68, 85, 111
Pusey, E.B. 57
Pyle, Andrew 62, 65, 165

Raeder, Linda C. 60, 62, 113, 166, 169
Raphael, D.D. 111–12
Reardon, B.M. G. 108
Rees, J.G. 64–6
Reeve, Henry 115, 149, 165–6, 169
Reid, Thomas 8, 140
Ricardo, David 7
Robertson, William 3
Robson, John M. 21, 24, 63, 166
Roebuck, J.A. 13, 24
Ross, W.D. 92, 113
Rousseau, J.-J. 71, 99
Russell, Bertrand 86, 111, 164
Ruston, Alan 21, 64
Rutt, J.T. 65
Rutty, John 3
Ryan, Alan 67, 81, 110, 169

Saint Simon, Henri de 71
Sánchez-Valencia, Víctor 21, 109–10
Scharff, Robert C. 108–9
Schelling, F.W.J. von 81
Schleiermacher, F.D.E. 14, 24
Schlipp, P.A. 111
Schneewind, J.B. 20, 66, 112, 164, 179
Scorgie, Glenn G. 66
Scott, Walter 11
Seccombe, John T. 152
Sedgwick, Adam 61, 87, 112
Selbie, W.B. 22
Sell, Alan P.F. 20, 22–3, 25, 61–6, 107–8, 112–13, 164, 167–8, 179
Semmel, Bernard 23, 49, 63, 66
Seth, James 86, 111, 113
Sewell, William 3
Shaftesbury (see Cooper, Anthony Ashley)
Shelley, P.B. 16–17, 61
Short, H.L. 25
Sidgwick, A. 60
Sidgwick, E.M. 60
Sidgwick, Henry 27, 60, 93, 114

Skorupski, John 20–1, 65, 67, 110, 113–14, 126, 165, 169
Socrates 89
Solly, Henry Shaen 27, 60, 162, 172
Southey, Robert 13
Spencer, Herbert 20–1
Spenser, Edmund 11
Spinoza, B. 178
Stephen, Harriet M. 158
Stephen, J.F. 46–7, 65, 171
Stephen, Leslie 20, 112, 126, 133, 158–9, 165–6, 171
Sterling, John 9, 14, 17, 23–4, 39, 63, 68
Stewart, Dugald 8
Stillinger, Jack 21
Stirling, J.H. 20
Stork, C.A. 8, 15, 23–4, 129, 166–7, 177, 179

Taylor, Harriet 1, 16–18, 24–5, 39, 43, 70, 127–131, 148, 155, 163, 165, 169, 174
Taylor, Helen 120, 148, 164
Taylor, John 16–17
Ten, C.L. 39, 63, 66, 113
Tennyson, Alfred 21
Thomas, W. 21
Thomson, J. Radford 91, 101, 107, 113, 115–16
Thomson, James 30, 61, 63, 146, 148, 169
Tinkles, John F. 25
Tocqueville, A. de 40, 64
Tulloch, John 12, 24, 71, 82, 107, 110, 145, 160, 169, 171

Tymms, T.V. 135, 138, 167–8

Upton, C.B. 5, 22, 25, 41, 64, 124–5, 137, 148–9, 155–6, 158–9, 164–5, 167, 169–172
Urmson, J.O. 112

V., B. See Thomson, James
Vaux, Clothilde de 70–2, 81
Veitch, John 67
Vernon, Richard 50, 66
Voltaire (Françoise Marie Arouet) 16, 123

Wainwright, Valerie 64
Walpole, Horace 11
Ward, W.G. 38, 42, 63–4, 98, 101, 115, 151, 170, 179
Watson, G. 66
Watson, Robert 3
Wentz, A.R. 23
Wesley, John 175
Westerton, Charles 61
Whately, Richard 68
Wheeler, J.M. 166
Whewell, William 88, 112
Whittaker, Thomas 79, 109–10, 114
Willey, Basil 157, 163, 171–2
Williams, Edward 37
Wilson, Fred 109
Woods, Thomas 165
Woodside, David 67
Wordsworth, William 11–16, 24, 81, 97, 130, 161, 172
Wright, T.R. 81, 107, 110

Select Index of Subjects

apologetics 33, 62, 176, 178–9
Arianism 6, 32, 64
associationism 8, 10, 78, 96, 104, 109, 162, 174
atheism 5, 18, 27, 29, 33–4, 46, 65, 119, 135, 178
atonement 32, 62, 157

Baptists 23, 37
Benthamism 1–2, 9–11, 19, 49 90, 113
Bible 31, 38, 54, 153

Calvinism 5–6. 22, 37, 42–3, 45, 69, 176
Cambridge Platonists 55
Church of England 18, 23, 36, 56–9, 68, 110
Church of Scotland 3, 61
common sense realism 73
Congregationalism 21–2, 37, 101, 107, 160, 171

deism 5, 36, 69, 135
determinism 10–11, 37, 40–2, 47, 64, 95–6, 124, 161–2, 174
Dissenters 36, 59, 61–2, 65, 102

education 100–04, 115–16
Enlightenment 6, 12, 100, 172
evil 5, 12, 99, 103, 119, 122–3, 126–7, 134, 167, 176
evolution 62, 97, 146, 164

faith 54
France 4, 7, 85
Free Church of Scotland 61
French Revolution 8, 81

humanity, doctrine of 105–6

immortality 27, 83, 146–7, 157, 163, 171, 176
incarnation 55
individual/ism 43, 45, 49, 51, 71, 93–5
intuitionism 51–4, 68, 119, 142–3, 174

Jesus Christ 153–8
Jews 59

Lutherans 23

Manichaeanism 131–3
Methodism 10, 18, 57
miracles 150–3, 157, 170
morality 30–5, 44, 46, 54, 83, 85–95, 97, 105, 107, 111–12

naturalism 126, 130, 141, 165, 176
nature 12, 32, 51, 121–8, 130–1, 133, 135, 137, 165–6
Nonconformity 18

positivism, 14, 35, 38, 61, ch. 3, 108–9, 148
prayer 96–7
predestination 42–3, 69
Presbyterianism 5, 64
psychology 78–9

reason 54–5
Reformation 6, 62
Religion of Humanity, 8, 50, ch. 3, 110–11, 119, 128, 134, 157, 174–6, 178
revelation 54, 56, 138, 149–50, 160
rewards and punishments 1, 10, 30–1, 83, 104, 170, 176
Roman Catholicism 18, 36, 42, 46, 49, 65, 69

Romanticism 10–14, 16, 18, 40, 90, 99, 129, 174, 178

Saint Simonian ideas 39, 45, 56
scientism 70, 107, 136, 167, 177–8
sin, 98–9, 116, 135, 157, 167, 176
supernatural 1, 32, 35, 82–4, 87, 103, 107, 147, 149,–51, 175–6, 178

theism 62, 119–146, 149, 153, 155, 160, 169, 176, 178

Unitarians 16–17, 21, 25, 27, 36, 46, 64–5, 160
universities 115
utilitarianism 3, 9–10, 14–15, 48, 50–1, 86–95, 97, 104–5, 111–12, 114, 157, 161, 173–4, 176

Mill on God

The Pervasiveness and Elusiveness of Mill's Religious Thought

ALAN P.F. SELL

Mill on God is Professor Sell's latest impressive study in a long list of substantial theological writings, and historical and philosophical works on religion. Drawing upon several of Mill's classic philosophical texts, his posthumous publications on religion, and a range of informal communications, Sell has produced easily the best available introduction to Mill's religious thought, the intellectual context of his religious views, and the reception of his ideas and arguments. This combative and elegant work of historical and philosophical interpretation teases out the important ambiguities and tensions in Mill's thoughts, and amply demonstrates the centrality of his concern with religion.

James E. Crimmins, International Academic Advisor and
Professor of Political Science, Huron University College, Canada

John Stuart Mill (1806–1873) was the most influential nineteenth-century British philosopher. Based upon a study of Mill's intellectual environment, life, critics – contemporary and subsequent – and the relation of his religious writings to the rest of his corpus, Alan Sell presents an invaluable introduction to, and exploration of, Mill's religious thought. Despite Mill's widespread failure to satisfy believers and non-believers alike, Sell shows that in his religious writings he raises issues of continuing importance, not least that of the appropriate starting-point for Christian apologetics. This comprehensive study represents an invaluable resource for students and scholars of philosophy, intellectual history and theology, as well as for those more generally interested in Mill.

Philosophy/Theology

ASHGATE

Ashgate Publishing Limited
Gower House, Croft Road
Aldershot, Hampshire
GU11 3HR, England

www.ashgate.com

ISBN 0-7546-1666-5

9 780754 616665